FREE
IS BAD

HOW THE **FREE WEB** HURT
PRIVACY, TRUTH AND DEMOCRACY

AND WHAT YOU CAN DO ABOUT IT

JOHN MARSHALL

Free Is Bad - 1st Edition

Marshall, John
Free Is Bad. - 1st ed. - 2020.
ISBN 978-0-578-78268-3

**Orthogonal
Thinking**

*For my parents, who gave me the ability to think,
and the confidence to do so.*

Praise for *Free Is Bad*

"We're all familiar with the adage "there's no free lunch." That applies to online content too. If you're not paying with money, you're paying with something else - like your personal information and privacy. John deftly explains the repercussions arising from "free" including the clear and present danger to democracy."
— Dr. Augustine Fou, Digital Strategist

"John Marshall walks us down the dangerous path we have taken to today with wit and a technical astuteness gained from years in the digital marketing industry. He also provides vital advice about how we can avoid continuing down this path to a potentially apocryphal future. If anyone can drive home the argument that Free is Bad – it's John Marshall."
— Gord Hotchkiss, Mediapost Columnist, Author and ex-search marketer

"The ability to control one's privacy enables social progress and innovation. Surveillance capitalism threatens both tenets. This book shows readers how to claw-back some of their private data from BigTech's "free" offerings."
— G Craig Vachon, tech investor and author of *The Knucklehead Of Silicon Valley*

"Nobody knows ad-tech and web privacy better than John. And he informs you in this clear, concise, readable, jargon-free, actionable, and enjoyable book: Free Is Bad has the words to live by for a better digital life."
— Richi Jennings, industry analyst and editor

"With a veteran's perspective and an incisive eye, John Marshall traces the evolution of key Internet technologies and media. From this exciting account we learn how things came to be the way they are, and what we can do to reclaim our personal and collective future. Highly recommended!"
— Tim Ash, keynote speaker & marketing expert, bestselling author of *Unleash Your Primal Brain: Demystifying how we think and why we act*

"Anyone who cares about the internet-related problems of our day (privacy, democracy, mental and emotional well-being, and polarization, among others) needs to read and understand what John Marshall lays out so eloquently in this book. The engines that have driven the growth of our technology tools and platforms have an enormous impact on how our modern society functions. If we are ever to fix our problems, more internet users/consumers need to understand what incentives created the problems in the first place. This book distills complex information about technology and advertising ecosystems into an easy-to-understand format. I highly recommend it!"
— Vanessa Otero, founder Of Adfontes Media and creator of the Media Bias Chart

About the Author

John Marshall is a serial digital marketing entrepreneur and a patent holder in analytics tracking. His companies built advertising and analytics tools and delivered the first distance-learning training courses in digital marketing.

After launching and selling three successful startups, John turned his focus to the insights he'd gleaned about the nature of web advertising and consumer behavior. He's since become a firm believer that our current relationship with the web as a free service has led to untenable compromises in service, information, and truth. However, he also believes the web can be a powerful tool that delivers quality services and information while still respecting our privacy. But only if we're willing to be the customer.

CONTENTS

PROLOGUE

HOW I GOT HERE

When I was 10, my parents bought me an electronics kit. I don't think they could have known how it would set the course of my life.

My imagination had already been inspired by hundreds of hours spent with Lego spread out on the floor. But these new building blocks of transistors and resistors just set my brain on fire.

A world of creativity was revealing itself before me—and I couldn't get enough. My Grandfather, a highly regarded nerd himself, encouraged me with loving appreciation for the radio sets and bistable oscillators I built.

It wasn't long before I'd hand soldered my first computer, with a whole 256 *bytes* of memory, and I managed to squeeze machine code programs out of my brain and into the primitive processor. I worked on Saturdays in the local electronics store to fund the purchase of more gear, surrounded by bits and parts and people who shared my passion.

Pretty soon I was writing 8-bit video games and selling them on cassette tape through ads I'd placed in computer magazines. By the time I was 16, I was making good money, and can recall being excused from school to meet with my accountant—ironically, missing an economics class.

My hobby became my business, my business became my obsession, and for better or worse I spent all my waking hours coding instead of studying. That's why I didn't get the grades I needed to go to college.

Combined with an adventurous and experimental spirit, all of this meant I wasn't destined for employment, but for entrepreneurship.

Silicon Valley

In 1992, the place for entrepreneurship was Silicon Valley. So off I went.

And I couldn't believe my luck. Everyone was a hyper-rational nerd, just like me. I really felt like I'd found my people.

When the internet came along in 1994, thanks to the indulgence of my family and to my early fascination with computers, I was quickly able to understand what went on under the hood and could find a place to participate in a meaningful way.

I landed at Netscape in the late 1990s, working as a product manager on the 3.0 release of the Navigator web browser. It was the only time I was employed at a big company.

My job was to teach companies how the groundbreaking future technologies we were working on helped people experience the web—and how the web could help their businesses. For three years, I had fun, learned a lot, made mistakes, and didn't make any enemies.

After Netscape, I returned to my entrepreneurial roots, launching three consecutive startups. One way or another, those companies were all focused on advertising or marketing. I'd developed enough savvy to bootstrap our growth and avoid outside investment, so the products, services and business models were entirely up to me and my hand-picked teams.

Building and running those companies taught me important lessons and brought valuable experiences that have come to form the basis of this book.

ClickTracks

I had an epiphany while reading a book that's become a classic among statistics nerds: *The Visual Display of Quantitative Information*. Inspired by Edward R. Tufte's landmark, I invented a unique way of displaying complex data, and launched ClickTracks Web Analytics in 2002.

Online advertising was already big business, but marketers needed a better way to measure success. ClickTracks built tools to help them understand how effective their marketing efforts were at attracting audiences to their websites. It wasn't the first to market, nor the most popular, but we did gain a devoted following—in part because we focused on data privacy.

Not long after we got ourselves established, Google released a competing product that was free of charge, so at first we thought our days were over. Instead our sales actually grew—because Google brought awareness of the market, and precisely because Google's tool was free.

Why? Well there were plenty of companies that wanted what Google offered, but they had privacy concerns, so didn't want their customer data ending up with Google. They were willing to pay us for a competitive product that delivered that extra level of security.

Thanks to our ability to prove there was a paying market for an analytics product that delivered the privacy that Google's free product didn't, we built a meaningful customer base. We were fortunate to sell the business, the patents and all the associated technology to a buyer who integrated it into a whole suite of powerful tools.

MarketMotive

After ClickTracks, online marketing continued to explode. Agencies were struggling to meet their clients' growing needs, and Fortune 500 companies were building their own in-house digital teams.

But neither agencies nor in-house teams could find enough experienced or qualified staff to implement whatever ideas they were cooking up, so I co-founded MarketMotive. We reached out to the thought leaders we'd met over the years, paid them to create videos explaining online marketing best practices, and packaged them into courses we delivered online.

We were effectively a media company, but at a time when such businesses were in trouble. We went against the received wisdom and charged a premium price for the courses, competing against free stuff on YouTube. We knew our courses were the best and were proved right when a larger online training provider acquired the business.

Algorithmic Ads

In the mid to late teens, display ads—or banner ads—weren't used much by small businesses, because they had a poor reputation and the industry had seen some shady dealings. Bigger companies still created them because they had agencies that handled all the messy details and helped them avoid any shenanigans.

At ClickTracks I'd already developed analytics that helped measure and optimize these kinds of ads, and at MarketMotive we'd taught people about their effectiveness. It seemed like I should be able to make them work for small businesses, if we could just cut out the ad networks and the sleazy salesmen who might not have a business's best interests in mind. The key was to make it do-it-yourself, push-button simple.

So I hired a team that developed AI "machine learning" technology that would create the ads without needing a graphic designer. It was a great idea with solid technology and it really worked, but those shady practices remained entrenched. Still, we found some success, proved our thesis, and were able to find a home for the company at a large online marketing platform.

AND HERE'S WHAT I LEARNED

Through the lens of my businesses, I saw the web and the digital marketing industry evolve.

I watched as the business of collecting and selling data became more important than the web content itself. I saw free products compete with and, in some cases bury, better paid products.

My experience wasn't narrowly focused on one high profile, Cambridge Analytica–style calamity, but rather on a whole series of business practices and outcomes. I had, as they say, a ringside seat at this inexorable commodification of personal data in the name of selling stuff. And maybe I had a hand in helping it along.

Now that I'm no longer head-down on launching and running another tech company, I've had time to think about the past decade. I've been looking long and hard at what online life looks like, how we ended up where we are, and how we as consumers contributed to the problems we're living with.

I see the mess we're in. It's a mess created by technology—especially data driven, advertising technology. And it's moving faster than society can adapt.

But it's in my nature to do more than simply clutch my pearls and wring my hands. I'm inclined to actively try to solve problems.

So I started with me.

I sought out solutions and took simple, practical steps to protect myself from advertisers' invasive data mining. And I modified my online behavior, to maximize the value I get from the web, and to minimize the negative psychic impact of divisive content and psychological manipulation.

As a result, "my" web is incredibly useful again, and my emotional well-being has vastly improved.

As I dug deeper and learned more, I came to realize that my choices were uncommon. Most people don't have my peculiar background. So either they don't realize what they're mired in, or they don't know what they can do about it.

This book is my attempt to fix that. I explain, from the trenches, why we're in the mess we're in, and the practical steps we can take to dig our way out of it—*right now*.

Because it's important to understand how these amazing, complex web of tools and services and content can appear on our devices for free. Not to mention what we might be giving up, in exchange for all this free stuff.

I think you'll find the journey both fascinating and vital.

INTRODUCTION

FREE IS BAD

There, I said it. Now that I have your attention, allow me to clarify:

Freedom is essential. As is free speech. Plenty of actions performed free of charge are also good, even noble—they are *pro bono*, or "for the good."

The open-source, or free-software movement is also good—it's based on all three meanings of the word "free." In fact, free software powers almost the entire internet, and is the reason you can read this book.

However all these niceties ignore the reality that in most cases someone needs to foot the bill. The internet upended the cost structure of many activities, but it didn't reduce those costs to zero.

You probably use a wide range of free services without sparing a moment's thought for how it's all paid for: the development, the maintenance, the management. If you do spare a moment, you probably shrug it off with "advertising" and get back to your TikTok or Facebook.

But executives at those companies are getting up early and worrying about growing their businesses. And in every company I founded—and those that I consulted for, and those that I taught how to think analytically—the path to growth and success leads through the acquisition and retention of happy customers.

But that's not you. You, dear reader, *are not the customer*. To use the classic phrase:

> **"You are the product ... *delivered to the advertiser,*** **who is the customer."**

—*Carlota Schoolman, Richard Serra*

Yes, Some Kinds Of Free Can Be Good

Let me save you the time and effort of posting counterarguments where free is, in fact, good:

- **Free speech:** As in, "the right to express any opinions without censorship or restraint." Yes, that's obviously a good kind of free.
- **Free software or open source:** Yes, good, also pro bono.
- **Free media:** such as TV, radio, podcasts and the like. Yes, they're OK, if consumed as entertainment.
- **Freemium and free trials:** Sure. Great tool for acquiring paying customers of software and services.
- **Wikipedia:** Definitely good, pro bono. It's funded through donations: I donate when they nag me. Because the readers are the customer, the readers fund it. There are no other customers.
- **Free lunch:** Probably no such thing. There's usually a catch. A timeshare pitch, for example.
- **Free everything:** As in communism? Nope: That huge social experiment was a disaster.

The key to understanding whether something that's free is also beneficial is *knowing who the customer is*. A business aligns everything it does around its customer, making sure they get what they pay for.

Wikipedia, for example, understands who its customers are. It's ad-free because, among many other legitimate reasons—concerns about bias, mainly—they know that, "Our customers are the readers and contributors and our product is an encyclopedia; we have to keep our customers happy in order to keep donations flowing. Once we switch to an ad-based funding model, the situation changes dramatically: our customers now are the advertisers, our product is the readers' attention, and it is this product that we sell to the customers."[1]

The customer is, as they say, always right. If the free service you're using is pro bono, and the clues revealing that are obvious, then it's most likely okay. The publisher has little motivation to build a sales force hungry for something to sell.

However if the service has commercial intent, it will operate in a marketplace. And almost everything on today's internet is like this, because operating at web scale requires major investment.

Marketplaces are characterized by three entities: Buyers, sellers and products.

The world of broadcast TV and Radio represents an interesting example of something being free, paid for by advertisers, but without the toxic nonsense that has sprouted on the web. We'll explore this in more detail in the second half of this book, but a little preview is the observation that Bob Hoffman made in his book *BadMen: How Advertising Went From A Minor Annoyance To A Major Menace*: "We used to have a pleasant enough arrangement with the ad industry. They gave us Seinfeld and in return we voluntarily gave a few seconds of our attention to their ads. It was a reasonably fair exchange."

It was fair because the consumer could see what they were getting, and crucially, what they were giving up. The same cannot be said of our online experience. It has become almost impossible to understand what you're giving up when your email, smartphone, web searches and news are all tied together. The knowledge behind how to exploit it is asymmetric and the data miners, content optimizers and targeting gurus are way smarter than us. We simply have no idea what's going on "in the cloud." The best you can do is escape with your dignity somewhat intact.

Self Regulation and Legislation

I know people who passionately believe that legislation or maybe industry self-regulation will make the world a better place.

There have been some small nudges in this direction with GDPR in Europe and CCPA in California. I'll cover those in the final section of the book, but I'm not optimistic about real change through legislation for a couple of reasons:

First, legislation is often slow to arrive and fixes the wrong stuff. This is inevitable when politicians lack specialized knowledge—they put half-baked ideas through the sausage machine of "policy."

Second, even if useful legislation were enacted, we would leave unsolved the problem of who would pay for the services. I mean, I'm sure we'd all welcome a completely free and private email service with no ads or data mining. But the big payouts from advertising would go. So with no ability to generate revenue, I can't imagine how that email provider could pay the bills, let alone thrive.

Someone needs to be the customer.

Reading The Book

Anyhow, we'll go deep on all of this in the following chapters. Here's what to expect.

Part 1: The first half of this book deals with the core technology products and services we use every day in our online lives. In each chapter, I'll give some context through history and an explanation of how we arrived at the present mess, then I'll help you decide if a service with built-in privacy is a good plan, or whether to stick with the current free-is-good world. I have no financial interest in the products I recommend, and links do not contain affiliate codes.

Part 2: The second half of the book covers media—more specifically, news. Naturally the history is longer and more nuanced, the present mess is deeper and more perplexing, and the way forward is less definite. So I'll give you guideposts to decide if the way you're getting news is important to you, and to look closer at the kind of news you're getting. Finally, we'll talk about what to do to make both better.

Be The Change

The web we have today could be so much better. We're all looking for positive change in content, access, bias, and influence. To make that positive change happen, we need to understand how our historical relationship with these tools helped them evolve into what we have today. And how we can play a part in improving them.

Ultimately I'm optimistic you can be the change you want to see. That's what @Ghandi would tweet.

NOTE: *The companies and technologies profiled here are in constant flux. Updates and corrections will be posted regularly to the website freeisbad.com*

Part I.

Information Wants To Be Free

1. SEARCH

Want to know something important? *Google it.*

What started out as a nonsense word became a brand. Then that brand got verbified—in much the same way as Photoshop, Rollerblade and Xerox.

Why does it matter? Because for most people, Google is search. They're one and the same.

Which is ... not true. I mean: It is, but it wasn't always.

Google didn't invent search. By the time Google even bought their domain name, there'd already been a dozen or more search engines. Some were obscure and technical, some were big brands in everyday use, and they did an okay job in those early days when search was finding its place in the web.

So why's Google the big dog now? It's not because they had first-mover advantage.

Is it because they invented the best ad-tech?

Nope. They licensed that from a tiny company you've never heard of. In fact, they didn't even want to run ads at first. The founders were dedicated to an early core principle of internet culture: "Information wants to be free."

Believe it or not, they truly believed ads would corrupt the quality of search.

And yet here we are: Google's an advertising behemoth that makes almost all of its money selling ads. How did this happen? Why is the act of searching for information so intimately tied to selling stuff?

It's because search doesn't come for free. And if you're not careful, it means giving up a lot of your privacy.

How much personal data you trade for search should be your decision. My goal is to help you make an informed choice.

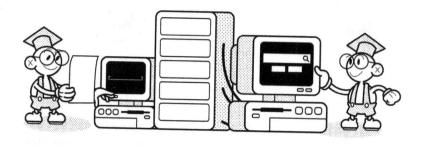

A BRIEF HISTORY OF SEARCH

Search engines have been around a long time. In fact, they predate the web. They were tools, not businesses, and were free of charge to help educational and research organizations navigate digital libraries and distributed databases.

Search Engines Were Like Phone Directories, But Worse

When Al Gore's 1991 High Performance Computing Act opened up public access to the "Information Superhighway," early search engines stepped in to make the vast amounts of information accessible.

But they were also utilitarian—mere extensions of the academic tools that came before. And they had funky names, like Archie, Jughead, VLib, Wandex, and Jumpstation.

These early engines were terribly slow and difficult to use. Some could only search one server at a time, and most merely returned site titles, not content.

Sometimes, if the search phrase didn't exactly match the site's title, you simply wouldn't get a result. Even if you did, it might not be very useful, because search engines usually just listed sites in apparently random orders—not even alphabetized like a proper phone directory.

Many of the biggest databases were curated by humans. If a site owner wanted to be listed in search results, they had to manually submit their site through a confusing and time-consuming process, submitting the address and description of each page individually.

Portals Were Like Malls

In the meantime, websites were getting bigger and more complicated. Some websites grew to be portals, and they were a big deal. They weren't search engines helping you find stuff elsewhere, they were like the mall: promising to have everything you wanted without you ever needing to leave. Portals worked like a "start page," where internet newbies could find news and sports, stock market updates, movie reviews, and even an email service—all under one roof.

There were a number of these portals early on. Some search engines, like Excite and Lycos, even added features to try to become portals. But maybe the most famous pure portal experiment was America Online, or AOL.

AOL provided a massive web portal built around a whole suite of compelling content and services, and they made sure that people didn't need to go outside the site to find whatever they wanted. The goal was to give users lots of things to do and lots of pages to look at, which meant lots of places for AOL to sell *display advertising*: big graphical image ads that flashed and scrolled like Vegas billboards. They made tons of money off those ads, plus users also paid a membership fee to use the site. Win win for AOL.

Portals still exist today, but as shadows of their former selves. It's hard to imagine now, but at the time they were as powerful as Facebook.

AltaVista's Portal Experiment

It's worth taking a minute to look a little closer at AltaVista's portal experiment. It's interesting in part because, like Excite and Lycos, AltaVista originally started out as a search engine. But also because of where they ended up.

The AltaVista search engine was developed by Digital Equipment Corporation (DEC) with the goal of providing services that made finding files on the public network easier. Thanks to its tech-focused parent DEC, AltaVista used a fast, highly efficient custom web crawler that could handle more web pages than were even thought to exist, running on advanced hardware.

It was a hit not only with casual surfers, but with professional researchers worldwide.

In 1998 DEC was sold to Compaq, who redesigned AltaVista as—you guessed it—a web portal. Its streamlined search page was abandoned, and new features like shopping and free email were added. The hope was to get some of that sweet, sweet advertising money.

Things didn't work out as they'd hoped. When the dot com bubble collapsed, layoffs followed and the company re-aligned. AltaVista gradually lost its portal features and refocused on being a quality search engine, leveraging its advanced tech and a new streamlined look.

AltaVista was eventually bought by Overture, a commercial search company specializing in delivering paid ads in search results, who you'll hear more about later. AltaVista's pedigree of advanced tech fit nicely into Overture's portfolio.

Remember the Overture name. It's super important later.

Yahoo's Portal Experiment

Originally called, "Jerry and David's guide to the World Wide Web," Yahoo was launched in 1994 by a pair of Stanford students as a manually collated directory of their favorite websites. The following year, they added a search engine called Yahoo! Search. Like most directories, it wasn't crawling and indexing the entire web, just searching its own hand-built index, but it was still plenty popular with users.

Unlike the other companies we've looked at, Yahoo never really thought of itself as a search technology company and was always more of a traffic-generating portal. Jim Brock was Yahoo's first attorney, served as principal outside counsel from its founding and then as a Senior Vice President overseeing a range of products, including Yahoo! Mail. I asked him how the company saw its mission in the early days. He says, "The Yahoo founders and management team were very technically astute, but I don't think they shared the vision of search being the central point."

With the rising popularity of true web-crawling search engines, Yahoo decided it needed to offer users a tool that looked outside its own directory. Since in-house energy was focused on building pages full of content and media, it was easier to just license someone else's search technology: Search "was always thought of as something you would outsource," says Brock.

And outsource they did, bouncing around from one search partner to another. They started early on by licensing AltaVista's engine, but then dropped it in favor of Inktomi, a back-end search tech provider that delivered search for companies like Microsoft and Disney. In 2000, they dropped Inktomi and licensed the up-and-coming Google Search. A couple of years later it went back to Inktomi and bought their search technology outright, but kept serving Google's search results to their users.

In 2003, Yahoo purchased Overture, whose portfolio not only included a powerful search advertising platform but also a number of successful search engine brands that now included, if you recall, AltaVista. Yahoo continued using Google for the portal while it worked on building its own new engine, plugging in bits and pieces of AltaVista, then dropped Google completely and the two became true competitors.

All along the way, regardless of whose search tech it was using at any moment, Yahoo was turning the newly acquired Overture's "paid placement" technology into a substantial profit center by efficiently selling ads intermingled with the search results.

Google's Search Experiment

Google was started in 1996 by two Stanford students: Larry Page and Sergey Brin. Like so many early internet projects, it was born in a dorm room.

Unlike other search engines, Google wasn't interested in creating a cluttered portal where search was an afterthought. It was strictly dedicated to building a better search that would bring users more relevant results. It didn't want to be a mall, it wanted to be the phone directory.

At the time, other engines ranked their results by looking at how many times a search term appeared on a given page. Page and Brin thought that a better way to assign value was to track the links between websites. The more times other sites link to a given website—called "backlinks"—the more relevance or value could be assigned to that website.

The patent for that backlink technology—*PageRank*—is actually owned by Stanford University, but Google has an exclusive license. PageRank remains an essential part of the algorithm used by Google.

At first they called their new engine "BackRub" because of the way its algorithms evaluated those backlinks. In 1997 they changed the name to Google—a nod to the massive number "googol" and the massive amount of information the tool could deliver.

Brock was still at Yahoo when Google launched, and says that the Yahoo team found Google's accuracy eerie. "Like reading our minds—because you had a page in mind or a website in mind and you put a query in, and then what do you know, it came back. ... People were amazed."

It didn't take long for millions of venture capital dollars to start flowing to Google—early investors included Amazon's Jeff Bezos. Page and Brin remained committed to their engine being an ad-free, transparent, academic tool in the belief that advertising was a bad idea for search engines—especially the idea of paying for better placements in the results.

In fact the pair presented a paper at Stanford outlining exactly how they thought search engines should work, saying, "It could be argued from the consumer point of view that the better the search engine is, the fewer advertisements will be needed for the consumer to find what they want. This, of course, erodes the advertising supported business model of the existing search engines. ... But we believe the issue of advertising causes enough mixed incentives that it is crucial to have a competitive search engine that is transparent and in the academic realm."[2]

Somebody Has To Pay For Free Search

But somebody has to pay for the servers, so Page and Brin ultimately lost that battle. In 2000, the AdWords network was launched, matching paid ads to users' search keywords.

However the ads were, and remain, text-only—to keep the pages clean and easy to navigate. Ad slots are auctioned, with higher payment getting higher placement. The non-paid results—"organic," as they're known in the industry—aren't influenced by payment.

Google had transitioned from being the phone directory to being yellow pages. Everyone was included, but advertisers that paid more got better placement.

In the following years, Google expanded its suite of tools—both by building in-house and acquiring other startups, including DoubleClick, Waze, DeepMind Technologies, and Calico. By 2015, those other products and services had grown to include artificial intelligence, drone powered delivery systems, autonomous vehicles, and more. So a new company was created called Alphabet, and the Google-branded internet related services and products are now gathered together as a subsidiary of that parent company.

Still, Google never became a busy, attention-grabbing portal. Its homepage today remains a tidy white void, with a single search tool in the center and small text links to its other products and services.

THE BATTLE FOR THE BUSINESS MODEL

We've only scratched the surface of all the search engines that have existed since the beginning of the web. Looking back, it seems like the people who created most of those early engines really just wanted to give users an organized way to find the most relevant information. They wanted, in a sense, to democratize access to valuable information.

Remember that early principle of internet culture—"Information wants to be free"? That free access depends on being able to find stuff.

Running a search engine is expensive, and investors like to see a return. Management always found a familiar solution in display advertising, but it wasn't enough to just sell a few banners on the homepage, like WebCrawler had tried. And it wasn't enough to stick ads right in the results, or to charge businesses for better rankings, like Overture did.

To sell a lot of ads, they needed an audience who did more than just search for something, find it, and leave the site. They had to give them other reasons to stick around, which led to building portals—to be like AOL, but making users pay with their eyeballs instead of with a membership.

Google and Yahoo seem to represent the two poles in the battle between pure search and multi-functional portals. Yahoo's experiment shows that users didn't want a portal without search, so it paid to license someone else's technology. Google's experiment shows that staying focused on fast, easy search technology—without all the clutter of a portal—can succeed if the ads are relevant, focused and impact the user experience as little as possible.

But neither model works *without* ads.

How The Advertising Worked

I talked with Dana Todd, CEO of Balodana, who has 25 years of experience in the digital marketing industry. She was the co-founder and principal at SiteLab International, chair of the Search Engine Marketing Professional Organization, and a board member of the San Diego Software Industry Council, so she's seen some things.

She and her teams were buying ad space for her clients way back in the mid-'90's, when search engines were evolving into portals, and they saw firsthand how that affected the cost, implementation, and effectiveness of advertising. "Lycos, Excite and AltaVista were being pressured pretty significantly to become portals," she says. "To make their shareholders happy, they had to come up with alternative ways to monetize that ... and they really heavily sold their pages chock-a-block with banner ads."

At that time, knowing how well an ad was working wasn't easy. There were no fancy algorithms for tracking a user's behavior or preferences, no way to read the content of their email: "We didn't have a lot of good tracking back then, so it was hard to gauge the effectiveness of anything."

Advertising Was Simply Context Related

What passed for ad targeting in those days amounted to choosing which section of the portal your banner ad appeared in. Selling something sports related? Put your ad in the sports section.

They were "treating it like an old school magazine," as Brock tells it. From Yahoo's perspective, it was "more like buying television advertising than it was like buying anything else. [We might sell] five featured advertisers across different parts of Yahoo during this time period and these slots."

Display ads weren't sold by the "column inch," the way newspapers had done it. Instead, they were sold either on a flat rate for a specified period of time, or based on how many people the ad was displayed to, measured as a "CPM" or "Cost Per Mille" (that's Latin for 'thousand') impressions.

This old-school display advertising model worked really well in the early days, when there were only a few advertisers experimenting in the space, and the ads weren't competing too much with one another for attention. But as the industry grew and portals were increasingly saturated with a patchwork of flashing, blinking advertisements all vying for the users' attention, the effectiveness of display advertising suffered.

Ads were hurting the user experience, and users developed "ad blindness." In other words, they just quit paying attention.

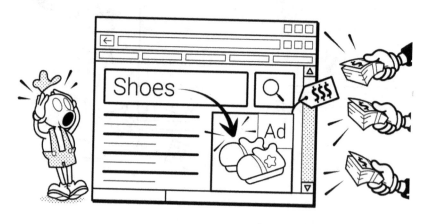

Context And Keywords Are King

Even if a user hadn't gone "ad blind," treating banner ads like TV or print ads meant they worked only if they were lucky enough to capture the attention of a random reader who happened to be in the market for their product. If a car lover likes to read about cars but is not in the market for a car, paying to show them a car ad alongside an article about rebuilding drum brakes is a shot in the dark—a wasted impression.

What advertisers needed was a way to show their ad to users who were actually interested in their product, and especially if that's why they were online when they saw the ad. They needed to know the user's intent right *now*.

The turn of the century saw a sea change in ad targeting. Letting advertisers use the search engine to target a user's specific search terms meant they could display a particular ad to that user in the context of what they were interested in at that moment.

If a user searched for "hot tubs," an advertiser could serve them an ad for hot tubs. While the technology was still new and relatively simple, it worked. There weren't a lot of advertisers competing for niche keywords, and ads were still sold by the CPM. A single keyword-targeted ad could get placed in front of a lot of qualified eyeballs fast. It was a feeding frenzy for smart advertisers who moved early.

"We were really excited," says Todd. "We'd never seen performance like that before. [For instance] we had a client who sold hot tubs. And to be able to have the only banner on the [search results page] for a term like 'hot tub'—I remember it was literally a 40% click rate." The click (through) rate is the percentage of all people who see the ad that actually respond and click on it. 40% is Holy Grail territory: it means your ad is ridiculously effective.

"It was insane—insane! If you had enough money to buy all the [keywords], you could literally own the entire category." Clients loved these new ads, Todd continues, "because the performance was so much higher than any of the other banner ads that we had done."

Keyword targeting marked the beginning of matching ads with user behavior and intent. It changed the game to pair what a user was actively showing interest in, at the very moment of decision, with an ad that matched that interest. And digital advertising went through a huge transformation.

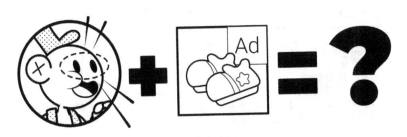

We Can't Measure Eyeballs

As we've seen, up until this point ads were sold in one of two ways: for a specific period of time, or by how many thousands of users the ad was displayed to (CPM). An advertiser might say "I want to be the only banner on a specific page for the next month." Or they could say "I'll pay $15 dollars for my ad to be displayed a thousand times."

But what neither of those models can do is measure performance. Data could show that the ad had displayed, but it couldn't show if the users actually noticed the ad—let alone whether they cared about the ad. Not unlike print or TV ads, the advertiser was paying to place their message in front of a black box: An audience whose interest was at best assumed, but certainly not measurable.

If your goal is simply exposure, getting a brand in front of a lot of eyeballs might be enough. CPM was perfect for putting the Coca Cola logo in the mind's eye of thousands of people.

But if an advertiser was trying to sell something *right now*, they needed something better. They needed to get the user to show interest in their offer and click the ad to start the purchase process.

What they needed was a way to pay only for ads that actually generated measurable interest in the offer: Ads that *generated a click*. In other words, they wanted to Pay Per Click (PPC).

PPC Beats CPM

One company had actually already pioneered that exact technology. But to understand where it fits in we'll have to back up a bit.

In the 1990s, GoTo.com owned one of the web's oldest search engines, called World Wide Web Worm. And they were well ahead of the curve with their targeting. As early as 1998, GoTo would "rank web sites based on how much the sites are willing to pay to be placed at the top of the search under a real-time competitive bidding process."[3]

But here's the kicker: The bid amount was not paid based on how many people saw it. It was only paid when someone actually clicked on the result and went to the advertiser's site. That meant the advertiser was only paying for demonstrated, measurable interest in their offer.

This technology was so advanced that GoTo was able to secure patents on the management and delivery of Pay Per Click (PPC) advertising. Remember that: It'll be important later.

In 1999, GoTo even offered a dashboard so advertisers could manage their own campaigns, define the keywords they were interested in, and bid in real-time to choose how much they were willing to pay for each click their ad got.

Now enter Google: In 2000, Google launched its AdWords platform, also allowing advertisers to target specific keywords. At first advertisers paid a monthly fee, and Google managed their campaigns; but then came the AdWords self-service dashboard, and advertisers could create and manage their own ads in real time. This was awfully close to what GoTo was offering, except that Google was still charging by the CPM, not the click.

Now here's where Google steps in GoTo's sandbox: In 2002, Google introduced a PayPerClick advertising model to AdWords, so advertisers could bid on the value of a click. GoTo—which had since changed its name to Overture—saw it as an infringement on its PPC patents. Needless to say, Overture filed a lawsuit against Google.

I mentioned earlier that in 2003, Yahoo purchased Overture. When it did, it also inherited that lawsuit. Sure enough, Google and

Yahoo settled the suit—in Yahoo's favor. Google paid Yahoo with 2.7 million shares of common stock, in exchange for a perpetual license under the patent. That means that Yahoo, not Google, owns the rights to PPC advertising. And Google, who went on to great success with PPC, did it on the back of Yahoo's patent.

PPC Performed Like Nothing Else

There's no overstating the impact the PPC model had on digital marketing. As Todd says, "It introduced a whole new category called performance marketing. ... The idea that you're only paying for a click seemed really enticing [and] was much more efficient. When pay-per-click first started, it was like nickel clicks. So it was cheap. It was cheap, cheap, cheap. So it was just too good to be true, frankly. It was a fantastic invention."

Brock concurs: "It wasn't until we saw the actual numbers that we understood that [PPC] was going to eat the internet. That was going to be the dominant and most effective advertising mechanism ... if you want clicks."

The beauty of search advertising is this: Users might type a keyword in a variety of ways, like "hot tubs," "soaking tubs," or "jacuzzis." If an advertiser was buying graphical ads and wanted to appeal to all those different terms, they'd have to build a dozen versions of their banner. But search engines let advertisers craft their ads in text, which meant they could easily build variations of their ad copy to match the variations of the user's search term. Which meant ads more accurately matched exactly what the user was searching for in their moment of decision, enhancing the idea that the thing you were searching for was indeed just a click away.

The search engine still has to work as a search engine, of course—delivering real organic results along with all the ads. Because the better the engine works, the more accurate the results are, and the more you'll trust it. And the more you trust the search results, the more likely you are to keep using the search engine—and to keep clicking more ads.

If both ads and results are relevant to your needs, you're more likely to click on them. And every time you do—even if you don't buy—you telegraph your interest to the advertiser, who logs your activity and probably starts following you around with more ads. All of which makes you a more valuable lead, whose likelihood to convert can be measured.

Users Want Stuff, Not Brand Relationships

It's fair to say that buying a banner ad on search and paying for eyeballs—CPM—was always a bad idea if you're trying to sell things online. The user isn't searching for awareness of a brand. They're searching because they want to find something and go there.

But the early days, the web had a dearth of content, so portals filled that void with pages of content loaded with banners. Advertisers understood old-school display ads, and sales teams understood how to sell them, so search engines inherited banners because, "That's how we've always done it."

The radical innovation that GoTo/Overture via Yahoo, then Google brought to the table with PPC was to sell *the onward click*, instead of the branding. This aligned perfectly with the core intent of a search engine: To find what you want and go there.

WHAT IT LOOKS LIKE NOW

Google, Yahoo and Bing remain the three most influential search brands in the US. But there are still plenty of other players, large and small, providing search around the world. Yandex is the leading search provider in Russia, Ukraine, Belarus, Kazakhstan, Uzbekistan, and Turkey. Baidu is by far the largest search engine in China.

Search advertising remains largely PPC based, although if you're just doing a branding exercise CPM is still an option. The platform names have changed: Google's AdWords is now Google Ads; Microsoft's adCenter is now Microsoft Advertising.

What hasn't changed is the rate of innovation: The ability to target users' interests has evolved fast since the introduction of keyword targeting and PPC, and continues to do so. Ads are matched with more than just the keywords you use in the moment: A lot of other data points are captured—painting an ever more detailed picture of you, your habits, and your interests.

In the early days, for instance, two searches by the same person were disconnected from one another. Let's say in the morning you searched for hot tubs. You spent 10 minutes finding the right hot tub, and then maybe you compared prices, bookmarked your favorites, and you were done. Then in the afternoon you searched for tennis shoes. There was no connection between the two—each search was its own little transactional world.

Today those two distinct searches are joined together and are known to have been asked by the same human: you. The advertiser knows you're in the market for a hot tub and that you're also interested in shoes. They might extrapolate that maybe you also need a pair of shower shoes for getting in and out of the hot tub.

They may also know which TV shows or books you've searched, which physical ailments you suffer from, which medications you take. Searched "foot pain"? You might get recommendations for orthopedic tennis shoes instead.

And that doesn't even count the data collected from other sources, like your browser, your phone, or even your car. All these data points get folded into a portrait of you, and all that information can be used to target search advertising at you in increasingly granular ways.

Google Is Curating Your Content

Google owns an overwhelming majority of search traffic, and it's now beginning to build a closed system—what some would call a walled garden. It's increasingly sending search traffic to its own properties and preferred content, even when superior or more relevant content is available.

Chelsea Rustrum, digital industry writer and co-founder of Instigation Protocol and Alchemy Spaces, wrote, "While Google seems like a public utility of sorts, you probably spend a fair amount of time interacting with the increasing limitations of it—missing out on the depth and breadth of information that exists or would exist if it showed up in your results. And it's not just users that are missing out—small businesses must close their doors if they can't be found. And many of them have."[4]

As Jonathan Tepper further explained in his article *The Death of the Internet*: "Even though competitors like Yelp might have superior local reviews, Google Reviews are given preferential placement in search results. Even though shopping comparison websites like Foundem in Europe might offer better results, Google can effectively blacklist them. Increasingly, Google offers snippets and previews of

Wikipedia and Getty Images [right in the search results]. Traffic to these websites has subsequently collapsed. Far from directing users to other sites, Google today starves content creators of traffic."

Tepper says Google is killing off technologies that would reduce the need to search using Google. "In 2013, the company announced they were discontinuing Google Reader, which relied on RSS. An RSS feed was a way for publishers to reach their readers directly without using Google Search." With Google Reader gone, he says, publishers are made more reliant on traffic from Google.[5]

Whatever Google's original vision for a free and open, more effective internet might have been, they are clearly down a new and different path of content curation—the ramifications of which are profound but mostly invisible.

Advertising Might Undermine The Public Good

Safiya Umoja Noble, associate professor at UCLA and co-director of the UCLA Center for Critical Internet Inquiry, shared with a Gizmodo reporter her thoughts on how search's reliance on advertising and content curation has hurt the public good: "The first search engines were, in fact, virtual libraries, and many people understood the value of libraries as a public good. As automation increased, and librarians and experts were replaced with AI, we lost a lot. The public good that could have been realized was replaced by massive advertising platforms, like Yahoo! and Google."

She says this resulted in users suffering from a "big gap between knowledge and advertising in search engines, especially when trying to understand complex issues. In some ways, search has undermined our trust in expertise and critical thinking, backed by investigated facts and research, and left us open to manipulation by propaganda. Search engines may be great in helping us find banal information, but they have also desensitized us to the value of slow, deliberate investigation—the kind that makes for a more informed democracy."[6]

Free Search Users Are Not The Customer

Search engines can still be valuable, and it's easy to think they're in the business of delivering their value to you and me because we're their customers and they should want to keep us happy.

The reality is: search engines have costs to cover. Even though their early intentions were altruistic, and even though they were driven by a desire to help us find stuff, in the end they've got to pay for servers, software and bandwidth.

And *we* don't pay the bills.

The sales team doesn't wake up in the morning raring to find new ways to satisfy you. If you don't get the results you expect when you run a search, there's nobody sitting at a red phone waiting for your call so they can fix it for you. No customer service, not even an elderly greeter in a blue vest to point you to the lost and found. You are not the customer.

The sales team wakes up raring to find new ways to satisfy *advertisers*. Even in an ecosystem that's largely automated through tools like Google Ads and Microsoft Advertising, there are sales and support staff available to help advertisers build better, more effective campaigns. That's where the red phone is. That's where the sales team puts its focus.

Because the *advertisers* pay the bills.

VISIONS FOR TOMORROW

Search is ingrained into the DNA of the web. It's hard to imagine the web without search, harder still to imagine paying for it. That would be like paying for cable TV, then separately paying for the remote so you could channel surf, right?

Nevertheless, people like you and me are becoming increasingly concerned with how our data is used, increasingly sick of ads, and are increasingly looking for alternatives to ad-driven search. According to a 2016 Pew Research survey, "86% of internet users have taken steps online to remove or mask their digital footprints [and] 61% say they feel they 'would like to do more' but are unaware of tools they could use."[7]

Dissent Among The Ranks

Let's not forget that in the beginning, way back when search was the way to tame the anarchy of the internet's wild west days, generating revenue wasn't the intention.

The intention was to provide a tool that allowed everyone to find everything they needed quickly and easily—no strings attached. As we've seen, today that heady vision is largely gone. Commerce, not academia, has won.

But the victory is not without its dissenters. Even Google insiders have become disenchanted.

James Whittaker was an engineering director at Google until 2012. He keynoted Google Developer Day events and Google Test Automation Conferences, and he wrote the book about how Google builds and tests successful software.

His years at Google were good years. Until, as he said in a pair of viral articles he wrote after leaving, they weren't.

In his early days at Google, advertising revenues felt like a necessary evil that subsidized a culture of innovation and creativity: "Our advertising revenue gave us the headroom to think, innovate and create," Whittaker wrote. "Forums like App Engine, Google Labs and open source served as staging grounds for our inventions." That innovation led to the creation of important and valuable tools like Gmail and Chrome. Whittaker and his colleagues believed that "Google was a technology company first and foremost; a company that hired smart people and placed a big bet on their ability to innovate."

That golden age of innovation didn't last forever. For Whittaker, Google's priorities shifted. Those tools he and his teams had created were being used to monetize the user base in ways he wasn't comfortable with. In his mind, Google no longer considered its users as customers: "Google's customers are its advertisers. What are those advertisers buying? Personal data of users of course. What are those users getting? Addiction to 'free' services."

Google's growing suite of interconnected, always-on tools had "trained users to login and stay logged in," he said, meaning "Google knows more about you than ever and guess what they are doing with that knowledge? That's right, using it to advantage advertisers."

Looking back now, he says, "Technically I suppose Google has always been an advertising company, but ... only in the sense that a good TV show is an ad company: Having great content attracts advertisers. [But] the new Google seems more focused on the commercials."

Whittaker doesn't hate Google. He uses and likes Gmail, Chrome, and Maps. It's the business model he hates. "Google has proved it is capable of building great products. Surely they are capable of providing value that people, not just advertisers, are actually willing to pay for." But, he added, Google has "backed itself into an everything-is-free corner. Can Google ever expect consumers to pay for any of their products given this history of free? If Google somehow invents the future, we're all going to have to watch a video ad before they take us there. And once there, we're going to have to pause from our work every time Google decides it needs to pay a few bills. Is this a future any of us want?"[8][9]

There are others who feel the way Whittaker does. And they're working to build a new way to search. A way that provides the same great, accurate, relevant search results you need and still respects your privacy.

Neeva Thinks You'll Pay For Privacy

Sridhar Ramaswamy was the executive who ran Google's $115 billion advertising division. But he grew disillusioned with the direction of the company, and left in 2018.

In a 2020 New York Times profile he said, "Google's focus on advertising growth had come at a heavy cost to the company's users. Useful search results were pushed down the page to squeeze in more advertisements, and privacy was sacrificed for online tracking tools to keep tabs on what ads people were seeing. ... I came to realize that an ad-supported model had limitations."

So Ramaswamy is launching his own ad-free search engine, Neeva. "We felt very strongly that there needed to be alternatives, alternative viewpoints, and alternative business models," he told The Times.[10]

The Neeva website states: "We built Neeva to feel like your personal corner of the web, designed specifically for you – always ad-free and private. Our mission is to serve our users, and only our users."

It promises not to collect your personal data, nor profit from it. And it won't run ads. Instead, it will be subscription-supported, meaning users will pay something less than $10 a month to use the tool.

Neeva will pull its results from a combination of existing sources like Bing, Apple Maps, weather.com and others. But it will still be personalized. According to the Times article, "When users link their Google, Microsoft Office or Dropbox account, Neeva sifts through personal files as well as the public internet for the right answers. And because it knows the people in your contacts, the retailers you ordered from, and news publications you received newsletters from, Neeva's search results will become more personalized over time."

So Neeva's still going to know an awful lot about you. It just promises not to ever sell what it knows. Will users be willing to pay for that distinction? Time will tell.

If It Protects Your Privacy Like A Duck...

DuckDuckGo is a privacy focused search engine that's been around for over a decade, driven by a simple mission: "Too many people believe that you simply can't expect privacy on the Internet. We disagree and have made it our mission to set a new standard of trust online."

According to Search Engine Journal, "DuckDuckGo uses its web crawler ... and up to 400 other sources to compile its search results, including other search engines like Bing, Yahoo, and Yandex, and crowdsourcing sites like Wikipedia."[11]

Like Google, DuckDuckGo is mainly supported by advertising: "Keyword-based advertising is our primary business model. When you search ... we can show you an ad based on the keywords you type in. That's it. ... Our privacy policy, in a nutshell, is to not collect or share any personal information at all. Every time you search ... it is as if you were there for the first time."

Controversially, DuckDuckGo asserts that search engines don't even need to collect all that other information: "Almost all of the money search engines make (including Google) is based on the keywords you type in, without knowing anything about you, including your search history or the seemingly endless amounts of additional data points they have collected about registered and non-registered users alike." So why does Google collect all that other data?

"Because Google is not really a search company; they are an advertising company."[12]

Startpage Promises Privacy

Startpage is another privacy focused engine that's been around a while. It was launched under the name Ixquick in 1998, and calls itself "The world's most private search engine." Its commitment to privacy started around 2006. The company questions why online companies harvest personal data, and is focused on building online tools to help users control their own personal information.

Search is the first tool it's built, but the plan is to add other private versions of common digital services soon, like browsers and email, "because it's our belief that personal data should be *your* data, not Big Data. Period."

Startpage doesn't have its own web crawler; it licenses Google's index for its database, then strips out all trackers and logs to provide you with more data privacy. They still make their money selling ads— but like DuckDuckGo, targeting is based solely on the keywords you use in that session. They don't track and combine your past searches, your browser history, cookies, or any other data points.[13]

Private Search That Puts Users First

Launched in 2003, Mojeek calls itself, "The alternative search engine that puts the people who use it first," and "The original privacy focused search engine." It's committed to user privacy, saying, "We don't want to know a single thing about you. That's because we believe it's your right to search the web without someone looking over your shoulder [and] we have a strict no tracking privacy policy."

Mojeek asserts that free search engines are not truly free: "These services are paid for with the integral part of what makes us all who we are, our identity. Your name, birthday, address, hobbies, emails, everything you've searched (and deleted), nothing is off limits in their pursuit of personal information. We think this is wrong, so we don't do it."[14]

Mojeek offers paid business solutions like an advanced search API for site owners, and an upcoming hosted/managed search service. It uses its own custom crawler, and with something like four billion pages in its index, it doesn't begin to approach Google's hundreds of billions. But it's a start.

More Privacy On The Way

There are plenty of other upstart search engines in the wings advocating for user privacy. I can't vouch for either their utility or their trustworthiness, because there just isn't time to research each and every one. But here are a few more for your consideration.

Ecosia is a privacy- and ecology-focused search engine that uses its profits to plant trees. "We use the profit we make from your searches to plant trees where they are needed most," says the site. "We don't sell your data to advertisers and have no third party trackers, unlike most other search engines."[15]

BetterInternetSearch, as of this writing, is in an alpha release. The site promises "We find the stuff you really want, no ads, no commercial bias, no personal data abuses."[16]

SwissCows offers "family friendly" search, stating, "Since we NEVER collect your data, we NEVER track your data! We respect your privacy!"[17]

Searx is an open-source "Privacy-respecting metasearch engine" that makes its code available to any number of search companies and organizations that want to develop private search.[18]

It's clear that search privacy is a legitimate concern among many users, and among many of the industry professionals who helped bring us to where we are. And there are lots of parties working on providing us alternatives to the big players we all think we need to use.

DOES ALL THIS MATTER?

Look, I get it. If you conduct any part of your life online, you use a search engine. I do. You can't really use the web without it.

But it doesn't come for free. Historically that's meant ads, and historically ads have meant giving up an awful lot of your personal privacy.

Admittedly, letting advertisers and networks look over our shoulders while we use our devices and services can provide some conveniences. You may be completely comfortable living in the Google ecosystem, and really enjoy having your browsing and shopping history bring you more accurate and useful search results. As Brock says, it's like magic when the exactly perfect site appears right at the top of the page.

If that's you—if you're aware of how the data is flowing and you're okay with it—that's your choice. And hopefully, now it's an informed and intentional one. There are four or five terrific and powerful search engines you might be interested in.

But we've learned that collecting all that data isn't really necessary to provide you the quality of results you need: Keywords are more than adequate to deliver relevant ads. All the other stuff they collect doesn't enhance the relevance—it's just used to chase you around the web with more ads.

So you might be interested in alternatives. Maybe, after hearing there are other perfectly viable search engines providing the same quality search results, many from the same sources, you've come to realize that you only use the engine you use because you didn't know your options—but now you want to make a change.

If that's you, it's time for a different intentional choice: It's time to move to a new search engine.

4 WAYS TO INTENTIONAL CHANGE

There is not currently a way for us to pay for an entirely ad-free, data-mining free search engine, and truly become the customer. And to be honest, I don't imagine there ever will be—Neeva's experiment notwithstanding. I don't believe there are enough people willing to pay for search to offset the significant cost of programming, servers, bandwidth, and everything else that goes into providing a quality search tool.

However, as we've seen, there are other options out there that mine your data to a lesser extent (and Google will even help you find them).

Step 1: Choose Your New Search Engine

Just type "DuckDuckGo" into the browser bar and your current search engine (Google, I presume) will come back with a link pointing to its competitor. Click it and try using it for some searches.

Works well, doesn't it? If you like, try some of the others too.

Of course, it's awkward to have to go through Google to use DuckDuckGo. But Google pays billions of dollars to browser vendors to make Google the default search engine, and it's banking on you not knowing what to do about it.

Fortunately this is easy to change.

Step 2: Change Your Default Search Engine

Once you've decided which search engine you want to use on the regular, you can make it your default. The details vary according to the browser and the OS, but it's pretty simple: Open preferences for the browser, find the "default search engine" option, currently Google, and change it to one of these: duckduckgo.com, startpage. com, or mojeek.com.

There's others you could put in there, but I like these companies as a starting place because they are privacy focused, supported by simple ads and have transparent policies.

Some privacy-focused browser add-ons will also change the default search engine for you, such as DuckDuckGo Privacy Essentials. We'll cover those in the Ad-Tech Chapter.

Step 3: Don't Let Popups Change Your Engine

Before we leave the topic, a word of caution: clearly this default search engine setting is highly coveted, as revealed by the amount of money Google is willing to pay to own it. That also makes it a target for bad actors and bottom-feeders. Some websites you visit might display a popup offering to change it for you.

The really bad guys even manage to make this look more official by masquerading as something the OS itself would display. Legitimate sites also make the offer (as startpage.com did during my research for this topic) but I'd rather you understood how simple it is to change yourself, and not risk getting fooled.

Step 4: Remember Google Will Always Be There

Finally, remember that once you've chosen a new default search engine, there's nothing stopping you from opening a browser tab, typing *google.com* into the bar and heading over there for a look at how things used to be, or maybe for some specific search where it actually does work better. If you do this, I'd consider using a private or incognito window so the browser prevents your data from leaking and feeding the beast.

WHAT'S NEXT

Search engines are designed to help us find information that's already on the web for anyone to find. So privacy isn't about the confidentiality of the information we're seeking, but rather it's about remembering that we did—linking us to the *act* of searching for it.

In other words, it's not that information about chronic health problems exist, but rather the fact that you searched for them. We may rightly have concerns about that kind of behavior tracking, but at least they're not mining data in our truly private interactions.

Right?

Maybe, maybe not. Next, let's take a look at something that we like to believe is private: communication from one human to another. In other words, email.

2. EMAIL

Everyone needs email.

Okay, that might be an overstatement. But it's fair to say that if any part of your life is online, you need email.

The business model for "free" email is either to show you advertising, or to harvest your personal data to target advertising at you elsewhere. I want to explain why that is—and what you can do about it.

We Still Love Our Email

You might not use email to stay in touch with family and friends. For that, lots of people prefer social platforms, text, and other kinds of messaging apps.

But chances are, even when you sign up for those kinds of things, you'll need an email address to get started—most services require email to confirm your new account. It's how they verify you are who you claim to be—or at least how they verify they can contact you when they need to.

More Than Staying In Touch

Email has plenty of other daily uses that aren't "keeping in touch," or "sharing chain letters."

You probably shop, arrange services, or pay bills online. And if you do, email is how you get confirmations of those purchases and payments. It's how you get updates on the status of shipments and deliveries, or hear about changes to terms of service. In your email, you get confirmations of things like tax payments and travel reservations. The entire history of all your financial transactions could be captured in your email.

It's also how lots of us manage doctor appointments, or get notified when test results are in. Our mechanic might send reminders about tuneups and oil changes.

Email is still a critical communication tool in business, despite the growing acceptance of text and chat in the workplace. Chances are, you depend to some extent on email for work—even if it's just to get next week's schedule from your manager.

And email's still the most effective way for businesses to nurture prospective and current customers. It closes new business, helps retain existing business, and assists in up-selling. This is the "transactional" email that says *thank you for your payment ... your order's on its way ... your warranty's expired ... don't forget your flu shot ... time to rotate your tires.*

Every day, between personal, business, and transactional emails, hundreds of billions of email messages are sent.

How, after all these years of evolution and innovation has good old email remained so critical to the web?

It's kind of grandfathered in.

A BRIEF HISTORY OF EMAIL

Like search, email predates the web as we know it. In the periodic table of internet tools, email is carbon: Stable and able to bond with many other elements, it fulfilled our desire to instantly exchange written ideas and information electronically, and was the foundation on which all online life was built.

Of course there were earlier technologies that let us communicate at a distance: The telegraph, Morse code, and the international telex network all delivered on the need to trade messages. But email got its start in the early 1960s. Later than the telegraph, but even before the internet.

In The Beginning There Was Arpanet

Although there had been email systems on large mainframe computers for about a decade, there was no way to communicate between these large host computers. But in 1971, a computer programmer named Ray Tomlinson created a system that sent messages across the prototypical internet.

In his spare time, he co-opted the @ symbol to link the name of the sender to the name of the computer they were using. His system was adopted by users of the Arpanet—the US Department of Defense's research network that grew into the internet.

The system was useful, but clunky. Users needed a better way. So in 1972, Larry Roberts wrote the first Arpanet email manager that let users file, reply to, forward and delete messages. It was better, but it wasn't the easy-to-use tool that we know today. Navigation was still a bit of a technical challenge.

That changed in 1988, when Steve Dorner invented Eudora, which brought an easy to use Macintosh graphical user interface (GUI) to internet email.

Email Joins The Information Superhighway

During the 1980s, the patchwork nature of the Arpanet gradually gave way to a more unified internet—and in 1990, the Arpanet project was formally decommissioned. Just a year later, the Gore Bill became the High Performance Computing Act (HPCA), and opened up a national connected network dubbed by Sen. Gore the "Information

Superhighway." The HPCA enabled cooperation between government, industry, and academia over the internet.

Internet Service Providers (ISPs) owned the high speed cables that had been providing the connectivity the early networks needed. When the public internet opened for business and everyone wanted to be online, ISPs went from an obscure backwater serving academia and oddball businesses to become a hotbed of innovation.

Now that ISPs were delivering the internet to the world, it only seemed natural that—along with the modems, cables and data packets—they would also deliver the carbon of the internet: An email address. Email promised to be the killer app everyone wanted, so ISPs bundled free email with internet access, hoping it would be an incentive to new customers.

Man, It's Clunky

Email from an ISP left something to be desired. The interfaces were clunky and awkward to use. Your email address would be something awful like firstname.lastname123xyz@att.net. And if you moved and had to change your ISP because a different company owned the wires—too bad, you had to change your email address. That meant emailing all your contacts to let them know about your new address, crossing your fingers, and hoping for the best.

In spite of all that, it worked. Customers loved the idea of having free email, even if it was ugly and difficult to use.

In 1996, Microsoft's Internet Explorer browser included a bundled app called Internet Mail and News, staking a claim in the world of email services. It had its limitations, not the least of which was that it ran locally on your computer. If you weren't at your desk, you didn't have access to your email.

Webmail Takes Over

At about the same time, a few companies like HoTMaiL and RocketMail were starting to offer nifty, free, easy-to-use web-based email that could be accessed from anywhere.

These services broke the relationship between your ISP and your email completely, because they didn't handle the dorky email your ISP gave you—they had their own email addresses, unique to their services, meaning you could keep it if you moved ISP. They also had interfaces that were easier to use, and generally just felt more modern.

Even better, they were *free*—because they were supported by ads. Needless to say, free web-based email, unencumbered by ISP lock-in and dopey addresses, was a hit.

Portals Embrace Email

Right alongside that evolution, companies like Lycos, Excite, Yahoo and Microsoft's MSN were defining web search and destination portal services.

In their quest to grow their audiences and provide cool new features that would keep users coming back, they were all acquiring as many startups as they could, including these free email services. In 1997 for example, Yahoo bought RocketMail for $97 million, rebranding it Yahoo Mail.

ISPs were still offering their own free email services, as if they were still an incentive to new customers. But the cost and complexity of providing email was becoming unmanageable. Running an email service requires servers and software and constant maintenance. Overwhelmed by spam, error prone protocols, and clunky, outdated software, ISPs just wanted the pain to stop.

That's when Yahoo stepped in and offered to let ISPs co-brand their Yahoo Mail service. The ISPs could pay Yahoo to take care of the technical mess, and still offer free email to their users.

At about the same time, Microsoft bought Hotmail for $400 million, seeing it as a way to capture users by offering email without having to go through the ISPs.

Free Email For All

As the 1990s came to a close, email as a concept and a tool already had a nearly 40 year history. It had now become an essential service, effectively our online ID, and in the bowels of its databases it held a deep history of all of our digital conversations, financial and otherwise.

Yet in all that time, we had never been required to pay for it—as far as we could see, it had no visible cost at all. Maybe, if we thought about it really hard while squinting into the middle distance, we could almost see that providing it must cost somebody something, but what mattered was *we* weren't paying for it.

It had always been free, and it would always be free. Right?

THE BATTLE FOR THE BUSINESS MODEL

In 2003, Yahoo Mail was the number one email service online. Although Yahoo gave it away free, it was still an important revenue stream, thanks to those licensing agreements with ISP partners. It was a big part of the bottom line, generating more than a billion dollars in revenue at its height.

The other big part of Yahoo's revenue came from display advertising—all those Vegas-like graphical banners and flashing picture ads we talked about in the previous chapter. As the most highly trafficked portal online, it had millions of eyeballs coming for its search engine, email, media, news, and information. So selling display ads was easy and profitable. Yahoo had hundreds and hundreds of employees in the sales force entirely focused on traditional display advertising rather than search advertising.

Not long ago, I talked with Jim Brock—an early Yahoo hire and its first attorney, with a perfect view of the industry's adolescence. "[We] felt more comfortable in that display advertising area, which is the traditional advertising industry," he says. "[Yahoo] was a great place to run a sophisticated ad campaign [and] you could almost guarantee that someone was going to see your ad that day if you were willing to pay enough."

It did try to strike a balance between advertising and user experience in the portal, learning early on that while anything was possible in terms of selling ad space, "You had to confront how advertising could either improve or degrade the user experience." So Yahoo invested heavily in the quest to get as many of their advertisers' messages in front of visitors as possible, without driving them away.

While Yahoo was happily generating email revenue through its ISP partners and display advertising revenue through its portal, it was also considering other options. It considered monetizing email by actually mining the *content* of users' messages and sharing that data with advertisers, but dismissed the idea as too complex.

"We talked about it quite a bit," says Brock. "But remember, the ability to use a set of data like your email for ad targeting was not that sophisticated yet. ... It was very early in the industry and the technology for that just didn't exist inside Yahoo. [We struggled just to] get data on who was coming to our site and what they were doing."

Then Came Gmail

Up to this point, Google had been getting really good at mining user data. But the only ads Google placed inside its own ecosystem were text ads on search results pages—no display ads appeared on any of their other properties. It was, however, using its data to grow a powerful display ad network to sell ads on other publishers' sites.

And like Yahoo, it was also looking for other advertising revenues beyond search and display.

Then in April 2004, Google launched the long-rumored in-house built Gmail service, and it was a game changer. Google had applied the same intense focus on technology that it gave its search tool, and that paid off: Gmail was light, fast, and easy to use.

"When Gmail launched, I'll never forget that day—that was a very difficult day," Brock remembers. "Just because it was so good. Literally the [Yahoo] engineers didn't really know how [Gmail was] that fast, how it was so responsive, how it could work that quickly." Further, he says it brought into focus the difference between being a media company or a technology company. "That was one of those media versus technology moments for Yahoo, and that's why Yahoo! Mail is [now a mere] junkmail inbox."

If Google's technically superior Gmail was going to start bleeding off Yahoo Mail's users, or damaging the value of partnerships with ISPs, Yahoo was going to need other revenue streams to offset that loss. Maybe by digging into users' email data.

Yahoo Declines To Mine

But as attractive as mining users' emails might have been, Yahoo was restricted by two problems.

First, they had clearly fallen behind Google due to a lack of technical development—they just hadn't really seen the size of the opportunity. "I don't think that there was an early recognition of [email] being an advertising medium in the way that Google thinks about it," says Brock. Whereas Google's early focus on the quality of its tools meant accessing and crunching all that data was built into its technological DNA.

And secondly, some people at Yahoo felt like it might be a move that had ethical repercussions—what Brock calls an "ickiness. ... There was a sense that we should let Google take the hit." So Yahoo decided to wait for Google to try email mining first, and see what kind of blowback it suffered.

Google was happy to take that risk, according to Brock. "Google made the first move on that by actually admitting into consciousness the idea that what was in your emails could be used to target advertising to you, and also to show you those advertisements in Gmail."

That first move was greeted like a terrible intrusion at first. But with time, consumers got used to the idea that their emails weren't entirely private. "There were lots of articles in the press about, 'Oh ... this is terrible,'" Brock says. But, "We've become so accustomed to this kind of information use and targeting now, that I don't think people bat much of an eye. People are either in or out, and most people are in."

Richi Jennings, industry analyst and email expert, agrees. He sees it as a generational evolution. "Kids who—all they know is probably a touch screen, not even a physical keyboard—they maybe intuitively understand there's information about them being stored in a huge tome somewhere, and probably don't care. They look at people born a few decades earlier getting distraught about privacy, and they're like, 'Get over it, granddad.'"

Advertisers, of course, weren't at all surprised by Google's move. Paid-search expert Andrew Goodman says, "I remember when it was novel that particularly targeted advertising would show up in a free Gmail account. And I remember thinking that—as an experienced advertiser who understands targeting across the board—it's just a method to show ads, it's not reading your email. [I felt that] people were willfully not understanding ... 'hey, this is why it's free.' So that aspect of Gmail never particularly surprised me."

A Quirk Of History

Of course, it's true that no person at Google is reading your emails, but technically they can, and algorithms certainly do. It's a quirk of the original design of email that the messages are sent in plain text. Back in the 1970s, nobody imagined the possibility that anyone would read them, and the compute power to algorithmically do so didn't exist.

It's as if the USPS went about its daily business of handling utility bills, medical reports, and birthday cards, but nobody had invented envelopes. "It's OK", says the mail carrier, as she hands you a sheaf of rumpled papers, "I didn't look at any of them."

As we're seeing, the nerds who invent something useful are often naive about how it could be exploited. The nerds did their best to close the loophole—messages are now often sent encrypted for their journey across the internet—but the plain-text origin persists. And with it, comes a fundamental lack of security.

We now have envelopes some of the time, but no glue to keep them shut. The algorithms entered the race with a huge trove of data to work on.

Traffic Vs. Data: And The Winner Is...

This moment in email history turned out to be an inflection point in the business of email. It had been a Battle of the Business Model—between "traffic as currency," and "data as currency." By which I mean ...

Traffic as currency: Luring millions of daily users to your media content and free email, so you can sell display advertising to reach them in your portal.

Data as currency: Getting users to stay for your technically advanced email and search, then harvesting their personal data to help sell advertising.

It meant deciding whether you were nurturing a user base that was visiting content and leaving behind journey data, or if you wanted them to stay and use tools, leaving behind their personal data.

In other words, whether you were a media company or a technology company: "The Yahoo story, in the long run," says Brock, "is all about a company trying to decide whether it was a media company or a technology company and never effectively committing to either. But [it became] mostly a media company, which ended up being not how you create a great valuation, and is why Yahoo is essentially gone now."

Google won the Battle of the Business Model—by providing awesome free email, retaining dedicated users who were willing to overlook advertising in exchange for that awesome email, and selling those users' data to the highest bidder.

That decision is what ultimately led to Google's domination of email.

Evolving The Email Harvesting Business

For thirteen years, Google happily harvested the data that revealed our interests and activities, and used what it learned to deliver personalized advertising—both inside Gmail itself and elsewhere.

And although the idea was initially met with dismay, users quickly became used to it and continued using Gmail by the millions.

Business users, however, wanted something with more privacy. So in 2006, Google launched a paid, ad-free email service, as part of a suite of tools with the dorky name of *Google Apps For Your Domain*, which is now simply G Suite. Inside G Suite, paying customers' emails weren't subject to data harvesting for advertising purposes, and no ads appeared inside the email tool. This made good sense for G Suite users, whose business and enterprise email needed an enhanced level of security.

Everyone Wants Security

Over time, though, some G Suite clients felt that the way Google was treating free Gmail users raised questions about the security of the G Suite tool. G Suite users numbered in the millions by this time, and the revenue they provided was not inconsequential. Google felt the heat.

So in 2017, Google decided it was time to treat free Gmail data with the same care as it did inside G Suite.

"G Suite's Gmail is already not used as input for ads personalization," said Diane Green, CEO Google Cloud," and Google has decided to follow suit later this year in our free consumer Gmail service.

Consumer Gmail content will not be used or scanned for any ads personalization after this change. This decision brings Gmail ads in line with how we personalize ads for other Google products. Ads shown are based on users' settings. Users can change those settings at any time, including disabling ads personalization. G Suite will continue to be ad free."

The move appeared to be designed to assuage the concerns of G Suite customers. Of course, it was relatively painless for Google to give up on mining your emails for advertising—in part because it could still track and analyze them for *other* purposes, such as improving your online experience.

Improving Service

Google's *Smart Reply* feature uses algorithms to guess your likely intent in an email, to suggest appropriate responses. Which, of course, means that Google's computers have to read all your email to understand how you think, and what you might really want to say.

The purpose of the harvest has just shifted from "selling to you" to "providing you improved service."

Google Is Everywhere

And it's not just your email: Nowadays if you're a Google user, you're probably using a whole suite of Google tools. You're probably logged in to one or more all the time, more often than not on a mobile device.

As Variety put it, "The Google app on your phone, for example, knows when your next flight is leaving, and whether or not it has been delayed, based on emails you get from airlines and travel booking sites. Similarly, Google Calendar has begun to automatically add restaurant reservations and similar events to your schedule based on the emails you are getting. Google also has for some time automatically scanned emails for links to potentially fraudulent sites, as well as to filter out spam."[19]

In the early days of the mobile web, you might have read lots of news stories about how location tracking was an insidious, invasive problem. It was easy to spin up concern that a mysterious *someone* knew where we were and where we'd been. The reality is, Google is constantly harvesting data about virtually every action you take, from your email, through your phone, to maps and more—cross-referencing it and sharing it across their entire ecosystem.

In this "always logged in" state most of us live in, that morning-til-night data harvesting across every moment of our lives poses a much bigger challenge to privacy than simply where we're standing at the moment, despite the conveniences it might provide.

Has Google Earned Our Trust?

But let's be realistic. Although Google has promised not to look at the contents of your email for advertising purposes, this wasn't the first time it changed the terms, and it may not be the last. It controls its own terms of service, after all, and it's entirely possible that down the line it'll modify them again in a way that makes your emails, historical or otherwise, fair game for mining with the intent to advertise.

"If I were a Google lawyer," says Jennings, "and a Google employee came to me and said, 'Hey, can we change the terms?' I'm sure I could find a way—whether or not it was intended five, ten years ago. I'd be amazed if lawyers for Google or for Alphabet couldn't find a way to do that—a way that they claimed was legal."

If you don't want your historical emails sitting in your inbox for Google to mine, you can delete them, sending them to the Trash folder until you click *Empty Trash now*, or they're automatically purged forever. (Alternatively, you can archive them, saving them for historical purposes and at least getting them out of your inbox. But so long as they're not completely deleted, it's important to remember that the data is still there, and it's still available to be tapped and used, should Google ever decide they want to do so in the future.)

Google Invited Strangers In The Back Door

As it turns out, despite claims of transparency, Google has a history of sneaking data mining in where you don't realize they've done so. In fact, they weren't the only player looking into your emails. All this time, they had also been allowing access to third-party developers who were creating apps that plugged into Gmail so they could provide enhanced features that Gmail lacked out of the box. And some of those third-parties were up to no good.

Now, it was Gmail users who were *choosing* to install these plugin apps, and they were accepting the terms and conditions—even if they weren't really reading them. So they felt confident that—like Google's own data practices—no real people were reading their emails.

That's what really seemed to matter: Users were okay with computers peeking at their data. But real people? Not so much.

Unfortunately, that confidence wasn't always well founded. Many plugin developers weren't leaving the scanning to the computers: Some had real, live people sifting through and reading the email.

Some plugin developers were even selling the data they collected to yet more third-parties—companies that Gmail users hadn't intended to have access—and who knows what their policies might be.

As Jennings says, "Maybe I don't care that a computer knows that I visit these websites every morning, but maybe I *do* care if a black-mailer knows I visit this particular website every morning."

Google, it turned out, was aware of all this secret data sharing: It was part of their agreement with the developers. This practice continued for another year after Google had announced their own internal changes to Gmail's data management.

The Political Hand Grenade

Then came the Cambridge Analytica debacle. The news that app developers had nefariously harvested data from millions of Facebook users for political purposes shone a spotlight on the issue of just how much access third-party developers had to user data, and what they were really doing with it.

When users learned that Gmail's app partners were using data in ways that felt too intrusive and manipulative, they didn't trust Google's apps any more. So in 2018, Google stepped in with sweeping changes to the way it worked with app developers. Google announced in part that developers "may not transfer or sell the data for other purposes [and must] meet minimum security standards to minimize the risk of data breach. Apps will be asked to demonstrate secure data handling."

WHAT IT LOOKS LIKE NOW

Google's free Gmail product has evolved. Partly because users started looking for more transparency, and partly because the growth of other revenue streams allowed Google to stop mining user contents. Now it focuses on mining user *behavior* to build better tools across its entire suite, such as the ads you click on, the purchases you make, or the sites you search and visit.

Yes, you'll still see ads in your free Gmail inbox, but they're no longer driven by your email's contents. Instead, they're driven by other online interactions you have.

The third parties that Google does allow into the data stream are much more strictly managed, in an effort to ensure they only take what data they need to deliver the features they promise. And they have to agree not to share your data with other players.

So does that mean that the world of free email is harmless now?

Email Is Not Free To Provide

Whether it's a behemoth like Gmail or Yahoo, or a smaller provider like ProtonMail or Zoho, offering an email service is complex and expensive.

Like carbon, it's grimy to handle: It's a terrible mess of codes and licenses and permissions and storage. But process it correctly, and it can become diamonds. That's what free email providers are doing behind the scenes: getting their hands dirty turning that internet carbon into the easy-to-use diamonds that we depend on every day.

But it all comes at a cost: There are startup costs, capital costs, and ongoing costs at every stage of the email-providing business. That's why the ISPs decided to get out.

Even a small niche provider has to rent big, fast servers connected to the internet via fast pipes. They can cost thousands of dollars per month, and they'll only support a finite number of email address-es and all their accumulated historical email.

The more storage it offers each customer, the more the cost ris-es. So to service a meaningful number of customers, it needs many servers and a lot of cash.

Plus there's the software that runs the email. Paying engineers to write and maintain a custom email platform gets expensive fast: Talented engineers aren't cheap.

A provider might decide to license its email software from some-one else, which comes with its own licensing fees, or use an open source solution. But neither of those paths come free. Whether us-ing licensed or open source code, a provider still needs someone in-house to manage the software, install updates, and fix all the hic-cups and glitches and bugs that are sure to come along. Which still means talented and expensive engineers.

Free Email Users Are Not The Customer

Big or small, your email provider has bills to pay. And like any business, they pay the bills by focusing most of their energy and re-sources on their paying customers.

When a service is free, you and I aren't the customers. In an ad-vertising ecosystem, the customers are the advertisers and data bro-kers who are willing to pay the email provider to reach you and me. Consequently, they're the ones the email provider pays attention to.

They're the ones the sales force wakes up every day, ready to take care of.

Of course, the provider does spend time and resources on new features and improved interfaces to make our experience better. But that's to keep the service easy to depend on and hard to leave, so that we'll continue to provide the data their advertising customers need.

And there's probably some kind of user support dedicated to helping us when our email goes wonky. But chances are the "help" page will point us at an FAQ first. Then at an automated chat bot. Then at a "community" forum—of other customers who work for free. Then at an email address. And lastly, at live help. Maybe.

Whereas if an *advertiser* wants to talk with a real person, I can promise you there's a red phone somewhere with a live sales agent on the line ready to take care of the customer.

So while providers may or may not be using our email contents to target ads, in the end they're still beholden to their paying customers. And no matter who's providing the service, when you're getting something for free, you're not the customer.

Where Email Is Not The Norm

I do want to acknowledge there are places in the world where email isn't ubiquitous. China is the largest example: There, instant messaging—largely via the WeChat app—is far and away more common than email. It's used both by individuals and by businesses.

In fact, WeChat takes the place of multiple apps: It can be used for shopping, exchanging documents, sending and receiving payments, and more. For larger businesses there's a corporate version called WeChat Work, as well as competitors DingTalk and Lark.

"WeChat, as a messaging platform, demands less formal working time than email," said Zhong Ling, of the Cheung Kong Graduate School of Business, talking to the BBC. "This informality makes people more likely to respond instantaneously. ... The demand for [an] immediate response is motivated by the cultural and business environment in China."[20]

It's not that people in China don't use email at all. It's just that those who do are far less likely to check it or reply, compared to their Western counterparts.

In the US, on the other hand, email is used by more than 90% of internet users—even more popular than online search. For those users, email isn't going anywhere soon.

VISIONS FOR TOMORROW

Despite the huge shadows that giants like Gmail, Yahoo Mail, and Outlook have historically cast, there have always been loads of other providers out there. Big or small, free or paid—or somewhere in between.

In the past few years, I've seen the internet winds blowing more strongly towards ad-free privacy, and more paid email providers who want to have you as their customer. It's a trend driven by people who have intimate inside knowledge of how the industry works, how the data flows, who the customers really are, and how the users are treated. They've got concerns about privacy and security, and they're dedicated to making a change by providing options that address the issues that more and more people are finding problematic.

Being The Change They Want To See

Hushmail is proof that we've always had alternatives to the free behemoths. It's been around since 1999—that's 21 years of offering a paid, private, secure email service that maintains your data integrity.

"Everyone is entitled to their email privacy," says Hushmail. "Take back control of your data and experience a clean inbox with no advertising. Choose which emails you want to send using our powerful encryption and keep your most personal conversations private and confidential." At the time of this writing, Hushmail doesn't offer a free service: All access is paid.[21]

More recently, in the summer of 2013, **ProtonMail** was founded by a group of scientists who met at CERN. "We are scientists, engineers, and developers, drawn together by a shared vision of protecting civil liberties online." says ProtonMail. "Our goal is to build an internet that respects privacy and is secure against cyber-attacks. We are committed to developing and widely distributing the tools necessary to protect your data online."

ProtonMail is a hybrid provider: It offers a basic free service, because it believes, "Privacy is a fundamental human right so we provide free accounts as a public service." It invites free users to support their efforts by "telling your friends and family about ProtonMail, or making a donation."[22] Paying customers get more features and storage, and the company nudges you in that direction.

Most recently, in 2020, **Hey** Email launched. It's from the same company that built Basecamp, a highly successful business management software suite. Hey is a whole new email platform designed specifically to protect customer data.

According to the Hey Manifesto, "There are lots of 'free' email services out there, but free email costs you one of most valuable things you have – your privacy and your personal information. We're not interested in your personal data. It's always yours, never ours. We simply charge a flat, all-inclusive fee. ... That makes our business work without having to sell your data, advertise to you, or otherwise engage in unscrupulous marketing tactics. We make a great product, you pay a reasonable price for it – that's fair for everyone."[23]

Clearly, email providers who view their users as customers aren't a new phenomenon. But it's a growing sentiment, and may represent a larger movement across a variety of internet services as business models evolve to respect our data and treat us as customers—in the truest sense of the word.

DOES ALL THIS MATTER?

If you've got an online life, you need an email address.

Historically the business model for "big email" has been either to show you advertising inside the tool itself, or to harvest your personal data to target advertising at you elsewhere.

Either that matters to you, or it doesn't.

If it doesn't—no worries. Some folks, perhaps especially younger users as Jennings says, are perfectly all right having their data mined, and appreciate seeing advertising they feel is personalized and relevant to them.

If this is you, what matters is that you aren't using Gmail or Yahoo Mail just because you thought that's how it had to be—because you didn't know you had options. If you've read this far, weighed all the evidence, and considered the risks, yet you've still decided to leave things be, then you've made an intentional choice.

On the other hand, your priority might be to protect your privacy, your data, and the content of your personal communications. You might see value in creating a balanced relationship between yourself and your provider, becoming the customer by paying for the product.

If that's the case, then you have another intentional choice to make: You need to decide where to take your email business.

Wait! Can't I Pay My Free Provider And Become The Customer?

It might seem logical to just offer your free email service money to pay for privacy. Sadly, that's not a likely option.

If you're with one of the big free email players, you probably don't have a reasonable option to pay for the service. At the time I'm writing this, for instance, there is no way to pay Google just for Gmail and get out of being the product.

You can pay Google for the entire G Suite and get ad-free email. But that's way more than just Gmail. It's a business solution, and it includes Gmail, docs, spreadsheets, remote meeting tools, forms, scripts, and lots of other things you might not need. Plus you'll have to bring your own domain name, like a business. So even if you pay, you'll still end up with a new email address that you'll have to update across all your online services, and tell all your friends and colleagues and your Dear Aunt Ethylene about.

Yahoo also offers paid versions of its email service: Yahoo Small Business Mail which offers customized domains but still serves ads "to keep prices as low as possible,"[24] and Yahoo Mail Pro, which is ad free[25] (good luck finding that buried on the site, by the way). As regards data collection though, I can find nothing promising either paid version of Yahoo Mail won't still mine your data.

FACILITATING INTENTIONAL CHANGE

I expect more than half the readers have just thrown down this book in despair, because this sounds like it's going to be too much work. But for those of you still with me, it's really not that hard. I've done it, and you can too. So if you're ready to find a provider who will see you as their customer, this is your roadmap to intentional change.

For the sake of clarity, we'll assume you're using Gmail, though the process is the same for any ad supported email.

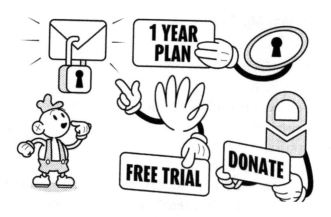

Step One: Choose A New Provider

First you need to choose your new email provider. There's a lot to choose from that don't sell your attention—we've talked about a few already. Most either offer a free trial period or a simplified basic version, and it's good enough for you to kick the tires.

I've summarized some good choices below to get you started, but this can't possibly be an exhaustive list, so doing some research on your own might yield even more options. After all, this is *your* privacy we're talking about, so you need to make your own informed choice that fits your unique needs.

Here's a selection of ad-free email vendors, offering a variety of prices and features.

Ad Free Email	Cost	Mailbox storage
Fastmail	$30/year to $90/year	2 GB to 100 GB
Gandi	Free (no ads); Multi-tiered pricing	3 GB (free), 50 GB
HEY	Free 14-day trial $99/year	100 GB
Hushmail	Free 14-day trial $49.98 year (Premium)	10 GB (Premium)
Mailfence	Free (no ads) €2.5/month (Entry) €7.5/month (Pro) €25/month (Ultra)	500 MB (free) 5 GB (Entry) or 20 GB (Pro) or 50 GB (Ultra)
OnMail	Personal Free (no ads); Premium options $5 to $20/user monthly	10 GB (free) to 1 TB
Posteo	€1/month to €1,45/month	2 GB storage (can be increased)
ProtonMail	Free (no ads); Multi-tiered pricing	500 MB (free) 5 to 20 GB
Runbox	Minimum (micro plan): $19.95/year or €14.95/year	1 GB (micro plan)
Tutanota	Free (no ads) €12 year (Premium)	1 GB Free and Premium, 10GB Teams. Can be upgraded to 10GB, 100GB, or 1TB.
Zoho Mail	Personal Free (no ads); Premium options $24 to $99/user yearly	5 GB "Lite". "Standard": 10 & 15 GB

CantSpyMy@email.private

Step Two: Choose Your New Email Address

One thing you'll immediately notice is that because these services are smaller, there's a lot more catchy names available. Instead of having to settle for johnnyonions7438@gmail.com you can be johnny.onions@fastmail.com or maybe onions@protonmail.com.

And don't be afraid to be creative. If you want an address that really represents you, go for johnnythewriter@fastmail.com or veterinarian.onions@protonmail.com. The email world is your oyster now. Your address will be a lot less generic, and there's a certain cachet to having a distinctive email address that's not @gmail.com.

Step Three: Install Apps Or Configure Clients

Your new email tool probably works just fine in a browser, and that's probably all you need. But if they offer any specific apps for mobile or desktop you might at least take a look. The apps might make the interface easier to use, especially on a phone.

Next you might want to configure your existing mail client; for instance Mail on iOS and macOS, Outlook on Windows. Your provider should provide a step-by-step guide to get this done. Doing so creates a single inbox across your old and new account, with both historical email and new incoming mail sitting in one place. But you might find keeping your new email inbox separate from your old email helps keep the transition sane.

Step Four: Update Your Contact Info For Online Services

I recommend using your new address alongside the ad supported one for quite a while, and gradually switching things over. I'm willing to bet you've got a lot more logins and passwords for all kinds of services and memberships than you think you do, and it doesn't need to be overwhelming. It's much easier to chip away at the job in small pieces than to tackle everything in one go.

For each online service you want to update, you'll need to login, go to your account settings, and change the email address. Sometimes you'll have to go through a confirmation process, where they send you an email to click on proving you own the new address. In that case, I'd add your new email address as a second contact email, confirm it when the confirmation email arrives, and then remove the old one.

Start With The Critical Financial Accounts: You may only have the energy or time to tackle a few at first, so start with the important ones like banks, credit cards, the IRS or your state tax board. Don't forget accounts like Amazon, Netflix, Hulu, or your phone service.

Anyplace where important financial information is stored, you make frequent purchases, or payments are automatically applied to active credit cards. The contents of those emails are especially sensitive as the presence of dollar amounts says a great deal about you.

Private health information is also critical, so put health provider accounts at the top of the list. And don't forget about things like legal services, utilities, or your department of motor vehicles. And of course from here on out, any new critical accounts you create should use your new email address.

Then Tackle Everyday Accounts: Then move on to the more everyday kinds of accounts like social media profiles, Craigslist, travel sites, your local movie theater updates, and all the other mundane places you've probably used your old free email. Again, you'll be surprised just how many there are once you get started. That's why taking just a few at a time will make it easier.

Check Your Password Manager: But no matter how good your memory is, you're not going to remember every single place you've used your email. So here's a tip: check your password manager. This is the widget that pops up when you register on a new site or log into an existing account, offering to remember the password for you.

Your browser or operating system may have come with one installed, or you might have added one somewhere along the way. They're very handy and safe, although they shouldn't be used for bank passwords.

If you've ever used your password manager, it can display a list of login IDs, which is often your email, for every site it's remembered. Spend just an hour some afternoon working through the list and updating all those lingering services. I'd make a spreadsheet somewhere to keep track of what you've changed, and what needs changing, just to make sure you don't miss anything important.

Oh, and by the way, now's a good time to make intentional decisions about just which of these sites and services you still really need, and to purge a few of those memberships and newsletters.

Step Five: Tell Your Friends And Family

Eventually you need to inform your friends and family of the new account, and this is surely the most involved process. Reminding Dear Aunt Ethylene for the 15th time is not to be relished.

Fortunately, there's a simple trick that will do almost all the work for you: a vacation auto-responder. You've seen these before, when you email someone and get an instant reply explaining they're at the beach for a few weeks. Your old email address very likely has this feature, so take a few minutes to find it, and insert a message telling everyone about your new email address. Then, when Dear Aunt Ethylene sends you a birthday greeting, she'll get an automated reply explaining that you've moved and how to find you.

After a few months, spending just minutes at a time, the majority of stuff is switched. If there are any remaining websites and services tied to your old email address, I'd assume they're the ones you don't plan on staying connected to, are rarely used, or easily ignored.

Step Six: Importing Your Old Emails

Your new paid email inbox is probably pretty empty and lonely looking. All your historical email is still sitting in your old free account. Now you have to decide whether you want to import them to your new service in a giant transfer, or leave them orphaned in the ad supported account.

Some people prefer to make a clean break, like selling their old furniture when they move, and others can't bear to part with that ancient, lovingly hand crafted, first email to a high school crush. If you think you really want those old threads in your new email account, you'll have to find a way to get them there.

Some paid email systems can be configured to suck the emails from the old ad supported account, but beware that this can expose your old login credentials to the new provider.

Another option is that the ad supported system might be able to automatically forward any incoming emails to your new address. This process leaves the old inactive conversations where they are, but forwards new responses to ongoing threads. And it doesn't expose any credentials, so it's less risky. But do keep checking your new spam folder, because some spam filters love to munch on forwarded mail (of course, you should be checking it anyway).

Step Seven: Should You Keep Your Ad Supported Email?

You might be thinking about keeping the old ad supported account as a dumping ground for junk—stuff like frequent flier newsletters, occasional free offers etc. And you might just be having separation anxiety from the decades of forgotten conversations stored there.

This is perfectly natural, but remember that being logged in to the ad supported interface also keeps you logged in to the advertising and search ecosystem. At the very least, log in only when you must, and log out when you're done reminiscing.

However, for a truly clean break, it's better to wean yourself off completely and have no free services at all.

What About Google Docs?

Many people use Google Docs, and it's a crafty way Google can keep you logged in and handing over data. So what happens if you give up your Gmail address?

Well, one option is to download all your docs and then you own them. If you can't, or still need to collaborate with others, here's a secret: Your Google account through which you access docs doesn't need to be tied to a Gmail account. You can change it to your new private email account where Google can't peek. You're still handing over some of your data, but less than if you stick with Gmail.

WHAT'S NEXT

Thinking this hard and this long about something as mundane as email may feel like a tale told by Macbeth's idiot—full of sound and fury, signifying nothing. And maybe it is.

But it's not just about email. It's about making intentional choices regarding how you transact your online life.

The thing I want you to understand is that you've got options. You always have. Way more options than "should I use Gmail or Yahoo?"

The option to protect yourself has always been there. And because you've got options, you get to decide what happens with your privacy, your data, and the content of your personal communications.

I also want you to know that the web of data mining is woven far and wide, and extends far beyond your email. The advertising technology (ad tech) industry, with its shared data and networks of ad distributors, keeps a close eye on all your online activity, and sells it to the highest bidders.

Because it can be harder to recognize that data harvesting when it's happening, it's important to understand how ad-tech works—so that's where we're headed next.

3. AD TECH

I know it's happened to you. You visited a website that sells shoes, clicked around a little, and then left.

You didn't buy any shoes. You might not even really be in the market for shoes. Window shopping is still a *thing*, right?

Then you hopped on Facebook or Twitter, or maybe surfed over to a news site—and lo and behold, there's an ad for those shoes from the site you just visited. Maybe there's ads from other shoe sellers too. They all know your personal business, and they all want to close that sale.

What The Hell? Are These People Psychic?

Not really. It's somewhat less mysterious than that. Your online life is peppered with data mining and tracking code, in obvious, subtle and even invisible forms, secretly monitoring your movements and collecting your personal data to make the ads even more invasive and creepy.

The thing is, advertising technology (ad tech) is super complex and specialized. Websites are in the business of publishing content, attracting visitors, and somehow making money, which almost always means ... wait for it ... selling ads.

So of course they want the ads, they just don't want to be in the difficult business of managing them. Even the advertisers themselves don't have the tools to make it happen. They're in the business of selling shoes, and really don't want to be messing about collecting data and figuring out which websites to advertise on.

Luckily for the both of them, there's an entire industry dedicated to the task of distributing ads around the web. Sharing and selling data about you and me—and using the data to find us online, inserting ads into whatever pages we're viewing—is big-league business.

Huge, in fact.

The Chase Is On

But maybe it's not so lucky for us, because we get chased around by shoe salesmen armed with our private information—and nobody likes that.

So who's responsible for this mess? It's easy to imagine a giant conspiracy, because it feels like we're under surveillance. But nobody planned it that way. The law of unintended consequences got us here.

To figure out how, let's start at the beginning.

THE WEB BEFORE THE WEB

Before the web we know today, there was another, very different project in the works. Like the web we know, it aimed to link all the world's documents and files, making them available for users everywhere.

Project Xanadu was the brainchild of Ted Nelson, an early pioneer in Information Technology (he was a philosopher and sociologist as well). In the early 1960's he wrote a series of papers outlining his vision for a system that would organize complex file structures and provide links between documents.

In his publications, Nelson coined the terms "hypertext" and "hyperlink," imagining the connection of specific strings of text within documents and accessible on a theoretical worldwide computer network (although he's rightly credited with the hyperwords, he "stood on the shoulders of hypergiants," such as Vannevar Bush and Doug Engelbart). We still use those terms today, but in a very different way and context than Nelson intended them.

Despite his counter-culture origins, Nelson recognized that protecting copyright and ownership is important, because information has inherent value (as we'll see later in the book, it "wants to be expensive"). Protection and attribution of intellectual property ownership is a *business* problem, and to solve for the business problem you must solve for the payment problem.

Payment Is The Problem

So Nelson also baked into Xanadu the idea of content monetization, using "a complete business system for electronic publishing ... with a win-win set of arrangements, contracts and software for the sale of copyrighted material in large and small amounts." Users could "jump from document to document, following links and buying small pieces as they go."

Xanadu would guarantee that the owner of any information was "paid their chosen royalties on any portions of their documents, no matter how small," through payments as small as a fraction of a penny ("micropayments").[26]

Xanadu would put content owners in control of their property, and its price. But 30 years later, the web still doesn't support micropayments, nor robust security. However, I'd submit that Bitcoin and other cryptocurrencies go a fair way toward that vision of secure, auditable transactions—they've certainly captured the imagination of a passionate following.

Project Xanadu imagined an elegant future web built on the simple premise of making content available with permissions, payment, and protection of ownership and authorship. However, it hasn't achieved its goals (so far). There are still a few websites dedicated to the project's history, and even a community hopeful that the vision might find a foothold. But it's unlikely to ever unseat the sort of web we have today.

What We Got Instead

Perhaps unfortunately, the web we know today wasn't built on Nelson's concepts of the protected distribution of content, but instead grew out of academia.

There's no business problem to solve, no "tracking and reimbursement" model to bake into the architecture to be sure the authors are paid for all their hard work. The academic model doesn't hinge on compensation going back to authors, and so the web we know didn't need to be designed to solve that problem—a choice that the Xanadu Project sees as "a diabolical dumbdown of our original hypertext idea. [It] ignored the fundamental issues of version management, rights management, and the origins of quotations."[27]

Rather than Nelson's code framework, the web was built using Hypertext Markup Language (HTML). That's the code all websites are built out of today—and your browser interprets that code to display the lovely sites you see.

As I hinted earlier, the process used to insert ads into the websites your browser displays had nothing originally to do with advertising. It's actually that unintended consequence I mentioned earlier: an artifact of the way web pages ended up being programmed with

HTML, and the way browsers display images. Think of it as a vestigial organ that can leave empty rectangles in the page—rectangles that advertisers were only too happy to fill.

To understand how that happened, you first need to understand how browsers interpreted that programming.

A VERY SHORT HISTORY OF BROWSERS

In the beginning, the web was an academic and research exercise.

In 1990, Tim Berners-Lee, the man considered the father of the web, built the very first web browser (more than a decade before Queen Elizabeth II dubbed him a Knight Commander). He named it **WorldWideWeb**, and it initially ran on NeXT computers—interconnected workstations used in higher education and business. (Be sure to remember Sir Tim's name: He's still highly influential regarding where the web may be headed in the future, and we'll be discussing him again.)

Mosaic Blew Our Minds

Then **Mosaic** came along, in 1993. As the first consumer-friendly web browser, it just blew things up. A project of the University of Illinois' National Center for Supercomputing Applications (NCSA), it quickly became the "killer app."

Mosaic was the first to integrate an easy to user graphical user interface (GUI) *and in-line images* into one browser. Yes, it's hard to believe, but 30 years ago, you had to open images in a separate program—they didn't show up on the same page as the text. Mosaic changed all that.

This web innovation—to deliver images in context with the text— was crucial, as we'll see later.

53%   **34%**   **4.3%**   **2.9%**

Now There Are Four

Since Mosaic made that important leap, there have been countless twists and turns in the browser market over the last 30 years. I *could* reel off a history of Line Mode, Midas, Viola, Lynx, OS/2 WebExplorer, Spyglass, Netscape, OmniWeb, Udi, Camino, and WWWを見る ... but I won't.

But I do want to note that some browser makers tried to charge money for their software—however, the market just couldn't sustain a paid browser no matter how good it was. From our perspective in the 2020s, it seems bizarre they would even try, but I promise you it was definitely A *Thing* that happened. And so were: browsers monetized by showing ads outside the page, browsers that sneakily replaced the on-page ads with their own, and of course the huge rise and crushing fall of Microsoft as the 800 lb gorilla of the browser market.

To cut a *very* long story short, there are now four browsers that own nearly the entire market.

Chrome Is King

Google Chrome comes in first, with nearly 53% of the market. It's free to install (and comes with every Android phone). It makes its money by auctioning off its search engine recommendations and driving data collection for Google's ad network. It's a revenue monster, defaulting as it does to Google Search, which directs web surfers to results pages littered with Google's ads.

...and So Is Google Search

Apple Safari is in second place with just over 31%. Apple provides its browser free, wrapped into macOS and iOS, reinforcing Apple's overall brand message of privacy and security. Since Apple has no search engine of its own, Google pays them to be the default in Safari, keeping Google Search entrenched.

The Plucky Fox

Next comes the open-source Firefox at 4.3%. The browser comes from the Mozilla Foundation—a non-profit that makes its income from corporate sponsorships, donations, and by selling its default search engine placement (mostly to Google, Yahoo, Yandex, and Baidu). Its DNA is from Netscape, a now-defunct company founded in 1994 by the leader of the Mosaic team.

800 lb Gorilla to Also-Ran

Microsoft crushed Netscape, once the dominant browser, by bundling Internet Explorer free with Windows, and I find it incredible that they have slipped from total dominance to fourth place. Today Microsoft Edge barely hangs on with 2.9%. Internet Explorer still clings to another 2.4% even though it's no longer in active development.

Microsoft's browsers are still free, and of course they direct what users they have to Microsoft's own Bing search engine, which collects search and behavioral data for their own ad network.

The remainder of the US market is split up among literally dozens of small independent companies like Opera and Brave, and volunteer projects like Basilisk and Pale Moon.

The Difference Is The Privacy

While the top four browser brands are in competition for your attention, they're weirdly interdependent as well. They all use bits and pieces and variations of the same code DNA. Their big differences are in the proprietary privacy and security features they each provide, and how well they control third-party products like extensions and plug-ins that can compromise your privacy.

So while it may feel like they're all different flavors of vanilla, one might be very much better than another, depending on your personal preferences.

HOW THE RECTANGLES CHANGED EVERYTHING

Okay, *now* for the advertising bit.

Remember that the first browsers were just designed to show text? There might be images associated with a document, but they weren't shown inline with the text—they were downloaded and displayed in a separate program outside the browser.

But the world of browsers changed: Mosaic brought text and images together, so we could enjoy an easy-to-drive browser with a friendly interface that turned all that HTML nonsense into a beautiful website, with words and pictures all magically arriving together like a virtual newspaper.

And this is where that accidental artifact comes into play: that vestigial organ of code that unintentionally opened the door for third parties like advertisers to insert their own messages into somebody else's website.

It's the images.

Images Can Come From Anywhere

Actually, what really matters is *where* the images are hosted.

We talked about the HTML code that web pages are made of. The HTML file contained everything the browser needed to decipher and display the page—everything except the images. Images are not text, they're huge blocks of unintelligible binary data.

Rather than shoehorn it into the HTML file, the web designer defines where the image should appear, how big it should be, and where the browser can load it from. The browser goes there, grabs the image, and inserts it into its spot on the page.

This is the holdover—the artifact from those early days when academics didn't mind waiting for charts and graphs to load. It remained valuable, because we were all on those slow, squealing dial-up connections. Text loads faster than images, so the text parts of the page would load first, leaving empty rectangles that would be filled when the graphics eventually appeared. Even if the image somehow wouldn't load, the page would maintain its beautifully organized design and the browser would simply display a gray square because it knew the size and position of the intended image.

But here's the thing: The image didn't have to be on the same server as the HTML file.

The image could actually be stored anywhere: even on another website's server, at a completely different address, owned by a different company. In other words, the images aren't restricted to coming from the "first party" that you see in the browser address bar—the party you've chosen to visit and are expecting to receive content from. They can come from a third party *anywhere on the internet.*

So what? That first-party versus third-party distinction has massive ramifications in how the ad business developed.

Sell The Rectangles

The internet had ushered in the era of free, but had failed to resolve who would pay.

As the internet grew, and as we searched with our free search engines and emailed with our free email and browsed with our free browsers, the websites we visited got more and more complex. The publishers—the people or companies that own websites and publish content onto them—knew they were in a race to suck in as many visitors as they could to satisfy their investors.

Just as with search engines and email and browsers, the cost of generating that content and storing all that data on banks of servers got more and more expensive.

And *somebody* needed to pay.

But consumers weren't interested in paying to visit these sites. Although in earlier decades they would have paid for cable TV or bought a magazine or purchased a newspaper subscription without thinking twice about it, they'd already been trained to expect everything online to be free. So the publishers had all this content going out, and nobody willing to pay for it.

Investors didn't care about all that. "Find another way to make money," they said. Luckily, because those rectangles on a web page could be filled from anywhere, publishers could insert revenue streams into them instead of images. So the publishers began designing their pages with empty rectangles, and selling the right to fill them.

Early Online Ads

The very first ever banner ads appeared on the Wired magazine website—at the time called *HotWired*—on October 27, 1994. Among these was an ad for AT&T, which essentially dared the user to click on it (not only was the entire concept of a banner ad new, but so was the clickthrough).

The hope was to show people how companies might provide value through advertising, and the landing page offered not only information about AT&T, but links to some of the finest museums in the world where users could take virtual tours right from their desktop. If you're curious what it looked like, it's archived at TheFirstBannerAd. com along with the landing page that it led to when clicked (warning: It's ugly, but then so was pretty much every web page in 1994).

One person credited with helping create that first campaign is Joe McCambley. Nearly 20 years later, in 2013, he wrote in the Harvard Business Review that in those heady days he and his colleagues had actually imagined advertising could be a valuable service. Small agencies like his were the first to experiment with online ads, and their angle of attack was experimental and almost altruistic.

As he recalled, "We knew that if we asked ourselves, 'How can we help people?' rather than, 'What can we sell people?' we could rewire people's brains to seek out brand experiences, rather than run from them."

Just a few years later, traditional advertising companies saw the business opportunity to be had online and entered the fray with their old-school thinking. Said McCambley, the industry was suddenly "back to delivering what TV spots, radio spots, and print ads had delivered for years: sales messages."[28]

Once again, we see an early internet technology that started out trying to make the online experience optimum for users, but succumbing to the lure of truckloads of fast money—no matter the cost to our experience.

In those first few years, advertisers simply paid flat rates to place their ads in the empty rectangles, much as they had for newspapers or radio. Yahoo was one of the first big online destinations that could sell its own empty rectangles, because it was one of the few big online sites that had its own ad sales force—and they sold those rectangles like crazy.

Dana Todd's ad agency worked with Yahoo a lot in those early days: "We had a personal rep [who was] very much like a standard media rep," she says. Yahoo treated advertising sales in the same way traditional print sales had been managed for decades before. There were standard ad sizes, and fixed rates for fixed periods of time. "You'd have a quick conversation, [Yahoo] would tell you their rates, and then we'd send an insertion order."

That old-school print advertising mentality, along with the built-in restrictions of HTML, web page designs, and empty rectangles, is why all the ads you see today have a few standard sizes from website to website—an advertiser can make an ad a certain size and know that even if it's placed in a hundred different sites, it'll work on all of them, without breaking the layout of their pages.

Let Someone Else Sell The Rectangles

That accidental ability to stuff rectangles with content from anywhere left the door open for anyone to insert ads. A publisher might find itself juggling relationships with dozens or hundreds of advertisers, so for lots of publishers, farming out ad sales and the insertion of the ads to someone else was an easy and attractive transition.

After all, most publishers really wanted to be in the business of generating content and building their audiences, not selling ads. For many, that meant getting rid of internal sales forces and delegating the sales of ads to a third party.

Since then, the business of delivering online advertising has become so convoluted, it's almost impossible to explain here. But I'll start with the most basic pieces and we'll see where it goes from there.

It Starts With The Data

The process starts with the data. If you've read this far, you know that search engines and email providers and browsers are constantly tracking and mining your behavior. You also know the data is used to target ads to relevant consumers like you and me.

If a publisher is gathering their own data and selling their own ads, they have the information they need to target us. But most publishers don't sell their own ad space anymore, they farm the job out to an *ad network.*

To do that, whatever data the publisher has gathered about their users gets combined with data from all the other places it's been mined to build as accurate a profile of you and me as can possibly be built. Data gets gathered up from our search history, our browsing habits, or ads we've clicked on before.

The data comes from companies you've probably heard of: Experian, Equifax, Mastercard, and so on. It also comes from companies you might not have heard of, such as Datalogix, TransUnion, and Infogroup.

These companies in turn supply the data to data aggregators like Quantcast, Eyeota, and Neustar. From there it can go through more hands, before it finally gets to the ad networks and exchanges.

Ad Networks Match Ads To Traffic

An ad network's job is to connect advertisers with publishers that want ads. There can be ad networks for TV, print media, and online, but the phrase is pretty much used exclusively for the online industry now.

Advertisers work with networks to target their ads to sites that cater to audiences the advertiser wants to reach. So if they're selling running shoes, they might target sites about jogging. (As the old saying goes: If you want to sell premium whiskey, advertise in golf magazines.)

Of course, it can get way more specific than that: Advertisers might define gender, income, location, credit score, whether the prospect is a homeowner ... all kinds of things. Thanks to all the data that's been gathered and shared, the ad networks have all the info they need to find the audience that best matches an advertiser's very specific criteria.

Traditionally, the advertiser pays the ad network based on how many times their ad is displayed—the Cost Per Thousand, or CPM. Alternatively, the fee can be based on how many times the ad is actually clicked—the Cost Per Click, or CPC. The network shares that revenue with the website owner, so if a jogging site has tons of visitors and any of them see or click an ad, both the ad network and the jogging website make a small amount of money.

Advertisers like this arrangement because they don't need to be in the business of finding the right websites and people to target.

Site owners like it because they don't need to have a Yahoo-sized ad sales team or manage ads themselves.

There are dozens of powerful, successful ad networks managing advertisements for millions of marketers, focusing on different niches or different media. They're all collecting and storing and parsing data about you and me every time we interact with an ad, and they're sharing that data back and forth to find just the right ads to match our interests and past behavior everywhere we go on the web.

All this happens in less time than it takes you to blink, and you'll never know the process took place. All you see is a website with ads for the shoes that you looked at last week.

A Picture Is Worth A Thousand Ad Networks

Everything I've just explained is painfully oversimplified, but you don't really need to understand the nitty-gritty of an entire industry to understand that *your attention* is being sold to the highest bidder—virtually every second you spend on the web.

In reality, your activity and marketers' ads are parsed and managed and matched by first-party ad servers, third-party ad servers, and supply-side platforms (SSPs)—plus of course the ad networks and the ad exchanges that aggregate them. To keep things ever so slightly more simple, I'm just saying "ad networks," but for our purposes, you can assume that phrase includes all the permutations of technology and services that drive the industry.

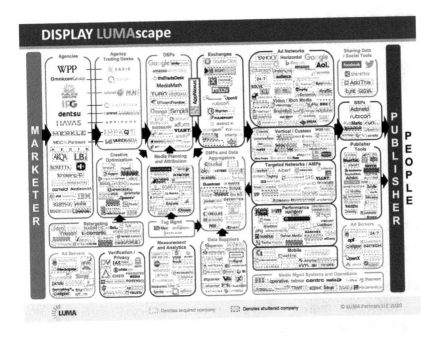

Source: LUMA Partners LLC. Copyright © 2020. All rights reserved.
lumapartners.com/content/lumascapes/display-ad-tech-lumascape

If you're interested in seeing the vast array of interconnected services that parse and share data to help marketers target customers, you can spend a minute or ten digging into this chart from LUMA, an investment bank that specializes in the digital media and marketing industry.[29]

THE BATTLE FOR THE BUSINESS MODEL

Ad networks are basically marketplaces, serving two players: Advertisers and Publishers:

Advertisers want to get their ads to as many qualified, targeted prospects as they can, so they're looking for empty rectangles that will be seen by as many people as possible who fit their target market.

Publishers want to generate income by selling their empty rectangles to advertisers, so they generate engaging content that will attract as many eyeballs as possible.

The better that publishers are at filling a particular niche and attracting a particular kind of reader, the easier it is for advertisers to understand what ads will perform the best.

In case it's not clear, the product being exchanged in this marketplace is *you*.

To be even more clear, it's your *behavior* being exchanged. We like to talk about how advertisers are paying for us and our eyeballs, but if advertisers are paying for clicks, they don't just want us to *see* the ad. They want us to take action and *click on it*.

As computer philosophy writer Jaron Lanier put it in *The Social Dilemma*, advertisers aren't paying for us, they're paying for the imperceptible change in our behavior created by their ads. Nevertheless, "eyeballs" is the shorthand we all know and use, so let's just say that we—and our eyeballs—are the product being bought and sold.

The business model for the ad network is pretty simple: Attract advertisers that have big budgets, and connect them with publishers that have specific audiences. The more spendy advertisers that a network has on tap, the more attractive it is to publishers. And the more quality publishers it works with, the more attractive it is to advertisers. If the publisher delivers good traffic with lots of impressions and/or clicks, it gets a cut of the network's fees.

How Ad Networks Compete

The way ad networks compete for advertisers' business is, of course, by offering competitive rates—mostly in either the CPM or

CPC models. But what's the point of paying to put your ads on sites if you're reaching the wrong audience or nobody's going to click?

The real differentiation for networks is in the quality of the traffic they can deliver, and how much tracking and engagement they can promise. That means *delivering people* like you and me, no matter where we are or how hard we try to avoid ads.

One network, BuySellAds, provides advertisers "sponsored content" opportunities that get the message out "without ... worrying about ad blockers."[30]

AirPush's HyperTarget tool lets advertisers target smartphone users, "based on their app download history, which reveals important information about their interests and can be leveraged by advertisers to better target their ads."[31] Yes, it knows what apps you're downloading, just so it can guess at what you're interested in. Fun, right?

Survata doesn't just know what you've been buying and where you've been visiting, it claims to know how easily persuaded you are, selling advertisers access to their "proprietary Persuadability Scores to focus on the exact individuals most likely to respond to your campaign."[32] Creepy.

Conversant Media's parent company Epsilon promises advertisers consumer data that includes "what they buy (online and offline), how they buy, the devices they use and the content they consume" and that "each consumer's online and offline activity is connected to a single ID *that your brand owns*."[33] [emphasis mine]

If you ever thought *you* were the one who owned all your personal online activity, I imagine you're seeing the light.

How Publishers Make Money

Ad networks cater to publishers just as much as they do to advertisers. Advertisers, of course, want to work with a network that can deliver a great audience.

For publishers, the business model is to create content that attracts visitors, surround that content with ads, and get paid when readers click. Because they're designing the layout of their sites, they can choose where their empty rectangles appear on the page, the sizes they want from the standard selections, and how the ads will behave as visitors move around the site.

Publishers can work with more than one network—there's no exclusivity. But they'll want to work with the ones that do two things: Pay the biggest cut of the revenue, and provide ads their visitors can't avoid and are likely to click.

Unfortunately, more and more visitors are trying to avoid ads, using things like ad blockers. It's up to the ad networks to not only provide the ads, but also the features that make it harder for visitors to escape being targeted.

If users manage to block ads, many networks provide an "ad-block recovery" tool to help avoid losing revenue. This tool helps the site automatically identify a visitor who's using an ad blocker, and fills the screen with a request for them to turn it off while they're on the site in exchange for a promise that the ads will not be obnoxious.

According to OptInMonster, 77% of people will turn their ad blocker off when asked nicely.[34]

Even if visitors aren't using ad blockers, they may not notice or interact with ads the way the publisher would like. Monetize Pros, a site that helps publishers choose the best places to put their empty rectangles to get the most clicks, published an article with over 100 tricks and tips for optimizing ad performance. It explains that if publishers make advertisements omnipresent "so that ads follow visitors around, you can increase their visibility on your site." (This advice probably works because readers will click on the ad in the hope it'll quit chasing them around.)

For mobile, they recommend a mobile anchor ad that "sticks to the bottom of a screen when a user scrolls." (Because what reader doesn't love giving up precious space on their phone's screen to an ad that won't go away? *Oh, wait.*)

Of course, once a visitor finally finds an article to read, publishers should know that "Placing text ads at the beginning of an article can result in high visibility for visitors expecting to begin reading a piece of content." (Yes, visitors are expecting to read content, but stuffing in an ad to circumvent that expectation doesn't make for a positive user experience.)

In fairness, Monetize Pros also warns publishers not to disrupt the user experience or put too many ads on a single page. But realistically—given that it recommends that ads should follow readers, hijack valuable mobile screen space, and intercept the content experience—those warnings feel like cynical lip service.[35]

Think Outside The Ad

Ads can also appear as "native advertising"—meaning they're designed and placed to look like part of the page's content.

It might be inline with the actual content, between two story paragraphs, rather than in the sidebars. It might share the same font and styling as the site's content, and it can be on the same topic as the story. The U.S. Federal Trade Commission defines it as "content that bears a similarity to the news, feature articles, product reviews, entertainment, and other material that surrounds it online."

Native ads are supposed to have something identifying them as paid advertising—usually you'll see the tiny words "sponsored content" above or below it. But it's easy for these ads to deceive the reader, either by accident or design. The FTC has brought cases against advertisers or publishers when it perceives the format of ads as deceptive. "The Commission has taken action against ads that deceptively mimicked the format of news programming or otherwise misrepresented their source ... including through an express or implied misrepresentation that it comes from a party other than the sponsoring advertiser."[36]

Nevertheless, publishers love native content because readers tend to view it as part of the article rather than an ad, and are more likely to click on it. In an article spotlighting prime examples of native advertising, MediaPlanet explained its allure: "For publishers, sponsored content is an important revenue stream. In fact, three-quarters of publishers and media buyers have embraced sponsored content to positively affect their bottom lines. Research also shows that 25 percent more of consumers look at sponsored articles than display ad units, and that native ads produce an 18 percent higher lift in purchase intent than banner ads do."[37]

Think Outside The Rectangle

Advertisers can do more than simply stick an image inside the rectangle they've rented. They can also add JavaScript code to put ads almost anywhere within the browser. And they can do things you can't see, like tag your device for tracking.

- You'll see popups—which are just what they sound like—that pop up in front of whatever you're actually trying to look at
- Pop-unders can launch behind the page you're looking at and are only revealed when you close or minimize the browser—*surprise!*

- Interstitials appear over the top of a page when it loads, after you've been on the page a while, or when you try to leave the page, sometimes forcing you to wait for a countdown before you can move on
- Sliders will swoop in from the side after you've been on the page for a moment, like they're sliding into your DMs
- Goalposts fill the space to the right and left of a page, when it's not completely filling the browser
- In-text ads are especially insidious—they highlight words in the content of the site so they look like links, but when you roll over or click them they actually launch ads
- Tracking pixels are invisible, transparent, single-pixel images that track and log your behavior for later use
- Tracking your device allows advertisers to identify and track you and your browsing without even having to display an ad or load an image (more on that later).

There's so much code, triggering so many actions on any given web page—actions you can see and actions you can't—that I won't even list them all here. What you need to know is that once a publisher decides to sell some empty rectangles, it seems their imaginations know no bounds when it comes to monetizing you.

Think Outside The Browser

I haven't even touched on the other places ad networks can stuff targeted ads, like inside your email provider (it's not just Google), inside apps, and even in newsletters you've agreed to receive. Imagine giving permission to receive a newsletter and agreeing to the publisher's privacy statement, then getting a daily, weekly, or monthly mailing with ads inserted that track your interactions and follow you afterwards?

Tracking you didn't agree to? Yup, it happens all the time and you might not even recognize the content as an ad.

Those Ads Are Watching You

For advertisers, the most valuable thing about ad networks might not be that they deliver tons of personal data to target ads to exactly the right consumer.

It might be that they track and report the performance of the ad in real time, allowing advertisers an opportunity to adjust and improve their targeting. The network reports back to the advertiser how many times the ad was seen, how many times it was clicked, and who it was that clicked and what they did afterward.

Did they browse? Did they join? Did they buy? Did they linger over the ad, or scroll away as soon as it loaded? The ad network collects that information and, where possible, attaches it to the rest of the data about you they've collected or bought.

The more current, extensive and detailed the information, the more accurately the network can target ads to exactly the right consumer. And the more accurately the ads are targeted, the more likely the consumer is to interact with the ad, which of course is better for the advertiser because they want more of us to click, browse, join or buy.

So the ad-tech industry has devised a few ways to sneak into your browser and gather ever more information.

Cookies: Following Prospects Around The Web

If you use the web, you've accepted cookies from strangers. Virtually every site tracks your behavior by inserting cookies into your browser.

Sites might or might not let you know they're doing so, depending on the laws they're governed by and how transparent they want to be. But where there's a notification, most folks just click *Accept* and move on, because they want to see the funny video. Much like accepting Terms and Conditions, it's the rare user who actually reads the fine print.

If you're going to continue clicking Accept, it's worth understanding what it is you're accepting and what you're not. So here's a quick rundown on cookies.

The web was originally conceived as user-centric and anonymous—the website and your browser had no relationship with each other—the site's server didn't know who you were. That worked great for academic papers and research, but once the internet became a transactional ecosystem, it didn't work so well for interactions where the server needed confidently to know who was controlling the browser.

Think banking transactions, for instance: Not only do you need to login, but the bank website needs to know that your subsequent clicks are also yours—and not somebody hijacking your connection after you typed your password.

So a method was devised that allowed IDs to be created during a visit and exchanged between the server and the browser. The IDs were bolted onto the web and given the name *cookies*.

Cookies are just data. They're like the token you get at a coat room: The number on it has no inherent meaning, but when you're ready to leave, it matches you to the same coat you left with the attendant, which has the matching, unique token.

To provide security, cookies are kept hidden from all domains except the one that issued them. So if your browser has a cookie in it from Amazon, for instance, Hulu can't see that cookie or gain any information from it. *Or can it?*

1st-Party vs. 3rd-Party Cookies

Here's the most important thing. It has to do with the permissions you give the site you're visiting, as opposed to the permissions you *don't* give to the ads on the site.

- First-party cookies are issued by the page you're looking at. That's the page you assume you're making an agreement with when you click Accept Cookies.
- Third-party cookies in the page are actually being delivered from other domains, like ads and trackers, but you're not agreeing to those cookies.

You're not agreeing, *because nobody asked.* You don't need to click on anything to activate those third party cookies—they get launched and stuffed into your browser automatically, via those third-party images sitting in the rectangles that were sold.

The ad network knows the ad has been displayed, and it knows the address of the page it was displayed on. From now on, if you visit another site where that ad network also has code, the network will recognize you as the one that saw the first ad, and show you more ads. (That's why you keep seeing the same damn shoes.)

I should point out that while publishers certainly have control over their own cookie policies, they have zero knowledge of the cookies that ad networks are planting on their pages; and by and large, *they don't care*—so long as they're getting paid.

With the lion's share of cookies owned and managed by ad networks, it's only natural that we've ended up with a concentration of data being acquired and stored by them.

Block Those Cookies—If You Can

You can choose to decline all cookies. But that means you're declining first party cookies, and lots of first party cookies are what's called "strictly necessary" for the site to function.

For example, without cookies you couldn't use your banking site, because it's the cookies that tell the site it's you who's logged in as you move from page to page. Without first-party cookies, shopping carts won't work, because it's the cookies that remind the browser that you have those shoes in your cart as you continue to surf around the site.

You *can* choose to decline third-party cookies. In fact, Google's planning on making that standard practice for Chrome in the future. But if you live in the Google ecosystem—and we all do to some extent or another—Google's cookies on all its properties are first party cookies. So you'll still be getting cookied by Google Search and any other Google properties and tools. Similarly, if you accept cookies from Verizon, and you visit AOL, the servers can exchange the cookie data because Verizon owns AOL.

Beyond The Cookie: Other Trackers

If third party cookies went away tomorrow, advertisers, publishers and networks would still be able to get plenty of data.

Publishers can enable Google Analytics in their sites, allowing them to track how you arrived at their site, what you do while you're on there, how long you stay, how many pages you view, and more. This helps them understand visitor behavior and adjust to make the site easier to use and more engaging.

Google provides plenty of other tools to combine tracking data from loads of different sources. If you click on an ad for new shoes on your phone and then physically walk into a shoe store, it's likely Google tapped your location, connected your online browsing to your in-store activity, and then let the advertiser know you completed your purchase offline.

Then there's "fingerprinting," which I hinted at earlier. Sites can recognise your browser by collecting information about your unique browser and device—like whether you have cookies enabled, your preferred language, the plugins you have enabled, the fonts your system has on it, and more. All those data points are put together to paint a profile of your particular configuration, stored online rather than on your device, and used to recognize you again later. All done invisibly, without installing a cookie or displaying an ad.

And it's not just websites that are gathering information about us. As ProPublica reported back in 2015, "Vizio's Smart TVs track your viewing habits and share it with advertisers, who can then find you on your phone and other devices." The TV analyzes what you're watching, when you're watching it, and whether it was live or recorded.

The Vizio snooping connects your viewing to your IP address, which can destroy any remaining privacy—it can increasingly be linked to an individual household, or at least to scarily-accurate demographics: "Experian, for instance, offers a "data enrichment" service that provides "hundreds of attributes" ... tied to a particular IP address."[38]

The Merging Of Online And Offline Data

In fact, merging online and offline data has been a kind of holy grail for advertisers—if only they could find a way around those pesky privacy issues.

In 1995, DoubleClick was founded as one of the first service providers for online ad-serving that tracked user behavior with cookies. About a year after their 1998 IPO, it announced a merger with Abacus Direct, a company that collected and sold personally identifiable customer shopping data for offline print magazines—names, addresses, and more. There was much concern at the time that DoubleClick would combine its anonymous online data with Abacus' offline information, revealing online customers' identities, but the FTC found no evidence this was happening.

Privacy advocacy groups sent letters to DoubleClick shareholders, urging them to reject the merger, suggesting investors "add DoubleClick and Abacus to 'screening' lists of companies that are to be excluded from investment based on social criteria, specifically a disregard for human rights."

The groups also complained to the Federal Trade Commission (FTC) about the privacy implications—at the time, the FTC was investigating the practice of profiling, in which corporations merge users' personally identifiable information (PII) and their web activity.

DoubleClick already owned other web properties including NetDeals, which collected PII—names, home and email addresses, and birth dates—when they entered contests. DoubleClick was up front about the bleed between those databases, stating on the NetDeals site that they "combine [NetDeals] information with other information about you that is available to us. ... This includes other personally identifiable information and certain non-personally identifiable information, such as the type of browser you use."[39] Sneaky, because DoubleClick owned NetDeals, so they were both considered first parties and anything shared with one was available to the other.

Despite all these concerns for privacy, DoubleClick flourished, and it was ultimately bought by Google in 2007. Google founder Sergey Brin promised at the time to keep DoubleClick's identifiable data and Google's anonymous data separate.

And Google kept its promise—for 10 years. But today, nearly 14 years later, during the 2020 Congressional antitrust hearings, Google CEO Sundar Pichai confirmed that he signed off on a 2016 merging of DoubleClick's data with Google's.[40] Its privacy policy once stated, "We will not combine DoubleClick cookie information with personally identifiable information unless we have your opt-in consent," But in 2016, Google had effectively crossed out those words.

(Google did offer users the opportunity to opt out of what it called "new features," but the wording of the notification was confusing and seemed irrelevant to most people.)

As a practical matter, this meant that "the DoubleClick ads that follow people around on the web may now be customized to them based on your name and other information Google knows about you. It also means that Google could now, if it wished to, build a complete portrait of a user by name, based on everything they write in email, every website they visit and the searches they conduct."

Google wasn't the first though: Offline data brokers were already merging their mailing lists with online shoppers. And two years before, Facebook had announced it would "track its users by name across the Internet when they visit websites containing Facebook buttons such as 'Share' and 'Like' – even when users don't click on the button."[41]

So, So, So Many Trackers

At this point, it's obvious that data mining is out of hand, and there's no way for a user to know who's tracking them, what information they're capturing, for what purpose, or who they're sharing it with. But some folks are doing their best to reveal the man behind the curtain.

Dr. Augustine Fou is an ad fraud investigator, and he's recently launched a tool that reveals just who's tracking you on any given website. At his FouAnalytics site he offers a free online tool that counts not only how many ads are on a page, but how many actual requests for data are spawned by those ads.

Those requests go out to countless connected entities like BrightCove, ChartBeat, and of course Google Analytics. Those services in turn send information to more services like DoubleClick, SelectableMedia and BounceExchange, which in turn are linked to more services like Company-Target, Openx and so on.

When I looked at one site, People.com, Fou's tool counted 258 separate ad-server requests and three requests for tracking. I'm sure a visitor knows none of them are there, and none of which any visitor intended to accept when they visit the page.[42]

The Promise And The Product

Like the web itself, advertising started out with somewhat altruistic motives, hoping to use ads to create meaningful exchanges between companies and prospects—to benefit both parties. As Lincoln might have said, we were not enemies, but friends.

Instead—also perhaps like the web—advertising followed the lesser angels of its nature, focusing on revenue. It strained and broke the bonds of affection with web users.

Which brings us to today.

WHAT IT LOOKS LIKE NOW

Today, we tiptoe through an online environment almost completely driven by advertising revenue.

Your free search is subsidized by advertising. Your free email is subsidized by advertising. Your free browser is subsidized by advertising. As Gilad Edelman said in a recent Wired article, advertising is "the underlying financial model of the open internet."[43]

So long as we're aware of it, if we're okay with seeing a bazillion ads in exchange for free stuff, what harm is there in it?

Subsidizing The Worst Content

Some say that advertising is paying for some of the most dangerous and damaging content on the web. For instance, advertising pays for platforms like Facebook that have become the distribution network for the sort of disinformation and propaganda that allegedly tilted the 2016 election.

"An algorithm that prioritizes keeping users engaged might therefore prioritize content that gets people riled up," said Edelman, "or that tells people what they want to hear, even if it's false." A free social network, he said, "makes money in proportion to how much time those users spend on the platform. More time means more opportunities to serve ads and to collect data that can be used to help advertisers target the right people. ... One thing that tends to hold people's attention really well, however, is polarizing and inflammatory content."

In some cases the ads aren't just paying for the platform, they themselves are directly responsible for disinformation. Particularly political ads, because Facebook has historically chosen to "exempt politicians from its fact-checking policies, including for ads—meaning elected officials and candidates are allowed to straight-up lie on the platform and target those lies to specific slices of the electorate. ... They can microtarget so granularly to individuals who are susceptible to believe it, without the benefit of the surrounding argument or the counterargument that exists if someone puts the ad on television for example."

Automated Disinformation

But let's not just hammer on social media—in some ways it's the least damaging, because to some extent we can see exactly what's happening and why. The bigger problem is automated ads.

The advertising networks of Google and many others are entirely automated by a technology called "programmatic advertising." Plug in an ad, tell the system how many people you want to reach and how much you're willing to spend, and off it goes to fill empty rectangles wherever they're found. Advertisers themselves pay little attention to where their ads end up getting displayed—so long as they're getting clicks, they don't seem to care from where. Even if they're helping monetize sites filled with fake news and dangerous misinformation.

Edelman shared a research study by The Global Disinformation Index that concluded, "Tens of millions of advertising dollars will flow this year to sites that have published high volumes of coronavirus disinformation and conspiracy theories [including] an ad for the British Medical Association next to a headline suggesting that 'compulsory vaccination' will genetically modify people, turning them inhuman."

This blind placement means that big brands are, knowingly or not, monetizing these propaganda websites. In turn, as is the case with social, brands reward the sites for publishing ever more absurd and divisive content to keep their audiences enraged—and engaged.

Write crazy crap, get more engaged traffic, sell more ads, make more money, start again. It's a race to the bottom, in pursuit of every last click.

Everyone's A Publisher

Google's original choice, way back when, was to stay away from banner ads. It only sold text ads into its search results and Gmail website.

I talked with Jim Brock about it—he was a very early Yahoo hire, serving as its first attorney, which gave him an insider's view of the industry's formative days. He says there was "a beautiful simplicity to Google's revenue model, which is extremely lightweight, very low cost of sales, and very powerful. ... Their ambition was large, they've succeeded like no one else really has in that area, and they built it on the back of a very powerful search advertising model—that Yahoo did not end up investing in."

When Google finally decided to tackle the business of banner ads—what we now call *display advertising*—it was from an entirely different angle: "Google's approach to display advertising was very different. They developed a network to put [display ads] on other places. You don't see display advertising on Googles own products [search, Gmail, etc.]"

Many advertising networks have minimum traffic standards a website must satisfy before they'll post ads on the site—some to the tune of hundreds of thousands of daily visitors. They don't want to waste their advertisers' time and money targeting tiny sites with tiny audiences. But Google has no such threshold.

Anyone with a website can drop in a line of code and start hosting advertisements through Google's automated AdSense program. Just be 18 years old, claim to post original content, and promise not to engage in click fraud. Then you can throw together a web page with some (allegedly original) words that are entertaining or shocking, leave empty rectangles for ads, let Google sell automatically targeted ads into those rectangles, and take a cut of the money. This lets very small, very niche sites start monetizing straight away.

During the 2016 election, for instance, Google's AdSense was gamed by teenagers in the North Macedonia city of Veles, which "was the registered home of at least 100 [political] websites, many of them filled with sensationalist, utterly fake news. ... The sites' ample traffic was rewarded handsomely by automated advertising engines, like Google's AdSense." These sites brought their owners levels of income that were massive for the former-Soviet region: In just four months, one young publisher made almost $16,000 by letting Google put ads on two political websites filled with fake and stolen content—more than 10 times the average income for the country.[44]

Vanessa Otero, founder and CEO of Ad Fontes Media, studies how the news industry is driven by advertising revenue. "A small, on-line operation run by one person," she outlined in a Medium article, "can carve out a space for itself that generates plenty of money ... by generating web traffic and social media engagement. Unfortunately, some of the easiest ways to generate those are by publishing news content that is hyper-partisan, extremist, misleading, sensationalistic, propagandistic, or downright false."

Content that generates fear, anger, disgust, and righteousness, she says, "is highly attracting and engaging. It can generate millions of page views on an individual site, and millions of page views can translate into tens of thousands of dollars per month or more in digital advertising revenue. In other words—polarizing junk news pays." She goes on to point out that advertisers, big brands with reputations to protect, have no idea where their ads are showing because cookies can't recognize quality content from junk.[45]

Google's commitment to advertising is even starting to hurt search results as it drives users toward its own properties rather than legitimate organic results. Rand Fishkin, one of the leading voices in the world of "search engine optimization" (SEO), talked in 2018 about "the shift in Google's behavior over the last few years." He said it had moved "away from an engine that drives searchers to other websites for the answers to their problems and toward self-hosted answers and solutions. That's made SEO much more difficult, as Google, for the first time in its history, is sending less outbound traffic."[46]

Although Google is the largest single display ad seller, they don't hold the same kind of market dominance that they do in search. There are lots of other ad vendors in the game, and plenty of them have even worse ethical standards than Google. The problems we face are a byproduct of everyone acting in their own best interest, and not in the interests of users.

Fraud Is Rampant

If publishers are paid by the click, it obviously behooves them to generate as many clicks as possible. Some small publishers who are just in business to generate ad revenue, and there are millions of them, can build a simple site with free software, "scrape" content from other legitimate publications to fill their site, and plug in an ad network like Google's AdSense.

Then they can turn the site over to an army of bots—automated software designed to reload the pages of the site over and over again, clicking on every ad that pops up. No real traffic, no real readers, no real clicks. Fou says bots can even game search ads too, by generating fake searches for specific keywords and then clicking on the ads the engine delivers.

If a publisher wants to claim a greater audience than they actually have, they can buy traffic, making it look like they have many more visitors than they actually do. "There are some websites," says Fou, "in their eagerness to grow ad revenues, they resort to buying traffic because you can't get a whole bunch of humans to do the same thing, like visit your website if they don't want to. [Even some] mainstream sites ... resorted to buying traffic to supplement their ad revenue because human audiences just don't grow fast enough and don't look at enough pages to grow that [revenue]."

Surveillance Marketing Doesn't Even Work That Well

Even if there were no fraud, surveillance marketing is not nearly as effective as was promised—no matter how much the industry claims it to be. "We have super granular data," they promise. "You can target down to the individual!"

Fou says that its effectiveness is largely a myth put about by ad networks and data brokers, to convince advertisers to work with them. He asserts that surveillance marketing only hurts the three original players in the game: The consumer pays with his or her privacy, the marketer pays with wasted ad spend, and the publisher pays with lost ad revenue, or death.

Sponsorship Diminishes Surrounding Content

Some websites don't depend entirely on visitors clicking ads to generate revenue. Sponsored-content providers will pay the site big bucks just to display their grids of stories, and get their hands on the traffic.

These sponsored content distributors charge other websites to advertise their content in the grid, sending them new traffic. So if a site has an article about what the stars of *Naked And Afraid* look like today and they want more viewers, they pay someone like Taboola or Revcontent to advertise the story on another site.

You've seen these grids of low quality, tabloid ads everywhere, I'm sure. Some people call them *chumboxes*—touting sordid stories about wardrobe malfunctions, iPads for $40, "one weird trick" to whiten your teeth, and crazy fruits that cure liver disease.

They're not just on entertainment and gossip sites; they're increasingly found on the sort of news sites that are struggling to make ends meet and stand ready to take anybody's money. While advertising this kind of low-quality content might not reflect well on sites trying to present a more legitimate aspect, money talks.

That's not to say all sponsored ads are bad. The trick for a publisher is to avoid ads that scream "I'm desperate for money"—and avoid the ad networks that carry them. The thing is, carrying this kind of clickbait content can hurt the perceived value of a site that's otherwise trying to project legitimacy and value. In 2016 Nathan Johns, a search quality analyst in Google's Search department, tweeted "Hot take: if you're going to report/complain about fake news, maybe think twice about those [chumboxes] on your site?"[47]

When legitimate outlets are struggling so badly to make ends meet that they're willing to take anyone's money and to risk sullying their image, something's broken—without a happy ending. As Fou puts it, "When you see a site [use chumboxes] you kind of know they sold out; their priority is to make money, not to serve their [users]."

VISIONS FOR TOMORROW

What would a future where users have more control over advertising and their data even look like? Is it possible to build an internet that doesn't run on ad money?

And if so, should we?

Give Users Control Over Their Data

Father of the web, Sir Tim Berners Lee, sees a future where users control their own data. "I've got a vision for an alternative world," he says, "in which that data does exist, but it's at the beck and call of the user themselves. Where the apps are actually separated from the data source. So when you use an app, it asks, where do you want me to store the data? And you have complete control over who gets access to it. It would be a new world. We're talking about a future in which these programs work for you. They don't work for Amazon, they don't work for Apple."

He also sees change coming in the form of users paying for content: "Maybe people will decide that they want to live in an ad-free world, and will do that by paying for it. ... There is a backlash coming, [and] there will be systems which are not advertising-based."[48]

Stop Surveilling, Start Protecting

Fou says the first thing on the agenda should be to, "End surveillance marketing with a three-step process:

1. protect consumers (specifically, privacy),
2. protect publishers (reduce ad tech), and
3. protect advertisers/marketers (from fraud and ad waste)."

But it might not be all that easy: "Too many incumbent forces are at work to preserve it, so the Badtech Industrial Complex can continue to rape and pillage from all three parties in digital marketing: consumers, publishers and advertisers."[49]

To move toward a better future, says Fou, we need to "flip the current notion of privacy upside down. Currently, privacy is what ad-tech companies think it should be. Consumers see 100 different privacy policies when they visit 100 different sites [and consumers] are forced to consent to them, even though 100% of them don't understand the legalese anyway.

One Privacy Policy To Rule Them All

Fou wonders what might happen if *websites* were the ones who had to consent to our privacy: "What if we flipped this notion of privacy on its head? What if there was one privacy policy instead—the privacy policy of the individual.

"Every site that the person visits would have to consent to it, instead of the other way around. If the site respects the user's privacy policy, then the user transacts with it and may even consider a longer term relationship with the site. A person's privacy policy as opposed to sites' or companies' privacy policies is exactly what is contemplated by CustomerCommons.org."[50]

Adopting Person-First Policies

As with search, we may see some change coming from those who helped build the broken model. Richard Whitt has a vision for a user-centric internet not unlike Fou's. As corporate director for strategic initiatives at Google, his job was analyzing policy and ethical issues. But as he revealed in a 2020 interview with the Ashoka foundation, he had become "concerned about the direction of large web companies — how tech platforms could be utilized against users, against the interests of citizens and voters." So he left in 2018, after eleven years. Today, as the founder of GLIAnet, he is advocating for a more human-centered approach to the internet.

"What we now have," Whitt says, "I call it the SEAM paradigm: surveillance of users, extraction of data, analysis of data, manipulation of users. ... I'm proposing an alternative way of thinking about it with GLIAnet: Instead of the SEAMs feedback cycles, we should start with the human being. What are the human being's autonomous and agential needs and wants, and how do we cater to that initially, rather than starting with the technology and layering the human needs on top of that? And so the idea of an overlay to me is important here again, the designed attributes of the web and the net are still there. The users at the edge and the end to end principle are still there. But what if we turn the end to end principle into something more radical? Which is to say, rather than power residing at either end, it's power at one particular end, which is what I would call the edge, which is where the end user resides."[51]

Huge changes are needed from big entrenched industries with truckloads of money on the line. This will be like turning around an oil tanker.

In the meantime, what can we do to mitigate the impact of ubiquitous ads and data collection on our well-being?

Block Third Party Cookies

Blocking third party cookies—the ones that aren't coming directly from the site you're visiting—represents a fundamental change to the ad tech industry. Safari and Firefox have already implemented this by default, but together they only represent about 22% of worldwide browser usage, so a little less than a quarter of users are having those cookies blocked.

Google, who owns nearly 60% of worldwide browser usage, continues to allow third party cookies by default, so the industry has so far been able to continue building their business by reaching nearly two-thirds of the audience. Now even Google is preparing to make the change, and in the next few years Chrome will also block third party cookies.

That means the advertising industry will have to find other ways to recognize visitors, collect data, and follow people around with ads for shoes. Like maybe giving their business to Google, whose network is still considered first party by Chrome, circumventing their own third party blockade.

Google is proposing a replacement for third party cookies it calls the "Privacy Sandbox." It's a set of tools that will still allow for collecting data on user interests and other contextual first party data points, as well as click-throughs. But they won't contain any identifiers that might enable connecting a click or a view to a particular user.

There are other alternatives being pitched by marketers and networks that are desperate to continue following specific individuals, including storing encrypted email addresses to attach behavior metrics to actual users. Which really represents a step backward in user privacy.

Premium Publishers Might Protect Their Readers

There's also the possibility that publishers, particularly premium publishers, will take more control over the first-party data they've collected on their users.

They've already got direct access to a devoted user base and have first-party data about their behavior and interests. This might put them in a prime position to dangle that valuable asset carrot in front of advertisers and networks, to take a more proactive part in the monetization circle.

Increase Browser Security

Browsers are beginning to push back with greater verve and dedication on all this advertising and data collection in an effort to protect their users and earn their trust again.

Apple recently announced new privacy features, including in **Safari**: The browser will sport a new "Privacy Report" button showing all the third-party trackers on a website, allowing you to block them from following you across the internet.

Google **Chrome** recently started blocking abusive notification prompts—classified as either "requests designed to mislead, trick, or force users into allowing notifications" or "fake messages that resemble chat messages, warnings, or system dialogs. It also includes phishing attacks, an abusive tactic that tries to steal or trick users into sharing personal information, and malware notifications that promote or link to malicious software."

Microsoft is also improving security in its **Edge** browser. NSS Labs reports that "Edge offered the most [phishing] protection, blocking 95.5% of phishing URLs. ... Chrome provided the second highest protection, blocking an average of 86.9%, [closely] followed by Mozilla **Firefox** at 85.9%." And Edge blocked "98.5% of malware. ... Firefox provided the second highest protection, blocking an average of 86.1%, followed by Google Chrome at 86.0%."[52]

The **Opera** browser website states, "You have the absolute right to privacy and security online. Opera's secure private browser is built to protect you, and your data, first and foremost. Opera's trusted and proven security features are built right into our safe browser, so you don't need to install third-party extensions for general, or enhanced, privacy. ... Opera's Ad blocker makes websites load faster and look cleaner by blocking ad scripts. It also includes tracking protection and stops cryptocurrency mining scripts for a secure browser."[53]

Google Stops Hoarding Data Forever

In June of 2020, Google announced yet another step in its data privacy evolution. As we know, they've been tracking our web and app activity, and our physical location, for a long time. And they were keeping that data for "an indefinite period of time"—meaning, as long as they wanted—unless you chose to toggle your privacy settings and have the data deleted.

Location tracking was always off by default, but many if not most users turn that feature on frequently, or leave it on all the time. That's how Google Maps can offer personalized recommendations about restaurants, for instance, because it knows where you've eaten before. And once you gave permission to collect that data, they kept it indefinitely.

Today, location data will be auto-deleted after 18 months. Or you can choose to have it deleted every three months or every 36 months. If you're an existing Google user, your web and app activity is stored for an indefinite period. But now you have the choice to have it deleted automatically every three or 18 months. If you're a new user, your data will automatically be deleted every 18 months; but you can also choose the three month option.

"We continue to challenge ourselves to do more with less, and today we're changing our data retention practices to make auto-delete the default for our core activity settings," Google CEO Sundar Pichai said in a prepared statement.

Reward Quality Content And Ads

Harking back to the Xanadu concept of providing small payments in exchange for content, a few browser providers are trying to move monetization from a "display any ads" model to a "reward quality ads and content creators" model.

Brave's new browser is dedicated to both protecting user privacy and rewarding responsible advertising. "Brave is on a mission to fix the web by giving users a safer, faster and better browsing experience, while growing support for content creators through a new attention-based ecosystem of rewards." With the "Brave Rewards" feature, users can send micropayments to their favorite sites by watching vetted, responsible advertisements on participating sites. And users can "tip" their favorite Twitter users, YouTube creators, Twitch streamers, and more.[54]

eyeo distributes the free ad blocking software tools, **Adblock** Plus and the Adblock Browser, which similarly permit ads that conform to acceptable standards. Ben Williams, an eyeo spokesperson, told me their model "still leaves the user in control, but it shows the users ads that have been approved by an independent committee."

eyeo also acquired a micropayment service called **Flattr**, a tool that lets you pay your favorite sites and content creators for doing great work. Regularly watching a weekly web series on YouTube? Give the producers a monthly cut of your Flattr subscription. See a great timely tweet that deserves some love? Drop some one-time cash their way.

How About Paying For Ad-free?

It seems obvious that there should be a way to just hand over money and make the ads and trackers go away. But I know it's not that easy.

That's why I'm especially intrigued by **Scroll**. I spoke to the founder, Tony Haile, who explained the origin of the company: "The question for me was, we've got this poor user experience [due to ads] where the media is dying. You have the rise of an unsanctioned user experience in terms of ad blocking and so forth. Could we take a business model and put it against that better user experience and see if we could find a new pathway for media?"

It's early days for Scroll, but they've signed some impressive names and are worth watching and my experience with the service was fault-less. One problem they face is the need to sign deals with individual publishing companies, which could prove limiting. By contrast, Adblock tools like those from eyeo are systemic, and work across all websites.

Reducing Obnoxiousness Through New Industry Standards

There are organizations advocating for less obnoxious ads, working to set standards that will allow publishers to monetize content while simultaneously protecting the user experience of visitors.

The Acceptable Ads Committee was started by eyeo, the company behind Adblock Plus and Flattr. The now independent committee has developed standards to allow publishers and advertisers to "Increase ... revenue by offering a positive user experience to ad-blocking users who are more likely to click on noninvasive, high-quality ads."[55] eyeo's ad blocking tools only show ads from whitelisted companies that agree to adhere to the guidelines of the committee, because, "Users deserve control of their web experience. Publishers deserve to monetize their content."[56] eyeo gives away their ad blocker tools for free; small publishers are not charged for whitelisting, but larger companies do pay to be added to the whitelist. Other ad blockers can also choose to unblock ads that adhere to the standards.

The Coalition for Better Ads has also developed a set of standards for less intrusive advertising: "Advertising helps support valuable free content, robust journalism and social connections across the internet," says their site. "Consumers, however, are increasingly frustrated with ads that disrupt their experience, interrupt content and slow browsing." Formed by a group of trade associations and online media companies, the coalition seeks to "leverage consumer insights and cross-industry expertise to develop and implement new global standards for online advertising that address consumer expectations."[57]

But I'm fairly skeptical of these well-intentioned industry attempts at self policing. We've already seen failures to solve even simple problems like third-party cookies. As far back as 2002 the problems were understood, so the W3C created a framework to give users more control over when, where and how those cookies got set and read. Unfortunately the framework, named P3P, or "Platform for Privacy Preferences Project," proved too complex for website owners and consumers lacked the knowledge to make sensible choices. It's now obsolete and nobody mourns it.[58]

Can't We Just Legislate Our Way To Privacy?

Ah, legislation. The solution that promises to over-complicate and befuddle whatever it touches. The EU tried it with first the ePrivacy Directive (ePD), which required websites and companies to get your consent before they can save and access tracking data on your devices. And, as is increasingly the case, if the tracking data is personally identifiable, the even more complex General Data Protection Regulation (GDPR) kicks in, to regulate the storage and processing of the data.

The result, years later, is suboptimal at best. Publishers and advertisers have done whatever they can to sidestep the requirement, or to outright trick users into accepting all kinds of nefarious cookies. According to a 2019 academic study, so-called "compliant" sites provide pop up notifications and some even offer the option of declining cookies. But the popups are often at the bottom of the page, and don't interfere with accessing the content, so they're ignored.

Other sites offer a big easy-to-click button that accepts all cookies, even those that are "privacy unfriendly," while only offering a tiny hard-to-see text link to more options that would actually allow users to choose greater privacy. Depressingly, "It is clear that the current ecosystem of mechanisms to prompt for user consent ... provides no real improvement for user privacy compared to pre-GDPR times," say the researchers. Predictably, they find publishers "often employ dark patterns to make people consent to data collection," leading users toward specific actions that may not be in their best interests.

In the end, you can almost hear the academics sigh with resignation as they conclude, "Our findings show that a substantial amount of users are willing to engage with consent notices. ... Unfortunately, many current cookie notice implementations [offer] no meaningful choice to consumers."[59]

I spoke with Aurelie Pols, a Data Protection Officer, Privacy Engineer, and Data Scientist hailing from Madrid, Spain. In Pols' estimation, it would require a combination of legislation and private sector institutions to even approach transparency and consistency. "I don't believe that legislation is the solution to everything ... but I do believe that legislation is part of it."

Pols thinks we'd need managing institutions and organizations to help society reach reasonable privacy goals: "I would imagine some form of an institution that would centralize these cookies and these trackers and define what these cookies and these trackers do, and make it transparent for the market. [This would mean] we all understand the same thing, interpret it in the same way, and agree on how it works. If we remain with ... the vagueness we have today, it doesn't mean anything. We have no trust relationship being built between individuals, and this is the real problem."

Ultimately I'm not optimistic. Neither legislation nor self-regulation will fix the mess we're in. Third party data collection, targeting, and optimization were never designed into the DNA of the web and will be very hard to design out. They are a distinct co-evolving life form that has a symbiotic relationship with the content.

In other words: Killing one could kill the other. Perhaps that's what should happen, but I doubt the proponents of legislation would welcome that.

DOES IT MATTER?

Change is coming. But what form it takes, and how it improves our relationship with the web remains to be seen. In the meantime, we have choices to make.

Are you comfortable with someone collecting online and offline data that could reveal your name, address or phone number? Do you accept obnoxious walls of ads because they're relevant to your interests? Are you confident that the sites you frequent aren't prioritizing clicks over quality or privacy? Good, then the system's working for you.

If, on the other hand, you're concerned about your privacy online and off, if you're tired of wading through a sea of advertisements that disrupt access to the information you seek, if you're tired of garbage content that's clearly only designed to make money by sowing division and spreading misinformation, then I'm with you.

The line is crossed when the exposed data concerns health, wealth, and family.

The challenge, as they say, *is in the how*. There's more we can do about some of these issues than can be done about others. But let's take a whack at it, and try to find the best possible way to enjoy the internet without losing our privacy or our dignity.

7 STEPS TO INTENTIONAL CHANGE

Perhaps I've scared you to the point you just want to hide under the comforter and wait for someone else to fix it. I get it.

But be assured there are some places online where quality exists, tracking is a smaller problem, ads are reasonable, and sanity prevails. You also can, and should, take steps to reduce how much of your data leaks out and feeds the beast.

Step 1: Choose A Browser

Start with your choice of browser—you've seen that it's central to the flow of information. Avoiding Chrome is the most consequential change because it will help keep you out of the Google ecosystem. By default, Chrome will login to Google sites on your behalf, which seems oh-so-convenient but should be avoided.

If you're using an Apple device of any type, it came with Safari, and that's a fine choice: It has a built-in password manager, smart third-party cookie blocking, excellent security, plus history and passwords are synced across other Apple devices. What's not to like?

Windows users can use Edge: it's excellent for many of the same reasons, and there's an Android version that syncs to your desktop. CEO Satya Nadella has turned the ship: The new Microsoft is innovating and treating you like a customer.

I would be remiss if I didn't mention Firefox which for a long time was a lone voice in the privacy/security wilderness. It does everything you could wish for, plus has the best tracking blockers and a nice Facebook sandbox mode that stops your use of websites from leaking into that black hole of data. My only hesitation is that you'll need to download it on all your devices and create an account, because that password and history sync feature is just so important. I've not used Brave nor Opera but they have a great reputation.

Step 2: Install A Tracking Blocker

Next, install a tracking blocker—the one I like best is DuckDuckGo Privacy Essentials. The exact installation and setup method will differ depending on the OS and Browser combination you're using, but they make all the important decisions for you, and the UI is simple.

One difficulty that tracking blockers face is the possibility they break websites in subtle ways. It's technically very hard for the developers to anticipate all the trackers and how they interact with pages and data, and some problems will always arise. Big companies with big reputations, like Apple and Microsoft, need to err on the side of caution. They can't afford to accidentally block a cookie that's essential to the functioning of a bank website. On the other hand a small, nimble company can push things a bit further, block more stuff, and if problems arise they can react quickly and rein it back.

An important detail about DuckDuckGo, Inc: Because its primary business is its search engine, its privacy tools will direct searches there. This is good for two reasons:

First—the revenue generation is obvious so you don't need to ask, "What's the catch with this free privacy tool?"

Second—earlier in the book, I already recommended that you use its search engine, so I just saved you the time and effort of changing the default search engine in the browser.

Step 3: Consider An Ad Blocker

I have mixed feelings about recommending an ad blocker—on the one hand, I obviously agree that ad-tech has reached an absurd level of craziness, beyond my ability to understand (and I've been deeply involved in this business for decades). I loathe being on the wrong side of an economic decision that I can't see.

On the other hand, I generally sympathize with the needs of businesses, because I've owned, invested in, and ran a few of them. I don't use pirated software, nor download movies from BitTorrent. I don't like the idea of cutting off the revenue stream of a small businesess I value. It would feel like showing up at the potluck empty handed and walking away without helping clean up.

However, I'm not going to judge anyone that's just tired of the ad-tech shenanigans and wants a way out. If that describes you, then my vote goes to Adblock Plus: In addition to the blocking the bottom feeders, they support legitimate businesses through their Acceptable Ads and Flattr initiatives.

Step 4: Don't Worry About Anti-Virus Software

I'm not recommending anti-virus software to beat tracking—even though those guys routinely tout the thousands of cookies and trackers they find on your computer. That's just marketing BS and scaremongering.

It also does little good to run a weekly scan and delete that stuff when your browser has been exchanging it with the bottom feeders in the meantime. Better it never got in there, by using a proper security focused browser and tracking blocker.

Windows users should probably stick with the built-in Defender tool for combating real malware, but the days of anti-virus software cookie scanning are over.

Step 5: Don't Use Social Logins

Finally, do not use Google or Facebook for login services on websites (especially Facebook). I know they're convenient, but you're just handing over too much data to those guys.

Instead, login with your own ID, usually an email address. That means creating and remembering a password—but that's OK because you're using a browser with a password manager, right?

Steps 6 and 7: For Power Users (Nerds Only)

The last two fixes are for power users. If your use of the web is occasional, and you open up a browser, buy more toilet paper on Amazon, close it and you're done, then stop here. But mentally prepare yourself for the shitstorm coming in the next chapters.

Using multiple browsers might be the power user's best defense. We already use different email accounts for work and private life, so just extend this thinking to browsers. Different apps for work and personal tasks is obviously more efficient than mixing it all together, and segregating these worlds between two browsers is even more efficient. I like to Cmd-Tab / Alt-Tab between the two, bringing all the relevant tabs in front and ready for my 100% productive focus.

I'm typing these words into an online editor from Zoho, inside a Firefox tab. Firefox has 24 other tabs open with various half-written chapters, my email for orthogonalthinking.org—also hosted by Zoho, since you ask—and other ... stuff. I also keep Safari permanently running, and it has 11 tabs with my personal stuff: hey.com email, a paid-for Seeking Alpha account for investments, Amazon in case I need toilet paper, and so on. Finally there's Chrome, where I'm doing research for this book, so I'm logged into a Gmail account, and I look at privacy practices and technical implementations of various websites. Crucially, that's also where I experience the full joy of unfettered data leakage and ads. A machine with 16GB of memory helps.

VPNs are worth an honorable mention—their use is surprisingly prevalent, partly to circumvent national licensing restrictions, such as watching ad-free BBC shows in the US, partly by visitors to China discovering the Great Firewall, and also by political dissidents in repressive regimes, where goons snoop on telecoms.

I have a friend who used to run a VPN provider. He visited a specialist physician at Stanford due to a rare condition, and at the end of the consultation the physician said, "If you Google the symptoms, first install this VPN software, so your IP address and identity are shielded from the consumer medical advice website. Otherwise they'll sell your data to insurance companies, and your rates will go up." Funnily enough, the doctor was recommending my friend's own VPN product.

If a VPN can save a journalist in Syria from getting disappeared, or your medical information from being exploited, shouldn't a privacy-minded citizen in a western democracy be using one too? Yes, but only if you're the customer. A VPN sits in a unique position within the internet ecosystem—while it hides your activities from some organizations, like a state-run ISP, it exposes those same activities to the VPN provider. I hope it's obvious that a free VPN provider can make money by harvesting the network traffic of someone who has implicitly said they have something to hide.

Worse, some of those nefarious VPNs masquerade as legitimate existing products. For example, at various times there were 50 lookalikes pretending to be the HotSpot Shield VPN, with identical names and icons in the Android Play store, all doing goodness knows what with the harvested activities. Clearly you need to choose carefully. My preference would be Hotspot Shield (the real one), TunnelBear, or Proton VPN.

WHAT'S NEXT

You've seen how unintended consequences led to the creation of surveillance capitalism. I've given you solid advice for escaping the worst of it. However there's one aspect we've not covered yet. It's so big, personal and embedded into our lives that it deserves it's own chapter.

Please welcome to the stage: Smartphones.

4. SMARTPHONES

Smartphones allow you to bring all your online activity with you: Search, email, browsing, documents, contacts, games, social and more—all in your pocket.

But that means you also bring all that data mining everywhere you go.

For better or worse, we love our smartphones. Most of us can't imagine living without them—especially those of us who grew up with them from childhood. Our phones are slick and elegant.

But most of all, we trust them enough to go to bed with them.

Dumb Phones

It wasn't always this way. Back in the 1990s, there wasn't much to love.

Before they were smart, they were utilitarian pieces of plastic, barely capable of making phone calls. They were clunky and ugly, with limited features, thanks to perverse economic incentives.

Now that we're married to smartphones, maybe we should check if the relationship still works for us. We deserve to be loved as much by our devices as we love them. Can we trust them or are they having an affair?

Maybe we need to know a little more about their past? So let's begin at the beginning.

A BRIEF HISTORY OF SMARTPHONES

In the 1990s, any cool, tech-savvy business wonk who needed a gadget for contacts and schedules carried a Personal Digital Assistant (PDA). Even before the term was coined, notable early attempts at PDAs include the 1984's Psion Organiser and 1991's HP 95LX.

In 1993, Apple's **Newton MessagePad** launched—the $100 million experiment that coined the term PDA. It was a modest success, but with some unfortunate bugs. But maybe its biggest drawback was that it wasn't a connected device. "We can now see that the key to Newton's lackluster performance lay in its disconnectedness," said MacWorld two decades later. "The infrastructure and technology simply weren't there yet. The MessagePad, in a sense, arrived too early to its own party."[60]

Palm Computing's 1996 **Pilot** PDA gave users all that personal organization goodness: address book, date book, memo pad, and more, all in one device—but limited by PalmOS's weird *Graffiti* pen based typing. Early pager-style BlackBerry devices introduced the iconic keyboard and connectivity in 1999, giving corporate users access to "email anywhere."

But still, none of these devices could make phone calls. So our super cool, tech-savvy business wonk also had a cellphone, and had to juggle two devices. Real convergence—the merging of personal organizers and cell phones together into one device—would have to wait.

In 1996, the Nokia **9000 Communicator** was an early entry, a mobile phone with a mechanical qwerty keyboard. It supported faxing, word processing, and a web browser, all running on a platform called

PEN/GEOS 3.0, bringing both real internet connectivity and mobile phone service to a multi-function PDA. But it was heavy and expensive, and maybe just too early for the market. Nokia's former CEO Jorma Ollila later told the Washington Journal: "We had exactly the right view of what it was all about... We were about five years ahead."[61]

Later in the same year, Microsoft launched a platform called **Windows CE**. Like Palm and the others, these devices weren't phones: They were marketed as "PC Companion" PDAs that emulated the PC experience—notably in HP's 300LX palm-sized laptop with a mechanical qwerty keyboard and LCD screen. Its apps included "pocket" versions of Word, Excel, Outlook, Notes, and a version of the Explorer browser that simplified websites for the small screen by reducing them to text only. Still, it wasn't a phone.

In 2000, Ericsson released the **R380**, the first phone actually marketed as a "smartphone." While it didn't provide a true browser, it did come with a touchscreen, apps, and internet access, using software DNA passed down the family tree from Psion.

In the same year, Handspring merged its PalmOS-based Visor PDA and a cellphone addin to form the rarely-seen VisorPhone. Two years later, the company launched the **Treo 180**, which was sold by a variety of carriers. The Treo did away with the weird Graffiti input method, in favor of a BlackBerry-style keyboard. Handspring merged with Palm, and a succession of Treo device launches continued into 2007.

In 2001, Nokia—previously five years ahead with its 9000 series—tried again with a new platform. This was the popular **S60**, a derivative of the Symbian software used by the Ericsson R380. The phones came with an impressive suite of third-party apps that made them a market leader: By 2009 they claimed nearly half the smartphone market.

In 2002, BlackBerry jumped in with the **5810**, a mobile phone that supported push email, text messaging, simple web browsing, calendar and more. Its successors became so popular they were dubbed "CrackBerries."

Microsoft's PDA-focused Windows CE went through a convoluted series of rebrandings, as smartphone functionality was added from 2002. Microsoft initially licensed the software to HP, Compaq, Samsung, Dell, and others, eventually making **Windows Mobile** the third largest operating system in the smart handheld market behind Symbian and PalmOS.

Carriers Control The Market

Consumers loved all this awesome new tech. But the phones were expensive and complex to buy and use.

It was a hands-on purchase; people wanted to touch and hold them, they needed a salesperson to explain the features and software, and manufacturers just weren't set up to sell directly to consumers. Even if they had been, most of the mass-market consumers they wanted to sell to simply couldn't afford to pay out a retail price of hundreds of dollars.

So what's a poor phone builder with warehouses full of $600 phones to do?

Sell to the carriers. After all, the carriers already had a direct relationship with the customers through their mall-based stores and their monthly billing. So manufacturers abdicated the relationship with consumers, choosing instead to sell their phones to their real customers: The carriers. The T-Mobiles and Verizons and Cingulars and Sprints of the world became the critical conduit between the devices and the users, and phones became nothing more than an incentive to lure customers to their service.

Cole Brodman, Chief Marketing Officer for T-Mobile, lamented the damage to the industry by carrier subsidies in a 2012 blog post. "Purchasing phones at steep discount (subsidized by wireless carriers) devalues the incredible technology innovations coming to market," he asserted. "It distorts the cost of devices and creates an uneven playing field for OEMs, carriers and retailers alike. Many Americans don't realize the actual cost of the phones they're purchasing with a two-year contract because the cost of that phone is included in the cost of their data plan and the fees associated with their contract."[62]

The carriers bought handsets in trainload quantities and sold them to consumers at a steep discount with low monthly payment plans. Cingular offered phones for $49.99 with a $49.99 rebate on a two-year-contract. Free phones! If you needed more phones, just buy one at $29.99 and get up to four more phones—*free!* If you didn't want a contract, you could buy a phone starting at $29.99 with no credit check and no money down and no deposit and pay-as-you-go for the low, low price of 25 cents a minute!

Both updates and upgrades came to you from the carrier as well. Time for a software update? It came through the carrier. Security patch? Comes from the carrier. New model, new features? Yup, it was the carrier who made the big announcement and offered deals on the new phones.

And those critical updates and security patches weren't much of a priority. It was up to each carrier to decide when to push updates out to their customers' phones, and that never happened in a consistent or timely fashion across all carriers. It meant consumers might suffer from delayed security updates, leaving them vulnerable. Or maybe they wouldn't get their cool new features, for weeks or months.

To rub salt in the wound, the carriers plastered their own logos all over the phones and in the interface, nearly erasing the manufacturer from the user experience altogether. The carriers owned the customer relationship from end to end and the manufacturers were completely dependent on their fickle whims.

Carriers Control The Features

Now that the carrier was the customer, they were in a position to ask for special treatment from the manufacturers. After all, they needed phones that were unique to them, something another carrier couldn't also offer.

They demanded that phones be locked to their service so they wouldn't work elsewhere. They asked for unique features that other carriers didn't have. They stripped other features out to keep them cheap. They were paid by third parties to load them with random "bloatware" apps that gobbled power, wasted memory, slowed down performance, and often couldn't be removed. They restricted the development of streaming technologies or full web browsers, to reduce the bandwidth the phones would use.

"Wireless carriers have treated manufacturers like serfs," Wired's Fred Vogelstein wrote in 2008. "[They use] access to their networks as leverage to dictate what phones will get made, how much they will cost, and what features will be available on them. Handsets were viewed largely as cheap, disposable lures, massively subsidized to snare subscribers and lock them into using the carriers' proprietary services."[63]

In possibly the most egregious example of manipulating services to their own ends, carriers blocked the ability to make IP phone calls over the internet. Forbidding callers to use free point-to-point calling services like Skype protected the carriers' lucrative long-distance and international per-minute fees at the expense of technological advances and customer convenience. Carriers even have a derogatory term for such services: *Over The Top.*

The phones, after all, were just bait to bring customers to the carriers, so why shouldn't the carriers pick and choose what they offered their customers? If a manufacturer didn't fall in line, the carrier could go to another maker who would be all too happy for their business. This toxic, codependent relationship between phone makers and carriers squeezed the consumer's voice to irrelevance and stifled technological innovation.

It was an ugly time, filled with ugly phones that didn't live up to their technological potential. It didn't give consumers the experience they deserved.

Apple Dips In Its Toe And Gets Bit

Throughout this period, Apple was conspicuous in its absence from the cellphone industry. As late as 2005, Steve Jobs questioned if Apple could possibly succeed in such a dysfunctional business relationship with carriers.

After all, Apple was a company used to calling its own shots, writing its own software, and manufacturing its own devices. It had been wildly successful forging direct relationships with its customers, it had a new hit product in the iPod, and Jobs didn't see a reason to suddenly give up control in a new industry.

"The problem with [selling] a phone is that we're not very good going through [carriers] to get to the end users," Jobs said. "Carriers now have gained the upper hand in terms of the power of the relationship with the handset manufacturers. So the handset manufacturers are really getting these big thick books from the carriers telling them here's what your phone's going to be. We're not good at that."[64]

He was also unsure there was a meaningful market for smartphones beyond what he called the "pocket protector crowd." What changed his mind was the looming possibility that cell phones with music features might eat into the iPod's growing popularity. So Apple grudgingly partnered with Motorola as manufacturer, and Cingular Wireless as carrier, to launch a phone that included iTunes software in an effort to plug that hole with the Motorola ROKR.

Motorola and Cingular took the lead on design and features, and the project quickly became a classic "design by committee" debacle, resulting in a clunky, awkward device that the market largely rejected as a failure. It was a learning experience for Jobs; he vowed never to allow another party to guide the design of an Apple product.

The head of Apple's iPod division, Jon Rubenstein, went one further. He insisted that there was no need for such a convergence of devices: "Is there a toaster that also knows how to brew coffee? There is no such combined device, because it would not make anything better than an individual toaster or coffee machine. It works the same way with the iPod, the digital camera or mobile phone: It is important to have specialized devices."[65]

Google Buys Android, Inc.

In the meantime, Google's interest in mobile phones was growing, and it found the platform it was looking for in Android.

In 2003, Andy Rubin and his partners had launched Android, Inc. Rubin had a long history of working in mobile technology. A decade earlier, he'd been an engineer at the Apple spin-off General Magic, where he helped build an early platform for hand-held mobile devices called Magic Cap.

While the Android software was originally intended to drive digital cameras, Rubin's team soon realized it had bigger applications for mobile devices. Business Week noted that Rubin saw "tremendous potential in developing smarter mobile devices that are more aware of its owner's location and preferences," also quoting him saying, "If people are smart, that information starts getting aggregated into consumer products."[66]

Gathering data on a user's personal behavior—and integrating it into products—dovetailed nicely with Google's existing focus on delivering web services personalized with behavioral data.

So in 2005 Google purchased Android, Inc., expanding its platform from web-based search and email into mobile. And it quietly went to work on Android.

Apple Demands Complete Control

Back at Apple, it was clear that the convergence of devices was inevitable. Even Jobs was convinced—eventually. But he remained determined that, if Apple was really going to get into the phone business, it wouldn't be a repeat of the ROKR debacle.

This time, Apple would control the process from end to end.

It partnered with Cingular—later *The New* AT&T—which, thanks to their shared ROKR experience, decided to trust Apple to design the phone as it saw fit. It didn't hurt that the carrier used the international GSM standard for mobile communications, opening the phone up to international markets. In exchange for free rein on design, Apple gave the carrier four years of exclusivity to carry the phone. As icing on the cake, they would also take a percentage of the revenue AT&T generated from every new iPhone contract.

Work on the iPhone began in 2004. Rather than using any of the existing platforms currently in the market, Apple developed its own: iPhone OS—later iOS. A team of more than 1,000 worked on the project—code-named "P2"—for nearly three years at a cost of $150 million.

Jobs Reveals The iPhone

The iPhone launched in 2007. It was a complete convergence of business tools, internet access, and entertainment, in a form unlike the mobile phones that had preceded it—although LG disagrees.[67] There was no mechanical keyboard, no sliding screen.

It was a PDA and a phone under a sleek slab of glass, which the user navigated without a stylus—just a fingertip and a grid of icons. At launch, it included a suite of apps: Messages, Calendar, Photos, Camera, YouTube, Stocks, Maps, Weather, Voice Memos, Notes, Clock, Calculator, Settings, iTunes, and a browser that loaded whole websites.

Steve Jobs revealed the phone on stage, downloading music, videos, and maps from the Internet. Mike Lazaridis, founder of BlackBerry's parent company Research In Motion, saw instantly that the iPhone was different. Not just because it had a touchscreen and no keyboard, but because it was clearly using loads of bandwidth. "How did they do that?" he wondered. "It's going to collapse [Cingular's] network."

Carriers had been doing their level best for years to limit the functionality of smartphones for exactly that reason: to throttle bandwidth usage. Now here was Jobs on stage with Cingular's CEO announcing their exclusive arrangement. "They put a full web browser on that thing," Lazaridis marveled. "The carriers aren't letting us put a full browser on our products." His co-CEO Jim Balsillie agreed. "These guys are really, really good. This is different."[68]

Tuan C. Nguyen says the iPhone "reoriented people's relationship with smartphones," which until then had been seen as productivity and organization tools for business professionals and technology wonks. In that moment the smartphone had become an indispensable tool for everyday people, "a full-blown multimedia powerhouse, enabling users to play games, watch movies, chat, share content, and stay connected to all the possibilities that we're all still constantly rediscovering."[69]

Consumers were instantly aware, with huge lines outside stores carrying the iPhone. They no longer accepted whatever the carrier's retail staff pushed at them. They walked in knowing what they wanted.

iPhone Forces Google To Adjust

Google was halfway through its new Android project when Apple launched its iPhone. And Jobs' demo threw the Android team for a loop.

Google's vision for an Android device was modeled after the Treo and BlackBerry, with a mechanical keyboard and no touchscreen. When they saw the iPhone's form and features it looked like it was light years beyond where Google was heading.

Team Android had to adjust their game plan if they were going to compete, and they quickly redesigned the platform to support a big touchscreen.

Google Cedes Control To Manufacturers

Unlike Apple, Google didn't have any direct expertise in building its own hardware, and it wasn't keen to get into the manufacturing business. So in marked contrast to Apple's policy of total control, the Android philosophy was effectively a lack of control over its market. Google decided to license Android to manufacturers and let them change the look and function as they liked.

I should point out here that unlike iOS, Android at its core is not a proprietary software. It's an open-source software based on a modified version of Linux, and other phone manufacturers besides

Google are welcome to use it. What Google did was build their own variation of Android, including an integration for their Google Mobile Services (GMS) software that delivers Google apps like Chrome and the Play store.

Plus, Google owns the "Android" name and logo. So if a manufacturer wants to include GMS, which of course is kind of the point of having an Android phone, it licenses Google's version of Android and has to sport Google's Android brand to boot. When you buy a phone that says it's running "Android" you're getting Android software that complies with Google's strict standards and Google's GMS.

Google Lets Anyone Build An Android

Google wanted everyone and anyone to be able to build phones with Android, so when the software was released to manufacturers Google offered no exclusivity. As Ars Technica's Ron Amadeo put it: "Google was starting from scratch with zero percent market share, so it was happy to give up control and give everyone a seat at the table in exchange for adoption."[70]

In fact, unlike Microsoft which always licensed its platform to manufacturers for a fee, Google simply gave Android away, knowing it would make more money from search and other advertising sources. Manufacturers, having wafer-thin margins and limited experience with software, were delighted to get on board with something that looked as good as an iPhone.

Like manufacturers, carriers were desperate for more smartphones with fewer restrictions than iPhones, and Google delivered. There were no limitations on carriers: Any carrier could sell the phones and modify the features and software as they liked.

HTC launched the *Dream* a/k/a the G1—the first Android phone—in 2008. It had a full-color touchscreen that slid back to reveal a mechanical keyboard, and a thorough integration with Gmail, Maps, Search, Talk, and YouTube, as well as syncing with Calendar and Contacts. The platform was soon updated to include an onscreen or "soft" keyboard and video support, on par with the iPhone's form and function.

Google might be a half a lap behind Apple, but now it was in the race.

Palm And BlackBerry Finally Fall Away

iOS and Android had radically changed the smartphone. And it left nearly all other platforms in the rear view mirror.

BlackBerry was too slow in refocusing from corporate users to everyday consumers and just couldn't compete with this new breed of smartphones "on which [consumers] could play games, watch videos and perform myriad other tasks that BlackBerrys were never designed to do," as Omar el Akkad put it, in Toronto's The Globe and Mail.[71]

BlackBerry suspended manufacturing, licensing its software to another company, TCL. But it too stopped manufacturing BlackBerry devices just a few years later.

Palm struggled as well, until it was bought by HP, which shut down the by-now unmaintainable PalmOS in favor of Palm's new webOS platform. A handful of smartphones were built with webOS before the software was sold to LG, where it powered "Internet Of Things" efforts, appearing in TVs, wearable devices, and refrigerators.

That left Windows Phone to stand alone against the juggernauts of Android and iOS. At least for a while.

Help Me, Windows Phone. You're My Only Hope.

Microsoft was hanging on to about 2% of the market—by the skin of its teeth. Things were looking dire. But then Verizon stepped in and offered a lifeline.

The carriers, you see, were getting tired of paying hefty prices to carry expensive iPhones and Androids that were eating into their profits. They wanted to go back to the good old days, when they controlled what the consumer could buy. If they could sell affordable, quality smartphones that were iPhone adjacent, they were sure they could force Apple's hand.

Microsoft, Verizon hoped, would be its savior.

Yankee Group analyst Katie Lewis said at the time, "Mobile operators are sick of taking orders from Apple, [which is one] reason why carriers like AT&T and Verizon are backing Windows Phone. ... iPhones are occupying an increasingly dangerous share of operators' smartphone sales."[72]

Verizon was sure they could turn Windows Phone into a real competitor and pose a challenge to Apple and Google. Verizon's CFO Fran Shammo told Reuters, "We're really looking at the Windows Phone 8.0 platform because that's a differentiator."[73]

The resulting phones were pretty fast, had some unique features, and were heavily subsidized by carriers. Microsoft, however, was too fickle with its exclusivity. Some models were exclusive to Verizon, some were also available from AT&T and T-Mobile. Some carriers promoted the phones hard, then suddenly dropped them. Microsoft also sold unlocked phones in its own store, but for some reason didn't offer financing—so if you wanted to make payments, you had to go to a carrier, who may or may not have the model you're looking for.

It didn't help that Microsoft's app marketplace was weak. App developers had little interest in building for a platform that held such a small market share, and buyers weren't compelled to purchase phones that didn't have a strong library of apps to enhance their experience.

Carriers struggled to keep customers once they got them. Microsoft might give a carrier exclusive rights to a new phone, then withhold the rights from that same carrier for later versions of the phone. So if a user was ready for an upgrade and couldn't get the latest version, they had to choose between switching carriers or switching brands. On top of this, Microsoft was still stuck in its past business model and charging for the platform.

"Windows Phone has struggled from day one with poor carrier availability and promotion, combined with a lack of real continuity," said Peter Bright in Ars Technica. "Customers who take an interest in the platform ... have been left with nowhere to go but Android or iPhone."[74]

In the end, the Windows Phone just couldn't compete. In 2017, Microsoft announced that Windows Phone had been retired, leaving behind today's duopoly: iPhone and Android.

THE BATTLE FOR THE BUSINESS MODEL

With only two viable platforms left in the market, there was a big pie to split. Apple's iOS was available exclusively in its iPhones, and Google's Android could be had in a wide variety of devices from a wide variety of manufacturers.

By now, even Apple was working with all the big carriers.

And everyone—manufacturers and carriers alike—had their eyes on profits.

Apple Ruled With An Iron Fist

Apple's control over the carriers extended beyond the form and function of the phones. They dictated how they would be displayed in stores, how they were represented in commercials, and carriers couldn't even put their logos on the devices. They were branded as Apple and Apple alone.

In 2011, AT&T's exclusive contract ended, and Verizon was able to offer the iPhone 4 to its customers. Verizon's expansive network increased Apple's reach and improved customer experience in the US. At around the same time, international adoption also skyrocketed. By the end of the year, the iPhone 4S was available in 70 countries and 100 carriers. A year later, iPhones were in 100 countries and on 240 carriers.

Throughout that expansion, no carriers were given any exclusivity, and no carrier was able to dictate how the devices should operate. In their final act of freeing customers from the tyranny of the carriers, Apple in 2009 forced AT&T to permit IP calling, allowing customers to use services like Skype, rather than pay the carrier's expensive long distance rates. It's hard to imagine now how it had ever been allowed to happen in the first place.

All these strict rules for carriers, and a carefully cultivated, quality brand, succeeded in cementing the iPhone as the must-have device. Apple built a strong relationship with a rabidly tribal user base who saw themselves as the iPhone faithful, not the carrier faithful.

Apple also had its own retail stores, selling and servicing its other devices. iPhones fit right in, giving consumers yet another way to buy directly from the manufacturer, from a real person, who was well-equipped to offer real service and earn customer loyalty.

As Computerworld reported in 2012, "To stay relevant, retain customers and gain new ones, carriers have no choice but to carry the iPhone, so they essentially can't turn down a deal with Apple. Because of this fact, carriers are losing control over their customers, the customer billing experience and the U.S. smartphone market overall."[75]

And what of carriers' terrible reputation for slow updates, sometimes withholding critical patches or features for months? Apple was having none of that.

Apple sidestepped the carriers and distributed their own updates on their own schedule—securing one more direct connection to its customers.

Apple's Apps Were Closely Monitored

Apple's App Store was equally locked down. Developers were charged an annual fee to offer their apps in the store, along with a percentage of any revenues generated from downloads. Keeping harmful malware out of the store and off their customers' phones was a priority. No app made it into the store without it first being reviewed and approved.

Apple removed apps that didn't work, represented harmful or illegal activities, were clones of existing apps, or that delivered pirated content. While developers often complain of the cost and heavy-handed approach, it's overall been good for consumers, with high quality apps and few security risks.

Google Embraced All Carriers—For A Price

Remember: Google had entered the race half a lap behind with no experience building its own hardware and no retail stores of its own.

As we already said, Google let pretty much any manufacturer make Android phones. Google in return got more people using its advertising and search services. The strategy resulted in a huge variety of brands, features and price points available from nearly every carrier.

Carriers were excited to boss around these new Android manufacturers. They had new merchandise for their websites and store shelves and something they could slap their logos on again. Consumers ate it up; the phones looked more or less like iPhones, they functioned more or less like iPhones, and generally they were cheaper than iPhones.

With all those phones with all those features being controlled by all those carriers, Google had no control over its updates the way Apple did. Manufacturers could customize the software as they liked, and carriers could demand exclusive features and models, so there were loads of versions of Android phones out in the marketplace. Each of those phones got a slightly different update, and each partner did its own testing before release.

Verizon developed an especially bad reputation for holding back on Android updates, but in truth there were other carriers who were even slower. As AndroidCentral put it, "When 100 different companies grab the source code and build 100 slightly different versions of Android, keeping the devices all up to date is a mountain of work. ... The extra cool features that phone manufacturers add are a double-edged sword – they make the software better, but they also make updating it a lot more work."[76]

Google Apps Had Little Oversight

The Google Play Store, then called Android Market, was no better. Apps could be added with little to no oversight, and could access personal information like your location without asking permission. Offending or non compliant apps were only removed when users complained.

The Android landscape was looking an awful lot like the days of old.

Google Controlled What It Wanted To Control

Yet there was one place that Google exerted great control. It had to do less with how the phone worked than it did with how the user traveled the web while using the phone—and Google's ability to track and mine that behavior.

We already know that when manufacturers licensed Android, it came with Google's GMS features on board, including Search and

Chrome. But it was possible to load other browsers and search engines on the phone, and that didn't make Google happy.

After all, Google hadn't gotten into the phone business to provide a vessel for competing products. It had gotten into the phone business—to paraphrase Android's Andy Rubin—to develop smarter mobile devices that can track its owner's location and preferences, and aggregate that information into consumer products.

So Google either pressured or paid manufacturers and carriers to exclusively pre-load Chrome and Search on their phones, sometimes withholding access to the Google Play app store unless they did so.[77]

In 2011, Google had bought Motorola Mobility, getting billions of dollars worth of intellectual property in the process. Motorola owned patents on all kinds of communication technologies, which now belonged to Google. When it sold the rest of the company to Lenovo two years later, Google kept all the patents, which it used as leverage to make sure manufacturers did as they were told.

As an advertising company that depends on tracking massive amounts of user behavior data to target advertising, getting their own browser and search engine into as many hands as possible was the goal. Giving the platform away, and working with as many carriers as possible, was the path to achieving exactly that.

WHAT IT LOOKS LIKE NOW

It's only been a few years now since Microsoft shut down Windows Phone, but in reality Apple and Google had been dominating for a decade. Today Android holds about 41% of the US smartphone market while iPhone has about 58%.

But Apple's share of new activations is on the rise, meaning more people are buying new iPhones than in previous years. In early 2020, iPhones saw an 8% increase in new activations, and a 12% gain in new adoptions overall in the past two years.

There are a few alternative platforms in play aside from Android and iOS, and we'll look at some later, but they effectively account for 0% of the market.

Apple Is Still In Charge

Apple still retains control over both its software and hardware—from end to end. Consequently, security and feature updates are timely.

According to Statista: "Apple significantly extended the life cycle of iPhone models over the years. ... Later models have gotten software updates for five to six years. The iPhone 6s was launched with iOS 9 in 2015 and will still be compatible when iOS 14 is officially released in the fall of 2020."[78] Meaning even older phones will see the benefit of updates without being aged out too soon.

Phones are still available both from carriers or directly from Apple's site, where you can get zero-interest payment plans straight from Apple itself, choose any carrier, and easily trade in your old phone.

The App Store remains tightly controlled by Apple. The company line is: "We take responsibility for ensuring that apps are held to a high standard for privacy, security, and content because nothing is more important than maintaining the trust of our users. ... We review every app and every update [and as] part of our rigorous app review process, we use a combination of automated systems and hundreds of human experts."[79]

In mid-2020, Apple announced an upcoming feature for its iP-hones and iPads that will require apps to ask users for permission before tracking personalized data to target ads in an attempt to provide its customers with more transparency regarding how their data is used. Interestingly, marketing associations backed by Facebook and Google argued against the move, saying that the apps "will now need to ask for permission twice, increasing the risk users will refuse," acknowledging that users, when given a choice, would rather not have their data mined.[80]

The release of this new privacy requirement has been pushed back to early 2021. According to an Apple statement, this will "give developers the time they need to make the necessary changes, and as a result, the requirement to use this tracking permission will go into effect early next year."

Also early in 2021, Apple will roll out another new tool to make it easier for users to understand an app's privacy practices before they even download it. App "nutrition labels" will use simple language and icons to explain exactly what data an app will gather, whether it will be linked to the user, and if the user will be tracked. Apple says developers will be responsible for identifying any data they or their third-party partners might collect, and for being transparent about how it's used.

Google Closes The Gap

Google, on the other hand, still licenses its software and GMS to a wide array of manufacturers, each of which exhibit varying degrees of reliability and trustworthiness.

In what is perhaps an attempt to emulate Apple's end-to-end control of the customer relationship, Google finally started designing and manufacturing its own Pixel handsets in 2016, after a half-hearted half-decade of selling Nexus devices to developers. Phones are still available from carriers, but now you also have the option to buy directly from Google with a zero-interest payment plan. As of this moment, the phones come in three flavors; bundled with Verizon service, unlocked for any service, or with Google Fi, which is their own branded carrier riding on the backs of Sprint, T-Mobile, and U.S. Cellular; an option not available at Apple.

As with iPhones, Pixel phones get updates directly from the manufacturer, removing the carriers from the equation. The usual cadence is monthly security updates, plus annual major releases of Android. Google guarantees at least three years of updates and new releases.

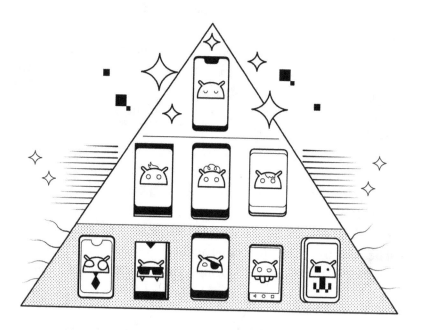

The 3 Tiers Of Android

This decision to become a manufacturer split the Android smartphone market into what industry analyst Richi Jennings calls the Three Tiers of Android:

- **Tier One** are "Pure Android" phones—Pixel branded (formerly Nexus) purchased directly from Google, and certified Android One devices[81] from manufacturers such as Nokia/HMD[82] and Motorola (certain devices only). The software is unsullied by bloatware, and updates are timely. In the case of Google Pixel phones, you are the direct customer of the manufacturer who provides both the software and the hardware. Usually you'd buy these outright and unlocked, adding your own prepay SIM card or SIM-only contract.

- **Tier Two** are "Trusted Impure Android" phones—mainstream Android phones from trusted manufacturers. These are manufacturers like Samsung, Sony, LG, or other trusted brands that have licensed Google Android. But they're *impure*, in that they add their own apps and enhancements to the operating system with various levels of success and reliability. Jennings recommends you opt to buy the phone outright and unlocked, rather than as part of a contract.

- **Tier Three** are cheap phones—suspiciously inexpensive Android handsets from brands you may have heard of only tangentially. At best, they're suspect in terms of their privacy: The apps and tweaks they've added might be less than trustworthy. You can find these phones on eBay, AliExpress, Amazon's third-party Marketplace, or even hanging next to the cash register at the convenience store.

Thanks to all these Android phones on the market, there are still struggles today with getting updates out on time, even for Tier Two phones. According to TechRadar: "After Android 11 launches, different smartphone brands will have their devices eligible for the finished Android 11 update slowly over time. ... Not all smartphone manufacturers upgrade immediately, however, and it will likely be some time in 2021 before all smartphones that can upgrade, have had the upgrade made available."[83]

Guessing which phones and carriers will get their Android updates distributed fastest has become something of a cottage industry, with experts posting ranked lists of the most reliably updated devices, showing that some take a year to update just 10% of their product line. Google's 2018-era *Project Treble* was supposed to have fixed this problem, but evidence of any meaningful improvement is scant. However,

Google has tried to gain some control over updates by distributing more fixes and "mitigations" within its own Google Play Services app.

There is a short list of Android devices that are guaranteed to be updated on time. If your company depends on Android security and updates, *Android Enterprise* devices and services meet Google's strict enterprise requirements. Manufacturers awarded Android Enterprise approval get extra support and training from Google and are recommended to enterprise users. This perhaps also shows Google's focus on pushing for improved service to its corporate users more than its consumer users. As you might expect, there's a large overlap in the devices available in this program and in Android One.

As regards favoring its own search and browser tools, Google is pulling back on its practice of forcing builders to preload phones with Chrome and Search, at least in the EU, and charges a license fee instead. But only under legal pressure: Google has been fined multiple times by the European Commission, most recently to the tune of nearly €4.5 billion, for "abusing the dominance of its Android operating system."

Choose Your Own Search Adventure

To further address this issue, starting in the summer of 2020, Google began allowing users to choose a preferred search engine for their phone from a screen that offers four options—one of which of course is Google.

To be one of the other three choices, search engines have to pay Google through an auction that's held every three months. Sources say that Google initially set the minimum bid price at $20 per user, but that it was adjusted down for the first auction. Reportedly the second round of auctions reduced the number of winners while prices went up.

Even auction winners like DuckDuckGo aren't pleased. According to its CEO Gabriel Weinberg, "Google is taking away all the profit of these search engines and profiting from it themselves." The result is that small startup engines are priced out of the game. DuckDuckGo's general counsel Megan Gray says if there's a fair solution, it's "getting rid of the damn auction. It should be a genuine choice – it shouldn't be pay to play. That would be the best outcome."[84]

According to testing, most users choose Google Search anyway, so offering the choice is a gesture seemingly aimed at appeasing the EU. The upshot is that Google is still tracking the search and browsing histories of the billions of mobile users in its ecosystem. And apparently enjoying yet another revenue stream to boot.

Google claims that it's imposing more oversight over Android apps—much of it by a "machine-learning based approach" called Play Protect that identifies, for instance, non compliant advertising and malware.[85] According to Google, Play Protect means Android apps "undergo rigorous security testing before appearing in the Google Play Store. We vet every app and developer in Google Play, and suspend those who violate our policies. Then, Play Protect scans billions of apps daily to make sure everything remains spot on. That way, no matter where you download an app from, you know it's been checked by Google Play Protect."[86]

Craig Vachon, Senior Partner at NextStage and Founder of Chowdahead Growth Fund, sees it differently: "Android has 2 million apps that they can't find who owns them. The email addresses when someone signed up are no longer connected to humans." Vachon says games can see your contact list, data usage, the other games and apps that are on your phone and which ones you actually use, all because you just wanted to play solitaire. "So, yeah, I think Android is a little scarier," he says. "I don't think Google cares, because it makes money ... and there's no real rationale for them to clean this mess up."

Two Distinct Sets Of Problems

Just looking at the business model, both historically and today, to me it's clear. With Apple you're unquestionably the customer and always have been. It builds exactly the phone it wants in the market, with no undue influence from service providers. You get software and security updates the moment they're ready—with no carrier standing between you and the manufacturer—and the App Store's policies offer protection from bad actors. It's true that Apple collects data, but as a rule they are aggressive about protecting privacy, and make extensive promises to treat customers well.

Computer consultant Todd Fraser puts it succinctly: "Apple's infamous walled garden approach unfortunately is currently the safest model for consumers. In which products can get rejected if they don't meet Apple's guidelines. This does suck ... but the products you do get ... tend to work rather well."[87]

When Apple attracts criticism it's generally not due to privacy or security breaches. The complaints usually fall into the category of "they make too much money"—and there is some validity to this. Apple takes a 30% cut of some purchases like audiobook sales. Amazon resists playing along, forcing the user to go outside the Audible app and to the website to make payment. Some companies, including Facebook, are even calling it out within the in-app purchase process, telling the user, "Apple takes a 30% cut of this." For the rest of us, it's tiresome to be inconvenienced when we're just trying to hand over money.

With Android, it's an entirely different kind of problem. Google's "embrace all partners" approach to software and hardware created challenges from the beginning—and that hasn't really changed.

Features and software vary from manufacturer to manufacturer. Distribution of Android updates and security patches are wildly inconsistent across both builders and carriers, and the carriers still largely call the shots on timing of those updates, unless you buy the phone outright.

Google is now doing a better job of protecting your privacy against invasive apps than they used to, but the bar was set low. Their fundamental plan to use the phones to put their search and browser in as many hands as possible means no matter which phone you buy and which carrier you choose, your online activity and behavior is being tracked and cataloged for Google's primary business: advertising.

Perversely, all this creates the opposite problem to Apple's— handset manufacturers make *too little money* and rush to market with poorly designed features, and don't support their products with updates.

VISIONS FOR TOMORROW

Change may come in the form of a complete separation between carriers and manufacturers, making smartphone users the direct customer of both service providers and hardware providers.

In 2012 Cole Brodman, then CMO for T-Mobile, had a vision that removed carrier subsidies altogether. "In the future, my hope is we will see the U.S. industry ... move away from the subsidy-only model. Not only would this help level the playing field and foster competition, it would also help consumers by keeping rate plans affordable, providing more transparency in how they purchase wireless and it could encourage a robust, consumer-driven market for affordable (yet still amazing) used smartphones and tablets."[88]

Or change may come in the form of another serious platform contender entering the market. On that front, Jennings isn't so hopeful: "People keep reinventing this idea—saying, 'I'm going to create this alternative platform and it's going to be privacy focused.' But they don't make any money doing it, so they fail. The only ones that persist are amateur efforts. And you're still faced with a problem of getting the security patches quickly."

So, are there any meaningful alternatives on the horizon?

Alternative Operating Systems

Open source software like Android can be modified and used as the basis of a new platform, without Google's oversight. Sirin is one such Android based platform, delivered in a device branded *Finney*, which they call a "blockchain smartphone." The Android core is layered with blockchain technology, and the phone includes a built-in "cold storage wallet" and "Safe Screen" technology for secure crypto transactions. Says Sirin: "Our vision is to bridge the gap between the blockchain economy and the mass market through multi-layered cybersecurity and a much-improved user experience." But this seems an extraordinarily niche operating system.

Non-Android software startups also exist, and some of them are seeing some success with millions of users.

KaiOS already claims to be the world's third largest operating system. They've got a focus on feature phones; budget devices with some smartphone features, but generally not as sophisticated - or expensive - as a true smartphone. Perhaps a perfect device for the emerging markets they're serving. Their software is in over 100 million devices around the world, with a focus on Asia, Africa, and South America. Their mission statement says that "KaiOS exists to empower people around the world through technology. We believe everyone should have access to the internet to unleash their potential."

Ubuntu Touch is an operating system optimized for touch-friendly devices like smartphones and tablets, that's also able to function like a desktop computer. It's an open-source operating system which can be used by any smartphone manufacturer. Maintained by a community of volunteers, it depends on donations to keep development underway. "Although Big Brother and others in the world may wish to spy on you and steal your personal data," says the team, "don't worry. With Ubuntu Touch – a safer system that respects your privacy – they will have nothing to see."

Tizen is another original platform built from the ground up. The project resides in the Linux Foundation, and like Ubuntu is developed by a volunteer community of developers. "Tizen is an open and flexible operating system built from the ground up to address the needs of all stakeholders of the mobile and connected device ecosystem ... Mobile operators can work with device partners to customize the operating system and user experience to meet the needs of specific customer segments or demographics."

And of course there's Huawei's Harmony OS. While they suffer from the politics of a trade war between the US and China, Huawei has seen success elsewhere and in 2019 was the world's second largest phone manufacturer after Samsung. The company is "committed to bringing digital to every person, home and organization for a fully connected, intelligent world." Harmony remains tiny and almost all Huawei phones ship with Android.

Whether one of these alternative smartphone platform projects, or any other, rises to the level of delivering real competition to iPhone and Android remains to be seen. It doesn't feel like that's something that could happen in the foreseeable future, unless or until some new technology sidesteps the current phone platforms altogether. For example, an exciting new AR goggle technology wouldn't necessarily need to run on either Android or iOS.

DOES ALL THIS MATTER?

For a long time, your activity and behavior have been tracked in lots of ways. From the way you search to the sites you visit, a snapshot of your online life is being built somewhere by someone.

Your smartphone takes all that data mining and puts it in your pocket, everywhere you go, along with an array of other kinds of information that don't exist on your laptop, not the least of which is your location at any given moment. There's the geotagging of your photos, whether you prefer portrait or landscape pictures. There's how many steps you take, how you hold your phone and whether you're prone to dropping it. There's the voice commands you use with your personal assistant, and the "accidentally" recorded audio when you didn't intend to wake the assistant. There's the apps you use, including the games you download and play.

Some of this data collection is aimed at making your experience better. Some of it is aimed at building out that personal profile, and using it to target you with advertising. If your phone permits sketchy apps and you've installed one, or it came pre-installed on your phone, then the scope for data mining extends far beyond these innocuous examples. Literally your banking details and anything else are up for grabs.

Not all phone manufacturers, or all carriers, provide the same experience. Some are dedicated to treating you like the customer, and some are ... not. Some collect more data on your activity. Some deliver updates and security directly to you, others don't.

You'd be surprised how easily your carrier can observe your activity, and even alter it. ATT has mused they would offer a $5 price cut in return for ads,[89] which is technically possible, if not ethically ideal.

However you feel about data collection, updates, and security, **make intentional choices** and find the smartphone and carrier that suit your personal needs and concerns best.

3 STEPS TO INTENTIONAL CHANGE

Now that you've thought about your priorities, you'll probably do one of two things: Keep the phone you've got and do your best to optimize for privacy and security, or make a change and switch.

Step 1: Is Your Current Phone Safe?

When you buy a car you're assured various guarantees from the manufacturer. Some are optional paid upgrades, like the infamously dubious "protective undercoating." But a considerable level of protection is mandated in law. For example, the manufacturer must supply parts at reasonable cost long into the future.

Your smartphone comes with guarantees too, but they pretty much end with a promise it won't catch fire or bend in your pocket. There are often *zero* guarantees the manufacturer will supply security patches, bug fixes, or software upgrades.

Security patches are especially important because hackers are constantly finding bugs and exploiting them to get nefarious apps onto your phone, often hidden in "free" products like games. From the time the hacker finds a bug to the time the manufacturer issues a patch, you're open to all kinds of mischief. Even after the patch is released, it can take months for the carrier to get it distributed and onto your phone, especially for low-margin, cheapo devices.

Eventually, all manufacturers simply quit worrying about delivering patches for older handsets. Not surprisingly, the higher quality and more expensive suppliers support their devices longer, but even then, nothing lasts forever. Once an iPhone or Tier One Android phone reaches three to five years old, consider upgrading just for the security and bug fixes. For Tier 2 Android devices, the longevity could be as short as one or two years. And for Tier 3, as the saying goes, *good luck with that*.

If you're not getting bug fixes or security patches every month or so, it's time to get a new phone—or you leave yourself at risk. Those risks are not some abstract dystopian futurism beloved by science fiction writers, nor are they cooked up in the basements of tinfoil-hat conspiracy theorists. As Dan Goodin reported in *Ars Technica*: "Over a Billion Android Devices Are at Risk of Data Theft."[90]

Step 2: If You're Keeping The Phone You Have

If your phone is new enough that it's still getting regular software updates, you may decide to keep it a while. But you'll still want to reduce data leakage and tighten privacy, and there's a number of steps you can take—for both iOS and Android.

iOS Users:

- **Use iCloud.** Think you need Google Calendar? Nope. iCloud does it. Reminders? Notes? Contacts? Stick with the Apple supplied stuff. Works great, synchronizes across devices, even to Windows. It's secure and private.
- **Use the Photos app** for your photos, sync them with iCloud, and use the built-in document editing tools.
- **Use Pages, Numbers and Keynote.** They work great and can read and write Office format files. Pay for extra storage if you need it.
- **Use Apple Maps**, which came preinstalled on the phone, and not Google Maps. Apple's product was a poor second for a long time, but you'll be surprised how good, and indeed better than Google, it is now. There are cases where it doesn't know about specific businesses but it's rare and I find Google Maps is equally error prone. I've not deleted Google Maps from my iPhone, but I stay logged out and I buried the icon in a folder.

I keep it as a last resort or when I travel outside the US where Apple Maps is not as good in some places. (Same goes for Maps on macOS.)

- **Use Safari not Chrome.** There was a time when the browser supplied with iOS was awful, so the first thing you did was install Chrome. However Apple (and to their credit Microsoft) have poured effort into quality browsers that are built around privacy. They have password managers built-in using hardware encryption. Safari does a good job blocking egregious third party cookies and trackers, security updates come frequently and best of all, you paid for it already so you're the customer. (Same goes for Safari on macOS.)

- **Change search to use DuckDuckGo**, or better still install the DuckDuckGo Privacy Browser.

- **Delete Google supplied apps** unless there's a compelling reason to keep them. This includes apps that might not obviously be Google's—such as Waze.

- **Delete apps you're not using** or should never have installed. Although on iOS it's very hard for an app to do something nefarious, and getting harder, some responsibility lies with you. Keep your phone clean, metaphorically speaking.

- **Turn off location in apps that don't need it.** Go to settings | privacy | location services and turn off apps that don't need to access your location. Consider turning off other data exchange between apps in the main privacy screen.

- **Chill out.** Buying an Apple product means paying a premium so you don't need to worry about hidden economic incentives that hurt you. The company works hard to win your trust and won't squander it. There are sometimes problems that are reported in the news, but that's because they're so rare it's newsworthy. I use Apple Pay because it's safer than a standard credit card transaction. I have no problem with Apple tracking my location using Maps because there's no business reason for them to sell that data. They make plenty of money and are better off promoting the privacy and security of the brand.

Android Users:

- **Fixes here are limited.** The platform is obviously built to keep you logged into Google across all the apps and services with a first-party cookie. A good basic option is to replace Google Search with the DuckDuckGo Privacy Browser. It's a full-fledged browser so it can keep you logged out of Google services, and searches come from their own engine that isn't built on tracking. They make money from clearly marked paid listings in the search results that are based on your search query in the moment and not historical behavior, much like Yellow Pages. DuckDuckGo also publishes some excellent guides with very helpful privacy tips, like this: https://spreadprivacy.com/android-privacy-tips/

Step 3: If You're Switching Or A First Time Buyer

Making a change means making a choice, and I wish we had more than two choices of smartphone platform for everyday use. Maybe one day Microsoft will return with something competitive, perhaps derived from Android so developers don't need to code for a third platform.

There are other options if you like compiling Linux kernels or flashing ROMs, but I don't and I assume you don't either. So it's iOS or Android.

The right time to consider switching platform is when you're thinking of upgrading to a newer generation of hardware anyway. Both Apple and Google provide apps that greatly ease the process of switching from the other guy.

Buying iPhone:

Buy directly from Apple, online or in the Apple Store. Their payment plans are reasonable, and you can choose your carrier during the purchasing process. The staff in the store are well trained, knowledgeable and enthusiastic, if a little zealous. If the phone ever needs to be fixed, you can walk into an Apple Store anywhere in the world and they promise to take good care of you.

If you must, buying an iPhone from a carrier is okay—the carrier isn't allowed to screw up the phone with bloatware or slow down updates anyway, so you're still getting an equivalent experience.

Buying Android:

I think you can tell my preference. But if you really must have an Android phone, it's best to buy a Tier 1 phone: a Pixel directly from Google—where you're closest to being the customer—or an Android One phone from the likes of Nokia/HMD. You'll be getting the core Android with the least bloat and the fastest updates directly from Google. You're best off buying an unlocked phone online—not from a carrier—and add your own pre-pay or contract SIM card.

If you do take a wrong turn and stray into a carrier's retail store and into the clutches of a salesperson, you need to figure out which Android tier the devices sit in. You'll want Tier One Pixel if it's available, because it'll have less bloat. But be aware that updates won't be delivered as quickly if you don't buy directly from Google.

If you're not going with a Pixel or Android One phone, let price be your guide. Only a third-party phone at the higher end, a Tier Two Android, has enough profit built in for the manufacturer to make the device and then continue to support it with bug fixes and security patches. At the bottom end, in Tier Three, they need to cut costs by limiting software updates, and generate revenue by modifying the platform and installing crapware that sells your data to the highest bidder.

WHAT'S NEXT

Clearly, smartphones aren't going anywhere. We love them too mulch.

But as long as we make smart choices about our phones, to get the security we deserve, what's the harm?

The harm might not come from the phones themselves, but from the way we use them. We don't really use them to make "phone calls" anymore. Today, we mainly use our phones for the apps. And the apps we use most often are social media apps: Facebook, Twitter, WhatsApp and so on. In fact, over 80% of the time we spend on social media is through our phones.

So despite how carefully we might choose the phone we use, our privacy and security is still at the mercy of the social media platforms we access through them. We're bringing those social apps with us everywhere we go—because we take our phones with us everywhere we go. And we constantly send our data to those social media platforms, through their apps.

Everywhere we go.

So let's take a look at our relationship with the thing we use our phones for the most: Social media.

5. SOCIAL MEDIA

We can't talk about ads, data mining and advertising revenue without talking about social media. The amount of time people spend on social platforms is staggering; for some, it's almost the only communication tool they use to stay in touch with friends and family. An alarming number of people even say it's where they get their news.

It's A Tradeoff

We all know that social media sites—Facebook in particular—gather huge amounts of data while we're on the platform. The amount of personal information we're willing to give up on social is staggering. It's the perfect storm of data collection and willing transparency.

What you probably don't know is how much stuff they gather outside the site itself.

A BRIEF HISTORY OF SOCIAL

There have been plenty of social media sites since the public web became a thing; I won't list them all here, but we'll look at a few notables. In 1997, SixDegrees tried its hand at social, offering messaging and bulletin board features between friends, but it only lasted about four years. They tried monetizing with ads but at the time, the adtech industry just wasn't mature enough to support the strategy.

MakeoutClub launched around the same time, in 1999, focusing on younger audiences and music, or as the site said, "indierockers, hardcore kids, record collectors, artists, bloggers, and hopeless romantics." Revenue came from advertising, but like other sites in the early days the ad-tech wasn't quite there. "Advertise on MOC: Email me for rates" the homepage stated.[91] How quaint. Believe it or not that little niche site hung on till 2017.

Friendster was launched in 2003, with a lot of the same core features introduced by MakeoutClub—sharing photos and personal updates, messaging with friends, and leaving comments on other people's posts. Like its predecessors, revenue came from banner ads, contextual advertising and sponsorships. In its first few months, it had three million users and grew fast from there.

MySpace Offered Users Flexibility

Over time, due to a combination of slow servers, poorly designed features and a management team that seemed uninterested in listening to their users, Friendster was squashed by the next competitor, MySpace. danah boyd, a technology and social media scholar who prefers her name uncapitalized[92] said, "MySpace evolved with its users, building a trusting relationship, figuring out how to meet their needs and cultural desires, providing them with features and really trying to give them what they were looking for. Friendster did not – it fought its users hand and foot, telling them how to behave."[93]

MySpace gave users lots of freedom to design their pages, post photos, embed YouTube videos, and even post classified ads. Revenues came from advertising, particularly from a 2006 agreement with Google that made the search giant the exclusive search feature inside MySpace. The deal was intended to give Google "a new outlet for the ads it sells via its AdSense program, and ... help MySpace.com increase its advertising revenue." For the privilege, Google had to make "revenue-sharing payments totaling at least $900 million."[94]

Facebook Offered More

Facebook was live at the same time, overlapping MySpace for a few years, but since it was limited to college students it didn't present competition. Then in 2006, it threw its doors open to the world and smashed MySpace with a vengeance. Within two years Facebook had become the number one social media site—in part, according to the Los Angeles Times, because it stayed focused on "features that enhance the social-networking experience, such as the 'News Feed' that matches the immediacy of Twitter's staccato updates." Facebook remained agile and responsive to its users, innovating by the day. "There are new things like Twitter that come along," said Charlene Li, founder of Altimeter Group. "What does Facebook do? It does Twitter ... and it does it better."[95] Today, Facebook is the world's largest social media platform, rivaling Google in advertising revenue.

Of course, Facebook's not the only social platform around. In the US, top sites include YouTube, WhatsApp, Instagram, Tumblr, Twitter, Reddit and LinkedIn. If we expand outside the US, there's WeChat, QQ, Qzone, TikTok, Baidu Tieba, Viber, Line, Telegram ... and some of those are gaining popularity in the US as well.

Yet no matter how you slice and dice the data—by age range, market share, or monthly active users—Facebook always tops the list. With a quarter-billion more Monthly Active Users than its next closest competitor, and an advertising platform that's threatening to topple Google, Facebook is the gorilla in the room.

So let's focus our energy there.

THE BATTLE FOR THE BUSINESS MODEL

In 2004, during Facebook's earliest days as a site for college students, it paid the bills in part out of the founders' pockets and in part by running a few ads. In 2008, Facebook had agreed to let Microsoft sell graphical and text ads on the site. Still, the company was cash flow negative and CEO Mark Zuckerberg seemed unconvinced that they'd found the path to monetization. German newspaper Frankfurter Allgemeine Zeitung quoted Zuckerberg as saying "I don't think social networks can be monetized in the same way that search did. ... But we are experimenting already. One group is very focused on targeting; another part is focused on social recommendation from your friends."[96]

Committing To Advertising Pays Off

Later that same year Facebook hired Sheryl Sandberg as its Chief Operating Officer. She held brainstorming sessions in an effort to decide on a long-term monetization plan, ultimately deciding that advertising would be a main source of revenue. Facebook immediately made changes to its advertising model to focus on profitability, and by September 2009 the company was cash flow positive for the first time.

Two years later, Facebook's revenues were $3.71 billion—mostly from advertising. And 2012 brought more ad formats in the form of Featured Posts that appeared inline with the organic content in the users' news feeds. In four more years, ad revenues hit $5.2 billion.

Fighting Ad Blockers Boosts Ad Revenue

Not all users were happy with seeing so many ads, and lots of them were using ad blockers. *eyeo*, developer of the leading ad blocking tool, Adblock Plus, got into something of an arms race with Facebook over the issue.

Ad blockers, of course, look for specific things in the HTML that indicate an ad. Because Facebook ran their own ad network, they controlled every bit of code around the ads. So they just camouflaged the ads to trick the blocker into thinking ads were organic user content.

So eyeo modified its blocker to find the hidden code. Facebook tweaked things and hid it again. And so on.

Facebook's VP of ads, Andrew Bosworth, defended the move: "Part of the mission of the company is to create connections between people and businesses. ... Ads on Facebook [pay for] a service that's free around the world." Facebook argued that users didn't need ad blockers because the site provided native tools that let users control the ads they saw. But eyeo responded that Facebook had taken the "dark path against user choice. But it's also no reason to overreact: cat-and-mouse games in tech have been around as long as spammers have tried to circumvent spam filters."[97]

It actually resulted in Facebook increasing its ad revenues because it got that much better at sidestepping ad blockers. In a 2016 earnings call, CFO David Wehner announced the company "had 18 percent year-over-year desktop revenue growth ... largely due to our efforts on reducing the impact of ad blocking."[98]

So let's recap: The 2004-era Zuckerberg said he didn't think social media could be monetized like search. A year later, Facebook committed to ads. Users didn't like it and tried to block the ads. Facebook finagled its code to fool the ad blockers, and in the process learned how to make ads even more aggressive and unavoidable. Users ended up seeing even more ads, and Facebook ended up making a boatload of money in the process.

Facebook, like Google, simply couldn't help evolving into an advertising company.

WHAT IT LOOKS LIKE NOW

Like I mentioned, Facebook doesn't use a third-party ad network to sell their empty rectangles: It manages the selling, placement, targeting and tracking in-house, functioning both as publisher and as ad network in one. It's a streamlined soup-to-nuts offering that's proven irresistible to advertisers. Just like Google is.

For the most, part users seem comfortable enough with the arrangement. Even after the Cambridge Analytica fallout and the resulting #deletefacebook movement, the site's not hurting much for users. Nearly a third of the planet is using the site.

That might be because it feels like a pretty straightforward transaction: "Here's my data, give me my Facebook." After all, it's not like Facebook's following us around outside the site or something, right?

Right?

Ads Everywhere Facebook Reaches

Today Facebook owns tons of other businesses, tools and apps, including Workplace, Messenger, Instagram and WhatsApp. And because all of them fall under the Facebook name, any permissions you give for first party access to your information extend to those other platforms. When you're using them, your activity there is collected and added to your Facebook-wide behavioral profile for advertising.

An advertiser setting up a campaign on Facebook can use a single dashboard, create one ad, and choose where the ad should run across all of Facebook's available properties. No juggling multiple campaigns or creating different platform-specific designs. Just click, send, and poof: Those shoes are following you everywhere.

The short list, from Facebook itself, goes like this: Ads can appear alongside updates from your friends in your news feed; on your Instagram feed; in the Marketplace; on video feeds; in the right hand column of the page; inside Instagram Explore; in your Messenger Inbox; in Stories on Facebook, Instagram, and in Messenger; in Video on Demand; in Facebook's search results; as a sponsored message in Messenger; or within an Instant Article.[99]

But wait! There's more.

Ads Outside Facebook's Tentacles

Like Google, Facebook doesn't just display ads in its own search results or on its own properties. Advertisers can choose to have their Facebook ads follow you into thousands of apps thanks to the Audience Network feature, which is a massive stable of partners Facebook works directly with to distribute its ad inventory.

"People spend a lot of their time on Facebook and Instagram," says the blurb. "But they are also spending time on other apps. Audience Network helps advertisers reach more of the people they care about in the other places where they're spending their time." Facebook ads will follow you on apps from "a wide variety of publishers and advertising networks that cover media, games, education, entertainment, sports and lifestyle."[100]

They'll follow you on interactive or social apps like Cupid dating, Daily Bible Inspirations, Simply Yoga, or Tumblr. On news publishers and aggregators like Flipboard, ABC and Fox News, and HuffPost. On widgets like weather updates and clocks, pregnancy trackers, even flashlight features. And of course, tons and tons and tons of games.

You're never alone—even when you're playing Solitaire.

Facebook manages this process end-to-end, in-house, without using any other networks or partners, capturing your activity and controlling the data all along the way. To entice advertisers to pay more to follow you everywhere, Facebook claims that people are eight times more likely to click if the ads follow them around than if they don't.[101]

The Call Is Coming From Inside The House

Not freaked out yet? How's this?

Advertisers can also create a "Custom Audience" by bringing behavioral and activity data from outside Facebook and loading it into an ad campaign inside the site. They just need to upload any kind of "identifiers" they might have—your name, email address, a phone number or your home address, say—and Facebook will match it with whatever they already know so the advertiser can target you.

Let's say you joined a loyalty club or a mailing list of daily deals. Or maybe you've visited a website, and they've cookied your browser. Or you might have downloaded and opened an app. Even if you've called or physically walked into a store and made a purchase. Facebook will do whatever it takes to find you on their site, target ads at you, and then follow you around—both on the site and outside of it.

Still insufficiently horrified? Advertisers can share those cross-identified lists with other advertisers. Meaning if a sneaker store has your identifying information because you bought a pair of shoes, they can share those identifiers with another advertiser who you've never done business with, say a store that sells sneaker cleaner. Awesome.

In fairness I should mention two things: Advertisers can share their lists but aren't allowed to sell them. And the identifiers they do have are "hashed" when they're uploaded to Facebook. That's a cryptographic security process that turns your information into randomized code. So although the original uploader may in fact have a readable version of your name or email address or whatever the identifier is, theoretically Facebook doesn't receive an actual readable identifier, and neither does any other business the list is shared with. Nevertheless, you'll still get ads from randos who you never agreed to get advertising from. Neat, right?

It's worth acknowledging just how aggressive Facebook has been about merging that online and offline data to know more about us, and what a change that represents from earlier players. Remember: Yahoo didn't want to peek inside emails due to the creep factor, and let Google do it, who reaped the benefits. Then Google didn't want to join up the data due to the creep factor, and let Facebook do it.

And boy, is Facebook reaping the benefits.

The Call Is Coming From Outside The House, Too

Ah, if only it were just ads and advertisers you had to worry about. But no—Facebook has cast a wide web of tools and tricks that capture your activity, whether you see it happening or not.

Have you ever been to a website and seen those Facebook buttons for "liking" and "sharing" the content? It won't surprise you to hear that if you click on one, Facebook knows, since it sends the "like" or "share" to your Facebook profile and tells all your friends what you did.

But what if you don't click the button? They'll never know you were there, right?

Wrong. If you're logged in, just the act of loading and viewing a page that has those buttons on it launches communications with Facebook, telling them who you are, what you're looking at, which browser you're using, and all kinds of other things. The website publisher might not even realize this—they just want you to share their content, they're not getting any of your data. But it's Facebook who wants your information, adding it to whatever they already know about you and your activity and building an ever more detailed portrait of your life.

The good news is that at least you're aware you're being tracked when you see the buttons. It's not a secret because now you know: Facebook buttons equal data mining, clicked or not. Being informed is half the battle.

Unless ...

The Invisible Hand Of Facebook

The site could have an invisible pixel. We've talked about these before: They're those tiny one-pixel-by-one-pixel transparent images that are buried somewhere in the code of the page. The image it-self lives on Facebook's servers, but is embedded in the page by the publisher.

Because they're transparent, your browser doesn't display them and you can't see them. But they're still loaded by the browser just like a Like button, so they still send information back to Facebook about your visit.

Exactly what kind of information gets captured is controlled by the publisher: Pixels are great for tracking all kinds of things called "events" that are valuable for them to know. Things like whether you added something to a shopping cart or wish list; if you saved your billing information during the transaction; if you registered for something like membership or a newsletter; if you used the chat fea-ture for customer support; if you customized a product by choosing a color or size; if you sought out a brick-and-mortar location for the business; if you searched for something on the site; if you bought a paid subscription; or pretty much anything else the publisher thinks is important to keep track of.

And everything that's captured is shared both with the publish-er and with Facebook.

The publisher uses that information to discover places where vis-itors lose interest and leave, so it can improve the site experience and get us to stay around longer. The publisher might notice lots of users searching for the same thing without success, so it can adjust the content to provide the popular items people want. Or it can see people add things to the cart and then click away without finishing the transaction, indicating that maybe the checkout process is too complicated, or the delivery's too expensive.

The publisher can also use that information to target ads. For instance maybe it'll target everyone who abandoned a cart with an ad that says, "Hey there, these shoes are on a secret sale—5% dis-count just for you!"

Facebook uses the data in much the same way, to help anyone else who might want to target you with ads for those shoes.

Logging Out Improves Privacy ... A Little

You could choose to log out of Facebook when you aren't on the site. Of course, you'll miss out on all your notifications and updates until you log back in, but at least Facebook gets a little less information when you look at a site with a button or pixel on it.

"If you're logged out or don't have a Facebook account," says Facebook, "and visit a website with the Like button or another social plugin, your browser sends us a more limited set of info. For example, because you're not logged into Facebook, you'll have fewer cookies than someone who's logged in."

Of course, that doesn't mean Facebook can't figure out whose profile to merge the information with: "[We still] receive info about the web page you're visiting, the date and time and other browser-related info."[102]

Ads = Free Facebook

Our relationship with Facebook is a business transaction: We trade our personal data in exchange for a free social media site. Remember, Facebook says, "Ads on Facebook [pay for] a service that's free around the world."[103] That's the mutual agreement.

If being tracked makes those ads a little less irrelevant and a little more focused on things we're really interested in, we might see that as a small trade-off for such a cool, free platform we get to play on every day. Besides, if we know how to find the right place in our Facebook dashboard—I checked, it's four clicks to get to the ads preferences—we can view and to some degree control our identified interests, what other kinds of information Facebook's collected, the advertisers and business who've targeted us, what kinds of data they used to target us, and which ad topics we want to be bombarded with.

So long as we know what we've signed up for and have some control over the transaction, being followed around by ads for the shoes *we're actually interested in* seems like a small price to pay for all the cat videos, pictures of food, and funny memes we can stand.

So what's the big deal?

Stolen Data And Dark Ads

2018 was an exciting year for Facebook.

First, the Cambridge Analytica scandal broke, revealing that millions of users' personal data was leaked and used to target political ads and disinformation.

Then Mark Zuckerberg testified before the US Congress to answer for the leaks and other concerns about user privacy and data mining. When asked if Facebook could just default all privacy settings to minimize data mining and let users choose what they want to share, Zuckerberg replied, "That is a complex issue that deserves more than a one word answer."

He went on to say that he would "tighten data policies, protect users from further leaks and become more transparent about who's advertising on his site," in an effort to rebuild users' trust. "We didn't take a broad enough view of our responsibility," he said, "and that was a big mistake. It was my mistake, and I'm sorry."[104]

Just weeks later, Facebook had to admit to the UK parliament that it had discovered untold thousands of fake "dark ads"—that is, ads targeted only at certain individuals and not shown in a time line. They ranged from ads scamming the elderly into investing their life savings in bogus cryptocurrency to suppressing African American votes. As TechCrunch reported, "It goes without saying there are far more – and far more murky and obscure – uses of dark ads that remain to be fully dragged into the light where their impact on people, societies and civilized processes can be scrutinized and better understood."[105]

Facebook claims to be unable to implement automated systems that might find and remove these bad ads at scale, so it leans heavily on its users to report them. But there's no easy way for users to see all the ads in the system. In response to the Cambridge Analytica debacle Facebook did enable a public, searchable archive of a sub-set of ads, in particular those labeled "Political Ad," but that means asking users to comb through way more than is reasonable.

Kremlin-backed political disinformation scams are really just the tip of the iceberg here. But even in that narrow instance, Facebook estimated there'd been 80,000 pieces of fake content targeted at just one election.

TechCrunch summed up, "Users are left performing unpaid moderation for a massively wealthy, for-profit business while simultaneously being subject to the bogus and fraudulent content its platform is also distributing at scale."

It's More Than Memes And Data

If we were just exchanging our data for a free Facebook filled with funny pictures and friends and family updates, it might seem like a fair trade. But a lot of us are using social media for more than cat videos and food porn. We're going there for at least some of our news.

A 2019 Pew report found that "social media is now a part of the news diet of an increasingly large share of the U.S. population"—more than 50% of people, in fact. Yet around 60% of Americans feel like social media has too much control over the kind of news people see—that there's some kind of invisible curation happening before the news hits their feeds.[106]

The news on Facebook is being scrubbed and filtered and targeted based on our shopping habits and activity from all over the internet. And as the "dark ads" phenomenon shows us, an alarming amount of Facebook "news" is coming from nefarious sources who steal data and write fake stories designed to divide and create upset and do harm, in much the same way Google enables fake news websites who use ad clicks to finance disinformation.

If the data we choose to share is just the shoes we like, that would be one thing. That's hard data—verifiable and measurable actions we take as we surf and shop. It's personal, but it's not Personal with a capital "P."

The data we're sharing on social media is "soft data." Social media is by definition Personal. It's where we share our feelings about current events, where we "Like" posts about politics, "Follow" pages that align with our feelings about vaccination, and "Share" stories about social injustice or governmental oversteps. It's where we share fundraisers for social causes. It's where we talk about our families, our love lives, our happiness and our depression. It's where we post pictures of our children and our pets.

Participating in social media is, for many of us, is a profoundly personal sharing of our soft and squishy insides. Yet it's a place that ironically has no interest in our personal privacy or protecting our anonymity because, in the end, it's an advertising platform that depends precisely on exploiting every single bit of personal soft- and hard-data it can ferret out, whether we expect that information to be exploited or not.

And yet.

But We Are Social Animals

And yet we're social animals, right? We like staying in touch with our family and friends. We like having conversations and sharing our thoughts and opinions. We like recommending great restaurants and our favorite movies and laughing at the cartoons our friends send our way.

Social media sites like Facebook are great for that. Especially when life places us far away from those we love (or at least like). I get it: I'm on Facebook myself, despite everything we've talked about here because I like funny cat videos as much as the next guy. Maybe more.

The trick in the long term is finding our way to a model for social media that does a better job at respecting our privacy. A social media that gives us more choices about managing our own data, and protects us from the fraudulent advertising, factious rhetoric, and harmful division that has become such a revenue stream for the big platforms who depend on us staying enraged and engaged.

Until that glorious day, the trick will be finding ways to use "social media as it exists" that help mitigate the intrusion on our privacy. A way to maximize the fun social entertainment factor and minimize the impact of bad actors who want to exploit us.

VISIONS FOR TOMORROW

Building a social media future that's completely free of data mining, advertising and abuse might seem like a pipe dream. But there are some alternative thinkers who are pursuing that dream, whether as a group of dedicated volunteers maintaining code on their own servers, or funded startups with long pedigrees in digital media.

Diaspora is a nonprofit, user-owned distributed social network dedicated to data privacy and independence from advertising. "Instead of everyone's data being held on huge central servers owned by a large organization," says the site. "Diaspora exists on independently run servers ('pods') all over the world. ... You own your data. You don't sign over rights to a corporation or other interest who could use it. ... Your friends, your habits, and your content is your business, not ours!"[107]

In an early 2011 blog post, the founder stated that "no big corporation will ever control Diaspora. [We] will never sell your social life to advertisers."[108] While the ideas are interesting, the somewhat geeky nature of the site, including its join process, restricts its membership to more technically inclined users. Nevertheless, it's an alternative for some.

Mastodon is similar, in that it's an open-source, distributed network, hosted on servers that belong to whoever wants to take responsibility for maintaining their node. Right now the site claims that nearly 4.5 million users are enjoying its ad-free platform. "Without an incentive to sell you things, Mastodon allows you to consume content you enjoy uninterrupted. Your feed is chronological, ad-free and non-algorithmic—you decide who you want to see!"[109]

It's much more similar to Twitter than Facebook in its features, so don't expect a Facebook knockoff. According to Make Tech Easier, "unless you want to set up your own instance, you still have to put some trust in the person hosting your account data." [110] Funding comes from individual subscriptions through Patreon. Like Diaspora, the concept requires a certain level of geek—and it's no Facebook killer.

Ello started out as a Facebook alternative with a set of similar features. Its early manifesto read, "Every post you share, every friend you make and every link you follow is tracked, recorded and converted into data. Advertisers buy your data so they can show you more ads. You are the product that's bought and sold. We believe there is a better way. ... We believe that the people who make things and the people who use them should be in partnership. You are not a product."[111]

Without ads, Ello struggled to find its path to solvency. For a while it even sold T-shirts. Today it's a marketplace that "connects brands, agencies and publishers with a global community of 625K creatives from 175 countries." Revenue comes from a freemium model that involves "the exchange of individual functions for small payments." [112]

Vero is a social app that feels more like Facebook's Instagram, but unlike either Facebook or Instagram, Vero carries no advertising and says it's committed to user privacy: "We made our business model subscription-based so we could be free of ads, making our users our customers. ... We don't mine your data, nor sell access to you, and because you control who sees what you post ... you can behave in a way that is more natural, which we believe ends up being better for you."[113]

The site saw a surge of users in 2018, after Facebook's Cambridge Analytica scandal hit the news, sending the user base soaring to nearly three million in a matter of days. Building the app was entirely funded by its founder, and while the intent remains to one day start charging for access, for now both the app and access to Vero remain free, and a small amount of revenue is generated "by taking an affiliate fee when someone buys books, movies, and other products they find on Vero."[114]

MeWe's founder Mark Weinstein was inspired to build the social site when he heard Mark Zuckerberg say, "Privacy is a social norm of the past." In 2016, MeWe was awarded "Start-Up of the Year" in the Innovative World Technology category at the South by Southwest festival, and was recognized as one of Entrepreneur magazine's top entrepreneurial companies.

MeWe maintains a "Privacy Bill Of Rights" that states, "You own your personal information & content. It is explicitly not ours. You never receive targeted third-party advertisements or targeted third-party content. We think that's creepy."[115]

MeWe's business intent is to remain free forever, and generate revenue by charging for upgrades. "We are classic capitalism as it's intended," Weinstein said in a 2019 interview. "You're our customer, and just like you might do at a restaurant, you can order some extra things." MeWe members have access to thousands of free emojis, for instance, but the site also offers custom emojis and stickers for a price. Users can also pay extra for more storage, live video streaming, and personal pages.[116]

The company has also spun off MeWePro, a suite of project management and communication tools for business not unlike Slack. MeWePro revenues will no doubt help support the social product, not unlike the way Basecamp's project management tools now subsidize the private email app Hey. In 2019, MeWe surpassed five million users, and projected 150 million by the end of 2020.

Change In The Wind

Is this a sea change? Not yet. Not even close. But it demonstrates that millions and millions of people are interested in protecting their data privacy and avoiding ads, and they're at least poking around at other social media options.

Some of these sites will always be niche, and that's how they want it to be. Others have their sights set on toppling the ad-driven, data-poaching monopolies of Facebook, Twitter, YouTube, WhatsApp, and Instagram, and good luck to them tilting at those windmills.

But if one of them manages to find quixotic success, or if billions of users really start seriously entertaining smaller niche alternatives, we may see a new leader emerge—or at least force meaningful change on the Facebooks of this world.

It should be interesting to watch.

DOES ALL THIS MATTER?

What's all this really mean in the end? Does It Matter?

Maybe, maybe not. If you're okay with trading data for free social media, you're probably thinking I've made a mountain from a molehill. It's not a big deal, and we should focus on more important things.

I don't disagree. As I say, I use Facebook, and I click on cat videos. Facebook knows I like cat videos, and I'm alright with that. If I end up seeing ads for cat toys because of it, I'm alright with that as well. If that's you too, then no change is necessary. You do you. Keep on keeping on. Your data—your choice.

On the other hand, if this has all been news to you, you might be feeling a little overwhelmed and freaked out. It's hard to know how upset to get about being secretly chased around the web and having our activities captured for advertising, but it sounds scary and intrusive and maybe even a little bit diabolical.

It might be upsetting enough that you want to throw in the towel, unplug from Facebook and jump to an alternative. Or maybe it's time to quit social media altogether and invest in stationery and stamps and wax and a signet ring to keep in touch with loved ones. If any of that's the case, you're making an informed decision and you're taking control. Good for you.

But chances are you're somewhere in the middle. Maybe you already knew about data collection but didn't realize how invasive it was. Maybe you've been thinking for a while that you'd like to take some control, and moderate what you're sharing while still reaping the benefits of cat videos and funny memes. If that's your path, again you're making an intentional choice—more power to you.

If you're ready to modify your relationship with social media, to establish a new transactional model you're more comfortable with, you'll need to think about two things.

First, decide what you want out of social media. How much sharing do you really want or need to do? Who do you want to stay in touch with? What do you want the experience to add to your life? Do you want to come away from a social media experience relaxed, informed, angry, or inspired? Do you want social media to enhance your family connections or expand your career connections? Think hard about this. It's very easy to log in every day and just consume whatever bombards your news feed without being *intentional* about what you wanted in the first place.

Then, decide what you're willing to give up in exchange for that experience. How many ads are you willing to endure? What kinds of ads? How much hard and soft data are you ready to share in exchange for them? How much work are you willing to do to become master of both your data and your social media universe?

Once you have those two decisions made, it's time to roll up your sleeves and make your intentional change.

5 STEPS TO INTENTIONAL CHANGE

Given the title of this book and my opinions about ad-tech and surveillance capitalism, I wish we had social media options beyond Facebook and Twitter. LinkedIn has expanded beyond its resume-focused roots, and there's interesting discussions going on and there are ways to pay, but it's very much business focused and lacking in cat videos.

There are a few other options that maintain privacy and even try to charge subscriptions, but they're just not that compelling. I've tried MeWe, and even my colleagues who are privacy advocates agree that's it's a wasteland. Nobody there, just crickets. Mastodon, Diaspora, Ello and others are all trying, but social media has strong network effects—nobody goes there because nobody goes there.

So. What to do?

Step 1: Pay If You Can

My personal preference would be to pay for social media and get rid of the data collection. Make it Netflix, not NBC. I've heard this idea was laughed off by Facebook because there's just so much more money to be made in the profiling and data harvesting, and I can't argue with that. Twitter seems to be more open to innovation, and according to rumors, they could experiment with a paid, ad-free option at around $50 per year.

Focusing on specialist niche interests could be a good strategy, as **Guild** in the UK is trying. I spoke to the co-founder, Ashley Friedlein, who described it as a combination of the networking aspects of LinkedIn and the communication ability of WhatsApp. Crucially it carries no ads because, "Guild is about what's good for us as humans. Free encourages bad behaviors. This philosophy carries all the way through the product." Professionals are willing to pay in order to get not just privacy, but confidentiality too.

However, for broad consumer type social media we have Facebook, Instagram and Twitter—I don't see how that's going to change. At the same time I'm not sure it *should* change. Despite the hand-wringing, it's just entertainment. I think you know that. We watch a horror movie and enjoy having our emotions manipulated and I don't think social media is much different.

Yes, your blood pressure might be rising right now because, "A lot of people get their news from social media *and that matters*," and you have a point—which we'll address in the next couple of chapters. But even so, I think most of us just like to pass the time and connect with people.

So let's figure out how to make the best of a free thing.

Step 2: Stay For The Cat Videos, Leave If It's Toxic

Rule #1, #2 and #3 of social media: **It's entertainment**. It's not news, it's not important, it's just a way to pass the time like a movie or a TV show. If your news feed is bringing you down and you're doom-scrolling through bad stuff, close it.

Maybe even delete the app. (Doing so will pop a warning about your data being deleted, but that's just the local copy of what the app is working with. All the important stuff, like your list of friends, is stored in the cloud.) After a break, if you want to use it again, just reinstall the app, login and it's back.

Step 3: Browse With Privacy

There are a few things you can do to make staying on Facebook better.

In earlier chapters, we mentioned Duck Duck Go Privacy Essentials. Besides making search and ads more private, it also blocks the ability of Facebook to harvest data from the websites you visit. So if you haven't already installed it, go do it now. I also like Firefox and their Facebook Disconnect feature, and I expect Apple to keep tightening the equivalent in Safari.

Step 4: Prune Your Friends List

Next is to prune your friends list and remove anyone that makes you unhappy. For me this is anyone who largely posts political opinions. I allow a certain amount of this because some of the conspiracy theory stuff is just hilarious, but that's my peccadillo. Over the years I've culled my friends down to just those who share my oddball sense of humor. I now find that Facebook makes me happy.

Step 5: Share With Intention

The final, and most important step, is to control what actions you take—i.e., sharing, liking, and commenting.

Take sharing. Let's say you just read a story about Elbonians running a counterfeit bagel bakery. Those crafty Elbonians removed the hole from their bagels and labeled them incorrectly. We've been duped. They're just lumps of boiled dough! Should you punch the Share button?

The fine people at Mozilla offer some excellent advice: Before you hit share just take a moment or two, understand your emotions, and consider why your emotions are up. Maybe the story is precisely designed to trigger your emotions. Then maybe next read the comments, and then consider fact checking. Go ahead, it won't take more than a few seconds. Also, consider whether sharing this will make people as happy as a cat video. No? Then maybe don't make people unhappy.

Next, just "like" stuff, don't "angry" stuff. When I like a post from someone, I really like it. I never use the anger emoticon.

Finally, your comments might not help. Be sparing.[117]

WHAT'S NEXT

Given the negative press surrounding Facebook, Twitter, et al, you might be surprised that I'm so relaxed about their impact on society. It's not that I don't care, nor even that I don't think Facebook has been harmful. It's just that they're not the problem.

It's Our Fault

We are the problem. It's us who share the errant falsehoods because we can't tell opinion from evidence from entertainment. It's we who are emotion-driven. It's we who form into like-minded tribes.

After all, Facebook doesn't create anything. We do, and so do people who want to manipulate us.

So let's turn our attention to the star of the show: *The Media.*

Part II.

The Media

"On the one hand information wants to be expensive, because it's so valuable. The right information in the right
place just changes your life. On the other hand, information
wants to be free, because the cost of getting it out is getting
lower and lower all the time."
—**Stewart Brand to Steve Wozniak, 1984**

TL;DR

Information wants to be free.
Information also wants to be expensive.
That tension will not go away.
—**Stewart Brand, 1987**

6. NEWS

Let's take a quick moment to recap what we've covered so far.

The web provides us all kinds of cool stuff: flight reservations, cat memes, updates on what our friends are eating, and frictionless e-commerce to get more stuff delivered to our doors. It's pretty awesome.

Tools like search and email and browsers and smartphones and social media have made it easy to find the stuff, view the stuff, share the stuff, and buy the stuff. Anywhere, anytime. Also pretty frikkin' awesome.

The relationships we have with those tools—search, email, browsers, smartphones, social media—have been defined by the business models that each were forced to adopt.

As much as those early internet geeks wanted to build cool tools and just give them away, the high cost of coding, hosting and maintaining them eventually required some kind of revenue stream. Since those services were initially free, we saw no obligation to start paying for them ourselves—heaven forbid.

So they went and found customers who were willing to give them money: advertisers. And we agreed they could collect and sell our data to those advertisers, so long as they continued to give us access to the tools for free—and we would continue to find and view and share and buy more stuff.

All of which is fine when what we're getting is flight reservations, cat memes, updates on what our friends are eating, and frictionless e-commerce. Virtually none of it is super important.

But what's the damage when the stuff we want is super important? What happens when we are the product that's being sold to whoever provides, say, the knowledge we need to be productive and informed members of a complex society?

What happens when we're trading our data for the news? If we're not actually the customers of the services that deliver the news, then does that affect the quality of the news we get?

I'm going to give a resounding *hell yeah*—it does.

Let's look at the reasons why.

HOW WE GOT HERE: A BRIEF HISTORY OF NEWS

Before the US even had a Constitution to add a first amendment to, the freedom of the press was challenged and defended multiple times as a cornerstone of liberty. In 1735, Brigadier General William Cosby, the British Governor of New York, sued, censored, arrested and prosecuted the printer of the NY *Weekly Journal* for publishing stories that were critical of his work. Ultimately, he lost the suit and the paper's right to criticize the government was protected.

The ruling, it was said, would "affect every free man that lives under a British government on the main of America. It is the best cause. It is the cause of liberty." As Thomas Jefferson later wrote, "Wherever the people are well informed they can be trusted with their own government."

Yet, nearly 300 years later, the inherent neutrality of the press is threatened because despite its alleged freedom, whoever pays for the news is who actually controls the news.

That truth has been in the DNA of news throughout its evolution.

Pamphleteering

Pamphleteering was brought to the colonies from England. Pamphlets were the twitter feed or blog of their day—small, independent publications created by anyone with a military, religious, or political message.

If you had access to a printing press, you could print your pamphlet, stitch it together and distribute it in the streets.

Finding And Motivating The Right Audience

Pamphlets were key to spreading messages in opposition to the British government leading up to the Revolutionary War. But like any kind of message, pamphleteers needed to find the right audience.

Thomas Paine's historical pamphlet, *Common Sense*, advocated for independence and an egalitarian government. He needed to get it to a wide audience that was interested and invested in the rebellion, so an ad for the pamphlet was placed in a newspaper that printed the text of King George III's speech condemning the rebellion. That put his pamphlet in front of a target audience already interested in politics, with a clear call to action: Buy our pamphlet.

The targeting worked, and they quickly sold hundreds of thousands of copies.

Delivering Popular Content: Sex Always Sells

People being people, titillating personal affairs and sordid political intrigue were also pamphlet fodder, and readers ate it up.

Alexander Hamilton had an extramarital affair with a married woman, Maria Reynolds. Her abusive husband James threatened to make the affair public unless Hamilton paid him hush money to keep the secret, which Hamilton did and Reynolds accepted.

Years after the affair, Hamilton wrote a series of essays under the pen-name *Phocion*. In those essays he dished dirt on political rival Thomas Jefferson, including his rumored relationship with one of his slaves, Sally Hemings. In response, a scandal-mongering journalist named James Callender wrote his own expose, accusing Hamilton of not only that earlier affair with Maria, but of an illegal scheme to defraud the government, in cahoots with Maria's husband.

Hamilton refused to be extorted and came clean in the *Reynolds Pamphlet*. In it he freely admitted to the affair with Maria, and declared that not only did he have no illicit partnership with her husband James, but that James had actually taken money to keep the affair quiet. Callender and Reynolds lost their leverage, folded up camp and backed off.

Though he cleared his name of the fraud allegations, the pamphlet cost Hamilton the presidency.

The Government Tried To Control Content

Despite the Founders' early embrace of press freedom, the young government was happy to follow in the footsteps of Brig. Gen. Cosby.

In 1798, when pamphleteers became too critical of the Federalists' dogma, John Adams signed the Sedition Act into law, criminalizing the publication and distribution of "false, scandalous and malicious writing or writings against the government of the United States ... with intent to defame the said government."

At the time, Thomas Jefferson was challenging Adams for the presidency and looking for leverage. (You remember Jefferson: He's the guy who said, "Wherever the people are well informed they can be trusted with their own government.") In an effort to "inform the public," he went to James Callender—the guy who wrote that expose of Hamilton—and hired him to write another pamphlet, called *The Prospect Before Us.*

It was a political hit job—a scathing assassination of John Adams' character. And wildly successful: Callender's publisher charged a dollar a copy, an outrageous amount at the time, and people were ready to pay.

That takedown of Adams was so scathing that Callender was prosecuted under Adams' Sedition Act, jailed for nine months, and fined $200. There were two other notable trials under Adams' Sedition Act: of Thomas Cooper and of Matthew Lyon. Interestingly, they too were charged with defaming Adams and his administration. The Sedition Act expired just a year later, in 1801, after Jefferson won the Presidency.

Jefferson of course denied subsidizing the pamphlet, but there are documented payments to Callender in the public record. I can't imagine a more compelling motivator to control content than influencing who will hold the most powerful office in the land.

This whole back and forth between political rivals shows us three things. First, that the press, in the form of pamphleteering, was highly influential in American politics. Second, that he who paid for the news controlled the content of the news. And third, that the press is only as free as the legislation allows.

And the legislators, remember, are empowered by "the people ... well informed."

Hmm.

The Growth Of Newspapers

Newspapers were growing pretty much alongside pamphlets. Early on, the colonies only had British newspapers, plus the occasional locally produced, single-sided "broadsheets" that advertised products, or announced events and proclamations.

Boston in 1690 brought us the very first proper multi-page newspaper, *Publick Occurrences Both Forreign and Domestick*. Its publisher, Benjamin Harris, had a stated journalistic intent and promised reporting that met the highest standards for research and accuracy.

The British Governor immediately shut down *Publick Occurrences* both for operating without a permit and, as though doing a test run for Adams' Sedition Act that would come a century later, for "Reflections of a very high nature: As also sundry doubtful and uncertain Reports." Harris was jailed, and nobody wanted to risk starting up another real newspaper for at least 15 years.

1704 saw the birth of the pro-British *Boston News-Letter*, which despite low circulation, was able to keep running thanks to subsidies from the colonial government. Notice that he who pays for the content controls the content, and can keep it going even when there aren't many readers.

The *News-Letter* was of course discontinued in 1776 at the beginning of the American Revolution. Still, other papers popped up in places like Philadelphia and New York. Like the pamphlets, they were highly politically biased, and by the time of the Revolutionary War there were about two dozen papers available in the colonies, propagandizing for both sides of the growing political divide.

Cheap, Fast, Entertaining News For The Masses

The 1800s brought steam-powered advances in paper making and printing technology, allowing for mass-produced, inexpensive tabloid-sized papers.

At just a penny—far less than competing broadsheet papers—the "penny press" phenomenon led to an explosion of cheap publications. Charging a single penny got more papers to more people, including new immigrants and the middle and lower classes—which as a side note, actually led to improvements in literacy.

The growing and dedicated readership made the penny papers more attractive to advertisers, so they were largely monetized by lots of ads. And it didn't matter if they were shared around, because more eyeballs meant higher advertising rates. To keep all these newly literate people buying, the papers were filled with crude journalism, from news and crime to gossip and adventure—all the salacious stuff people love so much.

Cheap printing and lucrative advertising meant papers could be released daily. That resulted in stories that were more current compared to other publications that were often just aggregations of stale news, weeks or months out of date.

The penny papers created many of the features we're familiar with today: banner headlines, illustrations, funny pages, and even sports coverage. For the less literate, "Pictorial" publications had "extensive illustrations of events in the news, as woodcut engravings made from correspondents' sketches or taken from that new invention, the photograph."

Then along came the telegraph, which further shortened the timeline for sharing information among reporters, and then between reporters and the papers. The combination of prompt reporting and powerful imagery was especially popular during the Civil War. The public had a bottomless appetite for news from the front; reporters' accounts of battles were eagerly anticipated, and readership increased even more dramatically.

Biased Reporting

Just like pamphlets, newspapers weren't neutrally reporting the facts. Politicians aligned themselves to specific publications that were financed by both the political parties they favored and the government. Editors "unabashedly shaped the news and their editorial comment to partisan purposes," as historian William E. Gienapp put it.

Newspapers gave one-sided views of the news. They reflected the wishes of their benefactors because—once again—he who pays for the news controls the news. This continued through the war and up to 1900. Top papers like Joseph Pulitzer's *New York World* and William Randolph Hearst's *New York Journal* were locked in a war for readers, sensationalizing news, fabricating facts, and delivering opinions over evidence in order to drive up circulation.

By the 1920s, the battle of garbage news had waned, as papers traded partisan reporting for more politically independent press coverage, to appeal to a wider audience. New publications popped up everywhere, subscriptions grew 12-fold, and the newspaper industry settled into its golden age.

Print News Finds Its Business Model

Even before the penny presses, advertising was a revenue source.

In 1704, the *Boston News-letter* was the first regularly published American newspaper to run ads. And in 1729, Benjamin Franklin's *Pennsylvania Gazette* dedicated pages and pages of space to ads for soap, books and stationery. By the mid-1800s, the US had 2,000 newspapers, running 11 million ads.

Of course, the more readers a publication could promise, the more desirable it was to advertisers, and the more the publisher could charge for their ads. Papers and magazines rarely enforced overdue subscriptions, and to pad their numbers even more, they gave away copies for free to coffee houses, reading rooms, and hotels.

Advertising really exploded during the Civil War. There was a new demand for uniforms, shoes, and other critical items, and women were out of the home, away from their traditional chores, working in factories and earning an income. Newspapers weren't taxed, and neither were ads, so publishers could afford to print pages and pages of ads for prepared foods, manufactured clothing, soap and stationery.

Crucially, the ads were no longer stuck in the back, relegated to a separate section. Now they ran inline with the stories—right alongside the latest news from the front, where the eyeballs were, taking up as much as 50% to 75% of the paper.

By the end of the war, advertising was readily accepted by readers, and had become standard in most publications—even respectable magazines like *Atlantic Monthly* and *Harper's Weekly*. And by 1880, newspaper revenues were almost equally split between sales and advertising.

Agencies Drive Even More Advertising

After the Civil War, advertising agencies blossomed.

Since agencies took their commissions from the advertisers, they made more money when clients bought more ads in more publications. The desire to sell more ads—wherever they could—drove agencies to promote the adoption of cross-publication, nationwide campaigns, guiding their clients to spend ad dollars in both magazines and newspapers.

Some agencies even took to buying ad space in bulk from the publishers at a cash discount and reselling it to their clients. That means they got their commission from the advertiser, and the markup on the ad space itself. Win-win.

They even became one-stop-shops, providing design, copywriting, market research and publicity. They knew all the publishers and understood rates and circulation data, so they could help their clients reach larger and more distant audiences (while adding nicely to their bottom line).

Print advertising ruled the world. For a while.

RADIO KILLED THE NEWSPAPER STAR

Then came radio, blowing a hole below the waterline of print.

Radio devastated newspapers' advertising revenues, which dropped 38% between 1929 and 1941. Many smaller publications folded in response. Larger papers, such as the The New York Times, The Washington Post, Los Angeles Times and Wall Street Journal, fared better against radio, thanks to their existing dedicated audiences.

Life magazine also did okay alongside radio, given its focus on photography—particularly through World War Two. Under new owner Henry Luce, it became the canonical photo magazine, delivering something radio couldn't deliver.

And Time magazine actually used radio to its advantage: Between 1924 and 1945, it produced the quiz show *Pop Question*, a series of 10-minute news summaries pulled from the magazine, and the weekly 30-minute *The March Of Time*—early examples of what we now call content marketing.

But these were the exceptions that proved the rule. Overall, radio became the new driving force in news and advertising.

We Welcomed Radio Into Our Living Rooms

Before and during World War One, radio was mostly a military technology. But after the war the airwaves were licensed to radio stations, and they began broadcasting directly into people's living rooms for free.

Simple "crystal-set" radios were cheap, and soon millions of listeners were getting news live from across the country and around the world. Literacy was no longer a prerequisite to being well-informed—anyone who had a radio was as up-to-date as the next person.

Thanks to the existing infrastructure they controlled, AT&T was well positioned to build out the first radio network. By the mid-1920s, it had 26 interconnected stations across the eastern portion of the country, and controlled news delivery from coast-to-coast. But they restricted other broadcasters from using their telephone lines, and this set them up for potential backlash from antitrust laws, so they sold off their network to RCA. That opened the door for others to use their lines, not only benefiting RCA, but soon the nascent CBS (RCA begat NBC, which later split in two to form ABC). By 1938, there were almost 700 stations across the country, 40 percent of them affiliated with a network or chain.

At first, broadcasters tried to get their news content from the same wire services the newspapers used, but the papers denied them. So "reporters" just read news stories from newspapers out loud, essentially amplifying someone else's content. Eventually,

United Press International (UPI) started selling its stories to radio stations too. Regardless, in those early days it turned out people who heard stories first on the radio went to the papers for more in-depth reporting, so for a while everybody won.

However, it quickly became clear that radio news provided something unique that the papers couldn't: the live, firsthand perspective of radio reporters. When the Hindenburg crashed in 1937, radio journalists were onsite providing a detailed, blow-by-blow description of the tragedy. Herbert Morrison's now infamous, "Oh, the humanity," made listeners feel they were right there with him, watching it burn.

Likewise, Edward R. Murrow and his "Murrow's Boys" team of reporters delivered reports during World War II. Their broadcasts from locations around the world, including a Nazi concentration camp, helped create the model for what would become foreign news broadcasts.

Radio also provided a workaround for politicians who might be worried about the biases of certain newspapers. That's why President Roosevelt chose radio for his "fireside chats"—to be sure he could reach as many citizens as possible without the filter of print bias.

Radio Finds Its Revenue Stream

In its first days, radio was seen as a way to bring "high culture" into American homes, with some stations run by civic groups, religious and educational institutions, government and military. At first, station owners just focused on advertising themselves or the other businesses they owned. Advertising was seen as compromising radio's potential as a cultural improver, with some groups lobbying to prohibit advertising altogether.

But since there was no way to charge listeners for the free airwaves landing in their living rooms, no subscription model, nor per-show payment mechanism, how would the industry monetize?

You guessed it: advertising. High culture be damned.

The first true radio commercial was a ten-minute talk from a real estate company, extolling the virtues of suburban living. Rather than call it advertising, AT&T coined the phrase "toll-cast." Stations were cautious about what they advertised, worrying that hygiene products might be inappropriate, or mentioning the price might be rude.

But it didn't take long for advertisers and broadcasters to realize that anything goes, even if they had to modify the content or rename the shows to satisfy advertisers. Big brands like R.J. Reynolds, A&P, and Kraft foods sponsored musical programs. Dramas and mysteries like *The Shadow* and *The Green Hornet* were brought to you by General Mills, RCA Victor, and Chesterfield cigarettes. Broadcasters turned their shows into sponsored content for Chevrolet, Quaker Oats, and Wheaties. By 1930, 90% of stations were selling advertising time to local and national advertisers.

Much as newspapers suffered when radio arrived, by the end of the 1940s radio suffered at the hand of television, and the radio shows that had been so popular for two decades were forced to the sidelines of the advertising economy.

BROADCAST TELEVISION ECLIPSES RADIO

Through the 1940s, "television receivers" were rare, so TV wasn't considered competition for radio or print news reporting. But the numbers grew fast: Everyone wanted a TV set in their home—by 1957, there were 544 stations, and nearly 80% of homes had a TV.

Television changed forever how we got information. It ushered in a radical shift in our collective understanding of the world. We didn't have to use our imaginations to fill in the blanks left by radio journalists. We could see what they were seeing, and go with them to places we'd only imagined.

To ensure that the information we received from this powerful new medium was balanced and fair, the Federal Communications Commission (FCC) enacted the "fairness doctrine" in 1949, mandating that broadcast licensees had to provide honest, balanced coverage of controversial issues that affected the communities they served.

TV For Social Good

During those first years, television was serving a social need. Stations broadcast major news events such as the 1951 Kefauver hearings on organized crime, and audiences were mesmerized. Students were sent home from school to watch as it unfolded live. A teacher of the period wrote, "I do not think any of you can possibly realize how much good it has done to have these hearings televised. It has made millions of us aware of conditions that we would never have fully realized even if we had read the newspaper accounts."

In 1952, both the Republican and Democrat presidential conventions were hosted in Philadelphia, just to accommodate the technical needs of TV broadcasters—drawing over 10 million viewers. Newspapers might still have denied television's growing impact, but others were beginning to recognize the importance and influence of the visual medium.

Entertainment TV Finds Its Business Model

TV had definitely found its people, and they were dedicated. Unfortunately, they were also watching for free. Just as with radio, there was no way for broadcast TV to require a subscription, and no way to charge per program.

Still, just like all the other things we've looked at, producing TV news costs money. It's expensive to buy all those cameras and those lights and pay the makeup crew and oh, let's not forget what it costs to send all those reporters to Dallas or the Kennedy Space Center. Where's that money coming from?

Yup. One more time: *advertising.*

The first commercial came early—way before sets were common in most homes. It was a ten-second spot for Bulova, broadcast during America's favorite pastime, a 1941 Dodgers and Phillies baseball game. But it would be years before advertisers were willing to commit real marketing budgets to television. TV ads were about 10 times the cost of print ads, and broadcast hadn't built a big enough audience or proven its effectiveness.

By the end of the 1940s, TVs were common in more homes, and audiences were gathering around the boob tube every night. As the 1950s dawned, advertisers saw millions of eyeballs glued to I Love Lucy, The Lone Ranger, Superman, Danny Thomas and Ozzie and Harriet, so that's where they put their money. Celebrity endorsements and brand sponsorships ruled. Frank Sinatra sang a jingle for Halo shampoo. Lucy and Ricky smoked Philip Morris cigarettes. In 1951, television had $41 million in advertising revenues—a staggering amount for the time. By 1953, that had skyrocketed to $336 million.

At the end of the decade, broadcast TV could reach 90% of American households, way more than any other medium.

Television advertising had come of age.

TV News Operated At A Loss

Even though big brands were shoveling advertising money into entertainment programs, news programs still operated at a loss. But networks weren't worried.

They still viewed the news as a public good, and entertainment TV was pulling in enough ad revenue to cover it all. William Paley, owner and Chairman of CBS, told reporters not to worry about news costs, saying, "I have Jack Benny to make money."

The powerful influence of TV became crystal clear during the 1960 Nixon-Kennedy presidential debate. Anyone hearing the debate on the radio heard a pretty well-matched pair of candidates, and listeners actually mostly favored Nixon. But on TV, Nixon looked sickly. He was pale and feverish with flu, he had an injured knee, and his five o'clock shadow looked unkempt. Kennedy, on the other hand, was young, charismatic, confident, healthy, well-rested and sporting a tan. To the television audience, Kennedy was the clear winner and weeks later won the Presidency.

Nixon later wrote, "I should have remembered that 'a picture is worth a thousand words.'" More than half of voters said they were influenced by the "Great Debate."

TV's responsibility to put public service before profits was proven on the day Kennedy was assassinated. From the announcement of Kennedy's death through his funeral four days later, all three major networks ran 50 hours of uninterrupted commercial free coverage. While this established a baseline of reporting that became the standard for breaking news events, it cost the networks as much as $100 million in lost advertising revenue.

News programs continued to be loss leaders for the networks through the 60s and 70s. But change was in the wind.

News Needs To Pull Its Own Weight

Two unrelated but concurrent events conspired to change the face of "news as a public good" forever.

In the mid-1980s, all three major networks fell under new leadership, with Capital Cities Communications buying ABC, Westwood One buying CBS, and Laurence Tisch taking the reigns as CEO and chairman of CBS. For all three, the expectation was that news programs better pull their own advertising weight, and budgets and production costs were now under closer scrutiny.

How could news programming hope to be as profitable as entertainment programming when it was, by definition, a dry and academic presentation of fairly balanced, unbiased, verifiable facts? Outside of the occasional and unpredictable "big news event," nightly news was a book report.

Luckily for producers, around this time the FCC overturned the Fairness Doctrine on the grounds that it discouraged the discussion of controversial issues and might even infringe on free speech.

Between new pressure from the inside to be profitable, and new legal freedom towards bias and opinion, news broadcasting was soon going to look very different.

News Leans Into Entertainment

To make their news programs more profitable the networks looked to what was already working and found it in CBS's 60 *Minutes*. This winning formula—a news show designed as a "magazine for television"—combined journalistic integrity with an engaging story-telling format that appealed to the audience's emotions.

It had been a success out of the gate, winning multiple awards, including a Peabody in its second year. News that told stories in an entertaining and captivating style did a better job of capturing the imagination of viewers, which translated into high ratings and high revenues for CBS. It was a dream come true for studio executives looking for ways to turn news into profitable, must-see TV.

By the late 1990s, revenues from news programs were subsidizing the entertainment programs—a complete reversal of the original business model.

Cable Television

Cable TV really got its start as early as the 1940s, providing a way to enhance access to local programming where over-the-air signals couldn't reach. Big mountaintop community antennas captured the signals, and households with no reception were connected, for a fee, to the antenna by cables so they could watch the local broadcasts.

That gave cable TV providers one huge advantage over broadcast TV: They could now control access, and charge a fee. No payment, no programs.

The cable companies could also pick up signals from far away, and they started delivering out-of-area programming, putting them into competition with the local stations. The FCC wanted to protect the local stations, so they clamped down on what the cable companies could transmit. No out-of-area programming, no movies, no sports.

That restriction lasted until 1972. As soon as it was lifted, cable companies were free to provide competitive content. Specialty entertainment networks like Showtime, HBO and Cinemax were delivered for an extra charge, with subscription fees split between the network and the carrier.

In the 1980s and '90s, news stations such as Fox, MSNBC and CNN were bundled into the standard cable service too, so while audiences were paying a monthly cable bill, they weren't paying extra for the news. That satisfied our ingrained expectation that *news should be free*, even if technically it wasn't.

Consumers were happy to pay up big for all this awesome new entertainment, and to meet demand the industry collectively spent billions licensing and producing new programming and installing wiring across the country to get cable TV into as many homes as possible. By the end of the 1980s, there were 79 cable networks, with 53 million households subscribed. Viewership for broadcast entertainment shows suffered and so did its advertising cash flow.

Today, subscriptions remain the primary revenue source for cable providers, but they also sell advertising. They can target particular geographies, so advertisers have the option of buying spots that run to everyone nationwide, in specific markets, on certain networks, or across a region.

And if you've ever actually read your cable bill, you know they're also adding on all kinds of surcharges and whatnot. These are mostly to offset the retransmission fees they have to pay out to the local stations to deliver their content.

Cable Newsertainment Proves Cheap And Popular

The relaxing of requirements to be fair and balanced, coupled with a new ability to deliver news programming for niche cable audiences 24x7, led to cheap, sensational opinion-based news commentary that could be shoveled into the feeding trough all day and all night.

Professor Michael Griffin writes that "instead of three channels (ABC, CBS, and NBC) dividing up a big, diversified national audience, cable TV came along and targeted narrow niche audiences. Instead of spending big money to reach a mass audience, advertisers could spend less money and reach the narrow demographics they were really seeking."

24-hour cable news programming pulled ad money away from the big legacy evening news networks, and if those news programs were going to compete they'd need to pump out news content faster than ever before. "Newsrooms didn't have longer periods of time to prepare content, check it, edit it, vet it, and then present it to audiences," writes Griffin. "Reporters were pressured to go straight to air with current events and any new information that was presented to them. That began to result in rushed and incomplete reports, inaccuracy, distortion, and misleading material."[118]

Once the gravy train of ad revenues was pouring in, it was time to improve margins. That meant cutting costs.

Cable networks discovered that it's cheaper to pay talking heads to spew uninformed opinions than to pay reporters to travel the world, embed in hot spots, and interview carefully cultivated sources. So news *commentary* became the rule.

As Pew Research said in 2013, "Traditionally known for its attention to breaking news, daytime cable's cuts in live event coverage and its growing reliance on interviews suggest it may be moving more toward the talk-oriented evening shows. This transition may cut the costs of having a crew and correspondent provide live event coverage."

That trend also appeared in local television, as the stations placed "even greater emphasis on traffic, weather and sports [while they] reduced the number of edited package stories on the air and shortened the lengths of stories, trends that may reflect the economic strains affecting the industry."

Pew had actually seen this trend develop years before: "A separate analysis of cable in late 2012 finds that, over all, commentary and opinion are far more prevalent on the air throughout the day (63% of the airtime) than straight news reporting (37%)."[119]

THE WEB THROWS NEWS FOR A LOOP

After the web arrived, every connected household soon had access to limitless content. At first, browser technology was primitive, and nobody had the bandwidth for streaming video.

But as the technology got better, so did the range of media and services: live updates, streaming video, music, secure payment systems, and more. The legacy industries of print, radio, and television had to respond.

Different outlets and industries had different responses, and their success at turning the web into a viable and profitable platform varied.

Radio Finds Its Provocative Voice

Broadcast radio already had a long history of opinion-driven news talk programming, with the first all-talk station launching in 1960. While politics may have been the subject at hand for most shows, they weren't driven by any particular party line and weren't the three-ring circus that came later.

Liberal hosts like Los Angeles' Michael Jackson, and conservatives like New York's Barry Farber, had partisan *personal* philosophies, but didn't make them the centerpiece of the shows. As Farber once said, despite his personal passions, it would never have occurred to him to attack the President.

When the FCC lifted its fairness doctrine, it freed radio to inject bias—just as newspapers and television could. That brought the Rush Limbaughs, Doctor Lauras, Al Frankens and Bernie Wards, all hosts with a much more partisan brand.

Then the web arrived, and suddenly firebrand radio hosts could reach much farther than their terrestrial signals had previously allowed.

In a 2015 Time Magazine article, Brian Rosenwald wrote that, thanks to the internet, a whole new audience could "hear what is said on talk-radio programs themselves. Hosts' words far more easily reach non-listeners than they did 25 years ago." That leads to swifter and more far-reaching audience feedback, holding producers' and advertisers' feet to the fire when hosts go too far. "Campaigns against a [controversial] host can build over time, and social media makes it easy to pressure station management and advertisers."

Rosenwald explained at the time that he ultimately saw provocative news talk radio as a poor fit for ad-dependent platforms online, and imagined that these shows would seek the relative safety of a subscription model to shield their revenue streams from boycotts and social shaming. Subscribers, after all, are dedicated fans who are not likely to bend to the outrage of outsider agitation.[120]

Today, radio-like news talk content is increasingly taking advantage of subscriptions and donations.

TV Embraced A Wider Audience

As bandwidth got better and video streaming became a viable medium, TV leaped at the chance to find more eyeballs. Fox News, CBS, MSNBC, ABC, CNN, NBC, and a plethora of local and international stations all staked their claims online.

Fox launched its FoxNews.com website in 1995, funded by ads and sponsored content. In 2009, it spun off Fox Nation as a viewer opinion website, which has since evolved into a subscription based news channel streaming on apps across all platforms, offering original programming distinct from Fox News.

MSNBC.com launched in 1996 and remained largely non-partisan and recognized for its journalistic excellence—even as its sister cable channel MSNBC increasingly leaned leftwards. So in 2012, it was renamed NBCNews.com, and MSNBC.com became the official address of the MSNBC TV show, where it could begin to reflect the progressive content of its TV namesake.

In 1997, ABC launched ABCNews.com. From 2011 to 2018 its news content was also shared on Yahoo's portal, giving them a larger audience than their own branded site could capture. Advertising was geo-targeted, inserting into the live stream one local ad for each three national ads, to help support local affiliates that feared being left out of the transition to web delivery.

In 2014, CBS launched CBSN, the first U.S. 24-hour online news channel. CBSN streams from the CBSNews.com website, and is available on a variety of cross-platform apps offering national and international news live, time shifted with a delay, or on-demand. Live-streaming local content is also available—e.g., CBSN Boston, CBSN Denver, CBSN New York.

Broadcast And Cable Are Losing To The Web

Broadcast and cable news are rapidly losing their audiences to online sources. A 2017 Pew Research poll showed that news consumers of all ages are increasingly going online. Even boomers, who are still nearly twice as likely to watch TV news over using the web, are slowly but surely turning to their devices. The trend is consistent, as a 2018 Pew poll reported that the number of adults of all ages preferring to get their news online was up 21% from 2016.

Large Newspapers Could Afford To Experiment

When the web appeared, big legacy papers seemed to grok that they had to have their own sites, even if they didn't quite understand why. Martin Nisenholtz, whose Times Electronic Media Company launched the New York Times' site, recalled, "We all had a sense that something important was happening, but at the time there were actually very few users."

They didn't really know what to do with the site, and toyed with the idea of creating a Yahoo-style portal to attract an audience. In the end, though, Nisenholtz said, "Publishing the newspaper on the web is what was expected. It's what the consumer expected. It's what was logical. It was low risk, in many respects. It didn't cost very much because we already had the content."[121]

For The Times, the path to making money online was simply to sell ads—like they'd always done in print. As we know, eyeballs are dollars, so to appeal to advertisers they needed to grow their audience.

It gave away free access for domestic readers, and for its first 18 months it charged international users to download stories. The paper was prepared to lose money in the short term, confident the experiment would eventually pay off as the web matured.

"I don't need to make money this year," said publisher Arthur Sulzberger. "And I don't need to make money next year. And I'd like to lose a little less money the year after that. [But] we're going to have to start seeing a financial return. And I don't think that's going to be as difficult as we think it is today, because I think the ethos and ethics of the web are changing."[122]

By 1996, The Wall Street Journal, The Washington Post and Los Angeles Times, had all joined The New York Times in launching their own online versions. The Wall Street Journal was the only one to charge a subscription for online access starting from day one, and they've been charging for access ever since.

Small Papers Struggled With The Web

Those big papers already had big audiences they could draw to their sites, and their print editions could subsidize their online experiments. That meant they could afford to wait and see where the profits might come from.

Small local papers didn't have that luxury. Despite radio and TV, they'd managed to keep a foothold in their local markets, delivering news, politics, sports, entertainment and editorials. Unfortunately once the web arrived, readers could find all those things online ten times over. Subscriptions suffered, readership suffered, and so did ad revenue.

Luckily, local papers still had local advertising to float them, such as real estate listings, employment ads, and classifieds. They were cheap, delivered high profits, and accounted for a large portion of revenue.

At least until Zillow, Trulia, Autotrader and Craigslist came along. These disruptive sites offered listings cheaper, easier, faster, and with wider reach, and they really hurt what was left of local papers' revenue streams.

That was especially true for Craigslist: The website offered free postings for rentals, items for sale, and more. The only things it charged for were car and real estate sales and job postings, which were all locally focused and offered advertisers way more words for a lot less money than newspapers did.

It hit local papers right in the pocketbook. A study by NYU Stern School of Business and Harvard Business School concluded that Craigslist cost the newspaper industry $5 billion between 2000 and 2007.

However, Craigslist founder Craig Newmark has long defended himself against claims that he single-handedly destroyed the newspaper industry, stating that the papers were on the decline long before he came along. "If I were to imagine a world where Craigslist was never invented," he says, "I do not think it would have made any difference." That might be arguable.

Still, today he's a staunch defender of legitimate journalism, warning that misinformation is an existential threat to democracy. And he's putting his Craigslist money where his mouth is. Forbes's Angel Au-Yeung, reported, "Since 2016, Newmark has given $170 million to journalism, countering harassment against journalists, cybersecurity and election integrity."

In Au-Yeung's interview, Newmark named those three "the 'battle spaces' of information warfare." He also recalled learning from an early age that, "A trustworthy press is the immune system to a democracy."

He plans to continue giving to the cause: "I have a lot of cash that I'll still be giving away as my twilight years progress."[123]

Why No Subscriptions?

Print newspapers were recognized, credible, reputable sources of news, and had always charged their readers for the product—either per copy or by subscription. There had been no rebellions, no boycotts, no letters to the editor questioning democracy. So why was *The Wall Street Journal* the only paper that stayed with that proven model?

In fact, other papers had tried to charge. In the early years and up to 2015, some publications started and eliminated their paywalls as many as 69 times, according to researchers at the University of Southern California.[124]

Papers expected paywall revenues to compete and beat advertising revenues, but that didn't always work. In 2005 for instance, *The New York Times* started charging for access to columnists' articles and its archives. It called the service *TimesSelect*, and it attracted some subscribers. Nevertheless, it eliminated the service two years later because advertising was more lucrative, and content sitting behind a paywall couldn't be discovered by search engines and monetized with ads.

Finally, in 2011, *The New York Times* implemented a paywall for *all* their content. As chairman Arthur Sulzberger explained, subscriptions would let the paper "develop new sources of revenue to support the continuation of our journalistic mission and digital innovation, while maintaining our large and growing audience to support our robust advertising business. And this system is our latest, and best, demonstration of where we believe the future of valued content - be it news, music, games or more - is going."[125]

Papers Simultaneously Failed To Innovate,
Fumbled Online Advertising

Failing to charge right from the beginning was clearly a mistake. In a 2009 interview, former newspaper editor and media COO Alan Mutter lamented, "The industry as a whole has done almost nothing right about taking advantage of its strengths, the ubiquity, ability to put out this unique product on people's doorsteps, and the original sin of giving away the content for free. [Papers should] create subscription content that's unique to the Web. There are all kinds of newsletters out there that people pay a lot of money for."[126]

Yet they didn't choose to charge. And that's fine—if you're going to rock at selling online ads then don't bother charging. But they didn't even take advertising so seriously. Papers felt certain that online ads wouldn't support their operational costs, but surely the big margins their print ads delivered would keep coming. And they didn't want to neglect their print cash cow by directing resources at finding new advertisers for their online properties.

So sales departments focused on what they knew and understood: selling ads for their print versions, to their existing print customers, with a taste of web advertising bundled in because ignoring the web entirely might make them look dumb. They hoped this would protect their print revenues, while still giving themselves and a few adventurous advertisers a way to experiment with this strange new web thing.

Unfortunately, existing print customers that were willing to try online ads just moved their print budgets to the web rather than spend new money. That meant the papers didn't create new revenue, they just transferred their revenue from profitable print ads to low margin web ads.

Too many papers were clearly risk-averse and chose to stay with comfortable, familiar ideas. But that low-risk approach meant no innovation in content, and focusing on print while bundling online ads to existing advertisers shows a lack of creativity in revenue models.

They couldn't even blame it on consumers' fears of online payments, because there were plenty of examples of e-commerce success:

Spotify, Sirius/Pandora, Netflix, Hulu and Amazon Prime were all doing just fine selling subscriptions for both physical items and streaming content. Clearly, people were willing to pay, even for content that was also available on legacy platforms like broadcast and cable.

Surely they would have paid for newspapers too—after all, they always had done.

Sadly the papers' lack of imagination and innovation torpedoed any chance they had of creating new markets and products to compete in the world of web advertising. By the time they realized Craigslist and other disruptors were eating their lunch, it was too late.

"Life today would have been easier," said Mutter, "if newspapers, magazines and other print-to-web media had recognized in the first place that their content was too valuable—and too expensive to create—to simply give it away on the internet."[127]

A Word About Jobs

I'd be remiss if I didn't mention that people worry a lot about the loss of journalists' jobs as papers shut down thanks to the web. And it's right to be concerned for people's jobs—especially in industries undergoing massive change.

There are two things to keep in mind about this though. First, according to Pew Research, newspapers were on the wane long before the web came along: Circulation as a percentage of households had been dropping steadily since 1960. And while jobs at traditional publishers have receded, much of the employment data doesn't count the new jobs created for journalists in outlets like Buzzfeed, Vox, or Bloomberg.

As Thomas Baekdal reports, "All these studies only looking at old media no longer represent what our world is like. And, as a result, we don't know how many people currently work in the media."[128]

And Here We Are

The publishers who've survived did so through conscious decisions that took advantage of the new opportunities provided by the internet. In the main, these innovators were able to make the successful leap to digital in three ways:

Expand from a city to nationwide: Certain cities have come to dominate the conversation, and publishers have exploited our focus on national issues at the expense of regional and local ones. Thus the New York Times and Washington Post have gained readers while The San Francisco Chronicle and Dallas Morning News have lost them. The internet enlarged our experiences beyond what was nearby and we want news to reflect that. The strategy has worked well for The Times: In Q1 2020 it added 587,000 new subscribers. That's almost three times the number of total subscribers of the Los Angeles Times. It's more than 70% of the total cumulative subscribers to Gannett's 260 media properties. The New York Times has more digital subscribers in Dallas–Fort Worth than the Dallas Morning News.

Build on existing loyal audiences: Some papers were already national, such as The Wall Street Journal, or international, such as The Economist. With no predefined geographic boundaries, they were much better placed to survive the boundless world of post-internet news. TV channels were obviously also well positioned. They simply doubled-down on their audience and message, as we've seen with Fox and CNN.

Build on shared language: The internet erased international as well as regional barriers, so a handful of publishers managed to jump to brand new markets. The Daily Mail and The Guardian were unknown to most US readers a decade ago, but through diligent efforts like hiring respected American execs, reporters and editors and creating dedicated US focused landing pages, they crossed over from the UK. They both now create specific articles for the US audience, reporting from a US rather than UK perspective. The BBC has done something similar, though its TV content and well known brand made the process easier.

Still, the classic newspaper publishers that have survived their transition online are figuring out how to make a business of it. Some are salvaging their revenues through paywalls or reimagined subscription or freemium models. Others are selling rectangles and hosting sponsored content. Still others are trying a combination of both.

But what's clear is that readers have grown accustomed to their "inalienable right" to free news that the web initially delivered—and they may not go back easily.

As consumers of news, we need to be aware of the difference between reliable, credible, evidence-based news, and sensational opinions designed to entertain and convert. Because one of those is going to deliver the unbiased facts we need to be productive, informed participants in society, and the other will leave us reacting emotionally to unfounded manipulations designed to generate clicks like Pavlov's dogs.

7. NEWS TODAY

In the previous chapter, we explored the history of news, who created it, who funded it, and how it responded to the influence of the web.

From here on, let's assume you receive all kinds of news, but it shows up in one place: your personal electronic device. If you still receive news on sheets of dried wood pulp slurry then I'm delighted for you. If TV is your thing, then nuke some popcorn and have at it. Still tuning in to AM radio? I have my doubts, but like, *whatever.*

The whole news industry—struggling to maintain relevance, dealing with fragmentation into micro niches, and striving to pay the bills—believes consumption via personal devices is the present and future. I can safely ignore TV, radio and newsprint, because I'm willing to bet you do, too.

Instead, I'm going to focus on news delivered online (in particular, stories and articles from legacy print publishers that moved online, or from born-online publishers that emulate newspaper journalism).

FIRST LET'S ESTABLISH A VOCABULARY

Before we dive in, I think it's important to define a shared vocabulary for some of the key terms we'll be using. We've discussed these ideas a little already but let's now put a stake in the ground for each of them—these are our working definitions for the rest of the book:

Evidence:

The available body of facts or information indicating whether a belief or proposition is true or valid: *The study found little* **evidence** *of groundwater contamination.*

Evidence works best with a neutral voice. It's characterized by lack of emotion, as in: "The Oakland Eagles beat the New England Revolutionaries 32-26."

Opinion:

A view or judgment formed about something, not necessarily based on fact or knowledge: *I'm writing about an issue that, in my* **opinion**, *is of great importance*.

Opinion is characterized by the use of emotion as the key lever, for example: "The Oakland Eagles are far and away the better team and deserved to beat the New England Revolutionaries." Often, as in this case, there's a tangential reference to the evidence—the Eagles won—but the driver is emotion. Opinions can also be total fabrications with zero evidence.

Entertainment:

The action of providing or being provided with amusement or enjoyment: *Everyone just sits in front of the TV for* **entertainment**.

Entertainment is something we all need, because we delight in having our emotions manipulated. The scary movie or the funny comedian or of course, watching The Oakland Eagles beat the New England Revolutionaries. When we have a favorite team, it can be highly entertaining to read the headline, "New England Revolutionaries Unleash Tweetstorm Blaming Biased Referee."

Clickbait:

Content whose main purpose is to attract attention and encourage visitors to click on a link to a particular web page: *Reports of the show's imminent demise are hyperbolic* **clickbait**.

The economics of internet business models and their optimization by some very smart people introduced us to Clickbait, and it's the candy of the internet. It's the sugar high we crave, in pure form. Not only is it emotion, but it's emotion that's highly targeted because it's driven by the desire to sell ads. We've already seen how ads are targeted at your needs, so it should be no surprise to understand that some businesses have optimized their news to meet those needs.

We could expect to read clickbait targeted to our support of the Oakland Eagles, claiming "New England Revolutionaries caught in child molesting ring in pizza restaurant basement" or similar non-sense. Whatever your implicit biases, there are words that can be crafted to match them, to extract the maximum ad revenue.

Okay, now we've got a shared vocabulary. So let's take a look at who's making news nowadays, how we're consuming it, what kind of news we're consuming, and why.

WHO'S MAKING NEWS NOW

Pick up almost any internet connected device and I'll bet you can get news in 10 seconds or less. There's no getting away from it.

It's all around us, day and night, on our phones and tablets and watches and laptops. It's seeping into our entertainment and our social media. It's so pervasive and there's just so damn much of it, that it's hard to imagine there actually are people behind the scenes, churning out all those words on the screen, or recited to us by talking heads.

But there are. There *are* people behind the curtain—writers and talking heads, programmers and producers and publishers, people who are employed by companies that figure out what we want and have turned that into a business.

Making sense of the endless stream of news and news-like content on your devices starts with understanding the two types of businesses that create that it all.

Classic News: Established Brands Who Thrive

Classic news organizations have been around for as long as 170 years—particularly among newspapers. For much of that history, due in part to self-imposed journalistic ethics and in part to the Fairness Doctrine for radio and TV, they could be relied on to do a good job of following established journalistic standards, delivering reporting that was balanced and neutral.

They did their research, checked their sources, checked their sources again, and ultimately presented objective findings. When they discovered they'd made mistakes, they printed retractions and corrections. Readers were subscribers usually. And they were loyal to the paper's voice and slant—whether long, detailed explanations or short highlights, a business focus or human interest, and even its policy bias.

When making the transition to online, classic news publishers stripped away the stuff that no longer worked, such as classifieds and event listings, and published the same editorial content they already had. They continued to make minor adjustments around the edges of the business, adding a section here, experimenting with formatting there, publishing email newsletters and so on.

But the core function of the operations didn't change much: gather evidence and explain it.

Most of us seem to want classic news, if we knew where to find it. This is confirmed in the Digital News Report 2020 from the Reuters Institute for the Study of Journalism at Oxford University. It surveyed 80,000 people in 40 media markets and asked about their news consumption habits and expectations. The report concludes: "Our survey shows that the majority (60%) still prefer news that has no particular point of view and that only a minority (28%) prefer news that shares or reinforces their views. Partisan preferences have slightly increased in the United States since we last asked this question in 2013 but even here a silent majority seems to be looking for news that at least tries to be objective."[129]

Neo-News: Born Online

So classic news publishers were occupied trying to migrate their established brands and dedicated audiences to the web, fiddling with paywalls, cutting holes in them, tearing them down and rebuilding them. Meanwhile, digital entrepreneurs spied an opportunity: Craft the news content that people—you—are vulnerable to, get you to visit the site, sell your eyeballs and sell your clicks. All the pieces were already in place.

First, there's the cash flow. It was clear there'd be no problem generating revenue—when we discussed ad-tech, we saw that targeted ads make the money pour in through those empty rectangles that Google sells. And it's scalable: Ads can be targeted more precisely and made even more profitable if the news itself is written to the biases of specific subsections of the audience.

Neo-news content would need to be short and shallow, but that means they could write more, post a lot every day, and keep you busy. They don't want you wasting time sitting on one page reading some long, boring article, they want you clicking on lots of small, entertaining, easy-to-digest chunks of targeted content.

More page views means more ads, which means more clicks, which means more money. Plus, let's face it, short shallow articles are easier to write. There's no need for a research staff.

Fact checkers be damned. No need for corrections and retractions, because who cares? The advertisers certainly don't, the readers don't. Save the money: Have the interns write more stuff.

These neo-news guys didn't hit the ground with an established audience that classic news publishers did. But that has its advantages. When there's no pre-existing expectations to meet, it's easier to experiment and try radical new ideas to capture interest and keep people entertained.

Of course, with no installed audience, the readers need to come from somewhere—and the natural place—the *organic* place—is search. People are already on Google looking for facts, so the neo-newsies just have to design their "facts" to match the specific topics folks are already seeking. And then, through the magic of search, the right audience shows up. We've seen how Google's data collection helps them match the search results to the individual, virtually guaranteeing the visitor will like this neo-news.

Then there's social media—*oh my*. With all the other elements in place, this is where the plan really takes off.

It's a match made in heaven. On one side of the coin, neo-news has all those short, emotionally driven articles that are free for anyone. On the other side, social media has groups of like-minded people who enjoy asserting their loyalty to the tribe. Just let the readers freely share the articles to anyone in their social circles and they'll bring their like-minded friends on board.

Neo-news has seen incredible, unbelievable growth over the past decade. Thriving, content-hungry audiences driven by social media, plus low capital costs, equals an ever growing array of publishers, creating billions of targeted words, catering to increasingly narrow interests. *Huffington Post* grew dramatically and became a darling of liberals, while *The Bulwark* set sail to conquer conservative lands.

So, we've basically got two camps making news: Classic news brands on the one hand, and neo-news content factories on the other—both of them generating a ton of news and news-like content, on all our devices, everywhere, all the time.

Assuming we're interested in consuming any kind of news at all, we're going to have to seek it out from one or the other. Which can be overwhelming, because nowadays there's a boatload of different ways we find and consume our news.

HOW WE FIND NEWS ONLINE

So there's all kinds of content out there online that presents itself as news, and it all shows up on your screens. And there's all kinds of ways we can seek it, find it, stumble across it, and consume it. Some, I believe, are better than others.

I think there are two things to consider when deciding how to consume your news: psychology, and technology. Let's look at the psychology first.

Foraging For News

For anthropologists, foraging behavior is a "hard-wired" mechanism that evolved to help animals—including us humans—use as little energy as possible to find and consume as many nutrients as possible. In the early 1990s, Peter Pirolli and Stuart Card, pioneers in human-computer interaction, correlated that behavior to the observed behavior of humans searching for information online, which they called "information foraging theory."

Because online information is spread out across thousands of sites, we have to forage for our news in much the same way we used to forage for food: by burning minimal "resources" (time and effort) to find optimal "nutrients" (quality information).

Gord Hotchkiss is president of Out Of My Gord Consulting, the former founder of Enquiro (now a part of Mediative), and author of The BuyerSphere Projects. He writes, "In today's digital world, information sources have disaggregated into profoundly patchy environments." Our task, when we're looking for information, is to "look for the best information 'patch,' which is determined by information 'scent,' the smell of informational relevance. The greater the scent, the greater the promise of an abundant information patch."[130]

That scent is the collection of signs that a site or piece of content gives us about its contents—a catchy or appealing title, keywords, images, a legit looking masthead, and so on. And from all those clues we make a split-second, gut-driven decision about how valuable it might be to us.

Hotchkiss says we have to "make a determination of which information we include in our diet. ... So we will quickly filter out low-quality information. In fact, if we think a patch contains only low-quality information, we'll exclude it from our diet."

Now that our news and information are "disaggregated" by being spread across countless online sources, we've got to find new, scalable ways to discover quality sources. Hotchkiss says that search engines are especially attuned to that foraging behavior. "Search engines give us the ability to create our own patches," he says, "somewhat like a spider spinning a web to catch prey. We see what we catch based on the scent, and if we don't like what we see, we quickly spin another web with another query."[131]

I feel somewhat less charitable than Hotchkiss about what kind of news a forager is willing to ingest. It seems that those foraging for news are more than happy to stay with a patch that delivers a shallow sugary high if that's easier than moving on in search of a more substantial meal.

And it was social media that really changed our quest for mental nutrition into a fast-food delivery service. Tasty stuff shows up at the door and we don't need to leave the sofa.

Searching For News

If we're not foraging, then we still want our facts on demand, and search is what we turn to—because it delivers everything we desire.

97% of adults in the U.S. conduct at least one search a day, according to SurveyMonkey. Among those who use search as a primary method, Google is the go-to source.

According to Edelman's 2020 Trust Barometer survey, when it comes to looking for news, 61% of people trust Google search results—exactly as many as trust traditional news outlets. The irony is, of course, it's increasingly *not* traditional news publishers writing the stuff that appears in Google—more often than not, it's neo-news.

Think about the last search you did. How many of the results did you look at before deciding what to click on? Most of us look at the first few results, maybe scroll down the page a little, but that's about it.

Survey after survey have shown that the first page of results receive the *vast* majority of traffic—almost nobody clicks Next—and the higher up the first page a result is, the more likely it is to be clicked. For news publishers to succeed, they obviously need to show up on Google, and being on that first page is money.

The results we get on that first page are designed to satisfy whatever level of neutrality or bias we insert into our query, because the publishers put keywords and "semantic trickery" in their content and headlines that let the search engines know which of our search phrases they want to show up for.

For example, a quick search for "2020 election"—a generic, neutral phrase with no emotional modifiers—yields over one billion results. The top five for me were for CNN (two listings), The Guardian, The New York Times, and NBC News. It shouldn't be at all surprising that the top news outlets monopolize those coveted top search results—their news has a solid foundation and far reach, and so does their advertising budget.

And what if I used more pointed search terms? What if I asked about a candidate's mental stability or fidelity—*did Crazy Candidate Sue cheat on her husband?* Suddenly those top slots expand well beyond "hard news" sources to include well- and lesser-known magazines, local news, entertainment outlets and sources with clear political biases. This has tremendous potential to be problematic because we tend to get "clicky" when we search, drifting away from our original inquiry to follow a more interesting headline (read: salacious). So even if we start out with the best of intentions to seek a reputable source, something else could just as easily capture our attention.

With carefully crafted content and headlines designed to match specific keywords and semantic intent, it's possible for a news story—true or false, left or right, fact or fiction—to appear at the top of a search. That means, theoretically, a search for a news story could yield results linking to something written by Hanna Dreier, Pulitzer-prize winning journalist from ProPublica and the Washington Post, or by Christopher Blair, a construction worker whose stream-of-consciousness fabrications are presented as news and have attracted enough viewers—and advertisers—to allow him to quit his job.

As Hotchkiss says, "Search has been remarkably successful in becoming the preferred 'patch' for a diverse set of information needs, but it still comes up short in one particular category. It doesn't do very well at helping us find information when we don't have a clear idea of what we're looking for." Search, he says, is not a very good "discovery" engine.

But it is a great affirmation engine, helping us find things we already know how to define. If our search terms and our search history are laced with unconscious bias, the results will be too.

So when we search for confirmation that Crazy Candidate Sue cheated on her husband, we'll find *exactly* what we're looking for.

News Aggregators

What if we just want to know what's currently important? We can't search for that. We need a starting place that gives us a bunch of articles, over a range of interests, deemed to be relevant by someone—or something. Even better if we can define a topic and get more news about that (and less about what doesn't interest us).

This idea of a single starting place leading to articles from multiple publishers is called an *aggregator*. Before we look at how they work, it's important to recognize that aggregators are not actually researching and writing anything: You're don't get online news from, say, Google News any more than newsprint subscribers get their news from a kid on a bike. The aggregator is a delivery mechanism that gets articles to you—or more specifically, to your device.

Thing One and Thing Two

Broadly speaking there are two kinds of aggregators: algorithmic and curated.

Algorithmic aggregators send out bots to crawl the web, looking for news content the algorithm thinks is worth sharing. When it finds something a reader might be interested in, based on what it knows about them, it adds the story to the feed.

Conversely, in a *curated* aggregation service, there are people involved. A range of publishers select articles and "push" them on to the aggregation platform, where human editors check quality and ultimately decide what shows up in front of readers.

The publisher is free to choose which of their articles appear and which don't—and of course those same articles might be available on the publisher's website for free, or hidden behind a paywall. This selectivity lets the publisher distribute certain articles as teasers while not being forced to give away everything.

Aggregators are becoming more popular for finding and filtering through news sources. It's worth taking a closer look to understand in more detail what you're gaining and at what cost when you use them.

Google News

Google dominates algorithmic news aggregation with its ability to instantly index websites, to personalize content by behavioral preferences, and to offer multiple languages. Its Google News service launched way back in 2002, so it has a good lead on its competitors.

It's free to both users and publishers, and selects content based on the authority and freshness of the publication, user clicks, geography and other predefined criteria.

The service doesn't deliver the entire news story, only a summary that links out to the complete story on the publisher's site. This includes content that lives behind paywalls, to the delight of publishers and annoyance to those of us who want to read beyond that first paragraph. Google keeps up with trends in the publishing industry and does what they can to help publishers monetize readers.

Since Google News is free to publishers, there's no guarantee that their content will end up on the service. But a publisher can increase the chances of being included by creating a free account in the Publisher Center, applying to be included in Google News, and submitting feeds, sitemaps, or videos directly to the system. Google says none of these steps are necessary for inclusion in Google News, however those sites that Google hasn't approved find very limited exposure and representation within the news results. There are also tools to help increase the chances of turning up in the News tab of a search results page.

Publishers could choose to exclude their content but no matter what gripes they may have with Google, no sane publisher would ever pull their content. Being included in Google News headlines is hugely advantageous as a foot in the door to the highly coveted search algorithm which is sourced by Google.

Marshall Simmonds, founder of Define Media Group, an SEO company specializing in strategic audience development, says publishers "want coverage in Google news because those stories and URLs flow into the greater search algorithm, the web search results and that Top Stories carousel appearing across the top of any breaking or trending news story. Those are good clicks. That is good traffic and publishers absolutely seek it out. We know of several news organizations with teams [whose job] is just to focus on getting Google News traffic."

Google News has two huge advantages over other aggregators: Google Search and tight integration with Android. Results from searches for newsy topics favor high-ranking news publishers, and tend to be displayed within Google News—reinforcing the perception as the go-to source. Moreover, our search histories help the algorithm deliver a highly individualized news feed, even guiding the order in which stories appear. Finally Android pushes notifications about news stories through notification alerts, raising their apparent importance.

It's actually a huge money-maker for Google: Although the news aggregation itself carries no ads, to read beyond the summary you have to click over to the publisher's website, where you'll be seeing ads that are probably served by Google. Better yet, those ads will be targeted to you personally because you're logged in to Google to get your nice personalized news. So it's win, win, win for Google. News Media Alliance estimates that this integrated approach delivered $4.7 billion in revenues from news content in 2018, including roughly $100 million generated by Google News.

Google News does offer a nod to subscriptions, by storing the login credentials for any paywalled publishers you might be subscribed to and seamlessly handling the login when you click through. It's also possible to subscribe from inside the Google News interface.

Google's relationship with news continues to evolve. Even as we were finalizing this book, CEO Sundar Pichai unveiled the details of the company's *News Showcase:* A billion dollar investment in partnerships with news publishers to protect and support the future of quality news. Under this latest expansion of Google's earlier investments in the news industry a growing stable of select publishers will be paid to curate their own stories and feature them in high-visibility "story panels" inside Google News. Google's made an initial three year commitment to the program, but Pichai says he expects to extend that commitment well into the future.

Why this huge investment into news? Pichai says, "We want to play our part by helping journalism in the 21st century not just survive, but thrive."

I think there are a couple of other less altruistic motivations for Google here:

First, it's kicking off this program in Germany, Brazil, Argentina, Canada, the UK and Australia—places where there's legal or regulatory blowback around Google's negative impact on news publishers. Shoveling money into the industry it's accused of harming is good PR.

Second, finding new ways to keep users inside the Google ecosystem is never a bad thing. It certainly *quacks* like a Trojan horse, and the easier it is to control and track activity, the better as far as Google's concerned.

Will the gambit work? Simmonds puts it, "There are still a lot of unknowns: What do publishers gain by participating in this new program? How does it help build their individual brand, grow their subscribers and contribute to their respective business models? This program feels like it's driven by General Data Protection Regulation (GDPR) and Google trying to play nice with international news organizations, because if that hadn't passed in the EU I don't think we're having this conversation. Ultimately publishers do not want to rely on Google to reach their audience. However, we need Google right now so we play by their constantly changing rules, lack of transparency and cryptic support."

Apple News / Apple News Plus

Apple News is much newer in the aggregator space, having launched in 2015 as an iPhone app, but it's an excellent example of news curation. The service benefited immediately from their built-in audience of 125 million monthly iPhone readers who, just like Google News users, can read articles for free.

Unlike Google, Apple doesn't just send an algorithm out to scrape any news it finds, but instead is curated by actual human beings, just like old-school editors. And articles are displayed in their entirety within the Apple News app, so readers don't need to click out to the publisher website.

Fans like the clean design and easy navigation and, if they've read this book, they especially like that Apple strictly controls those empty rectangles, stripping out obnoxious ads, trackers and ugly stuff. It does have its detractors—particularly publishers who loathe the way Apple controls not just curation but the empty rectangles too, and therefore the flow of money.

In 2019, Apple launched a subscription version called Apple News+. This version includes paywalled content, but a single monthly subscription grants access to all paywalled articles from all publishers. Apple keeps 50% of all Apple News subscription revenues, splitting the remaining 50% among participating publishers based on how much time users spend on their content. Plus Apple takes 30% of any publisher subscriptions sold through the app.

That's steep, even by Apple standards, but most publishers are okay with it, because they believe in Apple's reputation for success. They think they'll sell more subscriptions this way than directly on their own sites, so it's better to get half of something than all of nothing.

Simmonds notes that 50% is a "really high bar to compete," so it's up to publishers "to decide whether or not having long-term subscribers is worth giving up 50% of that revenue." He goes on to say that publishers really have to consider how offering a free service versus a paid service could benefit them best. This is particularly true for smaller publishers who may have to undercut their own prices to play in the same arena as the big names.

Some big, established publishers weren't interested in Apple's 50-50 proposal and opted out. *The Guardian* left Apple News in 2017, though it came back in 2020. And both *The New York Times* and *The Washington Post* declined to be part of Apple News+ from the start.

The New York Times chose to take a more aggressive stand against the revenue share in 2020, when they announced that they would no longer distribute any articles at all via the Apple News app.

The paper stated that Apple's service "did not align with [*The Times*'] strategy of building direct relationships with paying readers," and warned other news organizations of the risk of such a model to the future of journalism if they continue to encourage their readers to go elsewhere to get the news they produce. It's confident its global brand recognition, growing digital subscription base, quality content, and capable sales staff negate the need to split revenue.

Despite the human touch and incredible market penetration, the inclusion of Apple News on iPhones has done little to convert readers to paid subscribers. Even following the addition of local news and audio formats, the number of subscribers is far lower than, say, Apple Music.

Facebook News

To the extent that sharing memes that bash your political foes is "news," Facebook has been there from the start. However in 2019 they launched a true news aggregator, sourcing genuine reporting from the Facebook pages of publishers using a hybrid of curation and algorithms.

It claims to use humans who are "free from editorial intervention by anyone at the company" to curate the news, although they do receive help from machine learning and "thousands of signals" to rank content and "empower" users to curate their own content based on those editors' choices. Readers can also select their own preferences.

Facebook News curators will only include content from the pages of publishers who have registered in a news page index. Accepted publishers are required to "comply with broadly-accepted journalistic standards." Interestingly, they also note that "the amount of advertising and promotional content should not exceed the amount of news content," but how they measure that isn't clear.

When the site was first unveiled, Facebook said it would pay some of their participating publishers—for example, *The Wall Street Journal* confirmed that their parent, News Corp, would receive a licensing fee to allow Facebook to feature headlines from their publications.

But Facebook has a rocky relationship with the publishing industry. For example, at one point it began a collaboration with news publishers to promote their content called Instant Articles. However, it was simultaneously creating an algorithm that favored video, which promptly diminished the reach of Instant Articles. Around the same time, it started and abruptly ended its Trending Topics feature—after it was reported that the topics may not, in fact, have been trending at all.

As it approaches its first birthday, Facebook News is still finding its place in the news distribution business. The model of paying news publishers for their content supports journalism, but it remains to be seen if it's enough to support themselves.

In the meantime, for those people who claim to get their news from Facebook, that news might only be true for some of the people, some of the time.

Plus New Entries

News aggregation and delivery is on the rise, and we couldn't possibly go deep on them all. There are loads of other up-and-coming services and apps including Knewz, Feedly, Inoreader, Flipboard, and Pocket. So it's best simply to understand that aggregation is a thing, that aggregators have features good and not so good, and that they each have motivations for why they choose to deliver what they deliver the way they deliver it.

Aggregators Have Their Motivations

The design and implementation of all these aggregator sites and apps reflect the different philosophies of the companies producing them:

Apple, as per usual, encourages subscription, tightly controls aesthetics, advertising and privacy—and human curation drives what news stories show up.

Google, as per usual, is a free-for-all with algorithms running the show, collecting data and targeting ads—and subscriptions are an afterthought.

Facebook, I suspect, launched news as an attempt at deflecting negative publicity, but I just don't see the revenue generation model here and wonder how long it'll continue to pay up for quality news.

Much like all the other web services we've looked at, the aggregators are in a battle for the business model. It'll be interesting to see what wins out. But in the meantime, choose your poison.

Finding News Through Social: We Were Born This Way

The Reuters Institute report finds that an astonishing 48% of people in the US are getting their news from social media.

Gord Hotchkiss has some fascinating insights into why we act the way we do when we're interacting with news online—especially on social media. "Our loyalty to the brand and quality of an information provider is slipping between our fingers," he said in a recent MediaPost article, "and we don't seem to care. We say we want objective, non-biased, quality news sources, but in practice we lap up whatever dubious crap is spoon-fed to us by Facebook or Instagram." We're not really lying when we say we want quality sources—it's just that we're not necessarily seeking them out. The reason for that disconnect, he says, is because our brains work differently when we're seeking something, rather than stumbling across it. He says there are two ways that this manifests:[132]

First is the "top down" versus "bottom up" nature of our thought processes. "When our brain has a goal," he says, "it behaves significantly differently than when it is just bored and wanting to be entertained." When there's a goal, like looking for specific information on a topic—let's say Covid-19 information—the brain gets an executive order to round up all the parts of the brain and focus them together on the goal. "Suddenly the entire brain focuses on the task at hand and things like reliability of information become much more important to us. If we're going to go directly to an information source we trust, this is going to be when we do it." So, when we set out to research a particular topic we're much more discerning about where the information is coming from, and we make an effort to vet credible and authoritative sources.

But when the brain isn't pursuing a goal—when it's just rummaging around online looking for a distraction because we're bored—it works entirely differently. That's the "bottom-up" brain activation, and that is an entirely different animal. "We go to our preferred social channels," he says, "either out of sheer boredom or a need for social affirmation. We hope there's something in the highly addictive endlessly scrolling format that will catch our attention." In order for a news item to stand out from the rest of the endless content on our screens—the kittens and memes and shopping—it has to "hook" our brain's attention with something that feels familiar, such as a bias or belief, or maybe it has to piss us off and make us get defensive. That sudden intrusion on our semi-conscious scrolling grabs the attention of our lizard brain, because we're not thinking critically. "The parts of our brain that act as a gatekeeper against unreliable information are bypassed," he explains, "because no one bothered to wake them up."

Then there's what he calls the "priming" issue. When we're mindlessly scrolling, our brain takes in one random stimulus and primes our mind to infer a connection to the next. "Priming sets the brain on a track we're not aware of, which makes it difficult to control. Social media is the perfect priming platform. One post sets the stage for the next, even if they're completely unrelated." It's what we might call "going down the rabbit hole of the internet," where we start out looking at cat memes and find ourselves on YouTube watching tin-foil hat, deep state crockumentaries and wondering how we got there.

Because our brains are emotional, unpredictable and unreliable, and because we're more likely to be scrolling the internet in a "bottom up" mode, publishers and advertisers find us easy to manipulate.

So maybe social media isn't the best place to go for news.

Classic Local Newspapers Are Disappearing

Sometimes we're looking for specifically local news. It would be nice to think that local papers were still there for us, providing some kind of unique insight into the issues that directly affect our communities and families just outside the door.

Unfortunately, we've seen that local papers got crushed on all sides. They suffered huge legacy costs like pensions that needed to be paid and unions that needed to be negotiated with. Revenue was lost to online classifieds like Craigslist, while readership drifted away to better and more readily available reporting from the brands that went national. In large measure they've merged, been bought, gone bankrupt, or simply closed their doors. At this point it's hard to imagine that any can survive.

We're already seeing that far too many consumers have no source of local news, and that's not healthy for the communities they live in. The Hussman School of Journalism and Media, part of the University of North Carolina at Chapel Hill, conducted a series of reports on the impact of the web on newspapers, and it discovered a serious, near extinction of local publications. "In the 15 years leading up to 2020, more than one-fourth of the country's newspapers disappeared, leaving residents in thousands of communities – inner-city neighborhoods, suburban towns and rural villages – living in vast news deserts." News deserts, they explain, are communities "with limited access to the sort of credible and comprehensive news and information that feeds democracy at the grassroots level."

What happens when there's suddenly a vacuum in the delivery of news? Three things.

First, in some rare cases, entrepreneurial journalists start up their own local publications, with the support of the neighbors and readers who value their work. They're doing their best with wood pulp and digital to keep local journalism alive where they can.

Secondly, readers go to non-local outlets, like the sites of surviving papers in neighboring counties or states. Or, they go to social media. Neither of which provides the local news and insight they need to understand their own communities. As Hussman's researchers explain, "In the absence of a local news organization, social media and internet sites often have become the default media for reading, viewing and sharing news – as well as rumor and gossip – exacerbating political, social and economic divisions in a polarized nation."

Then a third thing happens—and this is where the really egregious stuff is happening. Remember when we talked about how easy Google makes it for anybody to create a site, publish bat-crazy fake news that attracts eyeballs, and get paid for advertising clicks? Welcome to the dark side of fake *local* news, where disreputable online players swoop in and launch websites that look like local news but are really just ad farms, designed to generate revenue and distribute disinformation.

Augustine Fou explained how this third phenomenon works: "Previously, if someone wanted to spread propaganda, they'd have to set up their own website, host their own servers, write their own content, all that kind of stuff. Now they can set up a fake website, copy and paste a few lines of code on there and start making ad revenue. All of a sudden, they have an ability to fund their disinformation operations. [Local news is] now being taken over by fake news outlets. CityOfEdmontonNews.com is a completely fake site spewing fake news. AlbanyDailyNews.com is another fake site spewing fake news. So as the dollars flow away from legitimate news organizations, they have to lay off reporters and shut down branches, [because] the funds are now flowing to fund fake news."

These fake news sites are pretty convincing to the untrained eye, and they leave people who live in news deserts thinking they're getting legitimate local journalism.

But hey, maybe some folks aren't looking at those sites. Maybe, as Hussman reported, they're going to social media for news. Or maybe they're not even looking for news on social, but just stumbling across it while they scroll through timelines filled with cat memes.

Is that a problem? Fou explains that yes, fake news is still a problem. "So let me now tie it to the bigger picture. Twitter, Facebook, YouTube cannot even handle [filtering it] because as a platform, it's a huge task to try to figure out what piece of info is actually fake news or real news, because they'll use the same keywords, right? An algorithm can't easily tell whether this piece of news is fake or not."

To the extent that any local publishers have survived, they make their articles available through the aggregators we already use, so their headlines and summaries drift past us along with everything else. Few of us are motivated enough to click through and visit the local publisher's website, and if we do, we quickly realize it was a mistake. The user experience is likely to be awful, with ads and popups jumping from all sides, ghastly design choices and blocky pages that won't render on mobile.

You Are Where You Eat

Clearly, different discovery methods are suited to delivering different kinds of news content, and different kinds of consumption experience. Some are well-suited for short and sweet content, others are better for long form reading.

Some are fast food, convenient and easy and unhealthy with hard plastic seats designed to make you leave as soon as possible. Some are organic farm-to-table cuisine, expensive and healthy, with comfortable seating and a chef who can make beautiful meals from quality ingredients.

In other words, it's not just about *how* you consume. It's about *what* you'll be consuming. That's why it's probably worth looking at the kinds of news that are out there waiting to be discovered.

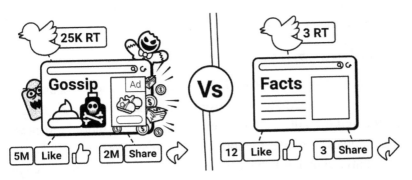

WHAT KIND OF NEWS ARE WE CONSUMING?

The Center for News Literacy defines news as, "Timely information about a subject of some public interest that is shared and subject to the journalistic process of verification by an independent organization that is accountable." Journalists, in fact, are held to a code of professional conduct that demands that opinion "must not, in the interest of arguing a side of a debate, misrepresent facts or the context that helps people make sense of facts."

The Society of Professional Journalists expects members to embrace a mantra of V.I.A.—verification, independence and accountability. The information they provide should be "accurate, fair and thorough." Reporting needs to "distinguish between advocacy and news reporting. ... Analysis and commentary should be labeled and not misrepresent fact or context," and journalists should "deny favored treatment to advertisers and special interests and resist their pressure to influence news coverage."

In other words: In a perfect world, news would be factual, be devoid of opinion, lack any bias, and it wouldn't be designed to reward special interests or advertisers.

That worked pretty well for a long time. Then along came the web, and in the online hunt for motivated eyeballs to sell to advertisers, evidence-based fact collection, multi-sourced corroboration, and reliable witnesses gave way to emotion-laden "opinion journalism," designed specifically to reward special interests and advertisers.

Because emotion wins the clicks.

Emotion Wins The Clicks

Charlie Beckett, professor at the London School of Economics, said in a 2015 talk that, because online publishers largely depend on traffic and eyeballs, they're compelled to create more "soft news" that appeals to readers' emotions and encourages them to engage and share. "Journalists have to fight harder than ever for every eyeball or ear," said Beckett. "Tugging at your heart strings is a tried and tested way to get your attention." Journalism has to work in a world, he said, "where it is blended into people's digital mobile lives alongside kittens, shopping, sport, music and pornography."[133]

Publishers are using the psychology of emotion to capture that traffic, and get visitors to not only read and click, but share with their communities. "Increasingly journalism is now distributed not by transmitters or newsagents but by social media. Getting people to share your content is vital and emotion is critical to making that happen. ... Luckily for journalists we now have the technology and the data to measure that process."

In the end, Beckett says we're no longer consuming news because it's useful or informative. Instead, "We are acting in an emotionally charged way in communication with our community or the wider networks."

"Outrageous is not only acceptable," wrote Hotchkiss in 2018, "it's become desirable. We marketers are enamored with this idea of 'viralness.' We want advertising to be amplified through our target customer's social networks. Boring never gets retweeted or shared. That's why polarization works. By moving to extremes, brands catch our attention. And as they move to extremes, they drag us along with them."[134]

Kevin Hartman, a marketing expert and strategic planner, wonders if outrageous divisiveness is destined to be the norm. As he explained, "I am curious if consumer trust has reached a point where more and more brands will look to intentionally create content that 'goes viral' due to its divisive or outrageous nature." Our resultant division, he says, may just lead to more division. "We're even more primed for divisive marketing as more brands break from safety and align themselves with causes."[135]

When the content we're viewing is sliced and diced and edited and optimized to a particular viewer at a particular moment, we're simply not all consuming the same information about a given subject. In *The Social Dilemma*, computer philosophy writer Jaron Lanier asked us to imagine that Wikipedia had multiple pages on a single subject, each optimized to different biases. You and I wouldn't be seeing the same page or getting the same information about the topic.

It's like we're each getting our own version of the facts. No wonder we're all having such a hard time communicating.

The proof of this trend is in the content. A 2019 RAND study looked at how news has changed with the growth of new online media platforms. It uncovered a shift away from traditional journalistic objectivity to "more opinion-based content that appeals to emotion and relies heavily on argumentation and advocacy." It found that classic news was "strongly characterized by the use of concrete objects, numbers, references to duration, connections to individual roles, spatial relationships, and retrospective reasoning." Neo-news journalism was characterized by subjectivity, immediacy, certainty, insistence, and argumentation that was based more on personal perspective rather than precedent.

In other words, traditional news was characterized by its use of evidence, whereas online news was characterized by opinion, leading to what RAND calls Truth Decay—the diminishing role of facts and analysis in political discourse.

So we're inundated with online content: cute kittens, sports highlights, videos of dads getting hit in the naughty bits, all of which appeal to our emotions to get our attention. News not only has to exist alongside all that, it has to stand out and compete on an emotional level.

For neo-news to win out over loveable puppies, it gets our attention by giving up on objectivity and reason, and embracing subjectivity and emotional immediacy. The news content is crafted and presented in a wholly different way online than off, at the expense of a century old commitment to the neutral delivery of evidence and facts.

Solely to appeal to our lizard brains.

We're Being Probed

Neo-news publishers are very good at finding the words and phrases that manipulate our emotions. They craft headlines with some staggering statistic or audacious claim or some other hard-to-resist draw to lure us in. Then they test it. If the headline doesn't work, they change it.

Even if it does work, they change it to "the latest update" to draw you in again an hour later. It takes just five minutes of testing on a high traffic site to determine which version of a headline is more clickable. If it's a big enough story, they change it again and again and again until the algorithm tells them to stop.

In fairness, this type of A/B testing is common practice across all kinds of news outlets. Classic news organizations use it to measure audience engagement, in their efforts to cultivate a more informed audience. Editorial staff is typically involved in providing feedback, keeping a "buffer" between the news and the technology that promotes it.

Amazingly, 60% of links posted on Twitter were never clicked—not even by the user who posted it.[136] Many people simply don't read past the headlines for any type of news. As appalling and lazy as that is, and it saddens me, it's a behavioral truth that news publishers have to accommodate.

Both kinds of news providers, neo- and classic, have their reasons for testing and changing and recycling their headlines. One for more clicks, one to reach and inform more readers. One for evil and one for good. It's on you to be able to determine which you're responding to.

Maybe it'll help to look behind the curtain at how they operate.

OpinionFacts vs. DullEvidence: A Monetization Parable

Imagine two news publishers. One we'll call *OpinionFacts*, launched by a group of digital entrepreneurs in 2011 with a splashy website and app. The other publisher we'll call *DullEvidence*, and let's say it's been around since 1869, and still sells news on wood-pulp, but of course it now also publishes via a website and app.

The sales force at each is tasked with one job: growing revenue. But their editorial approaches are very different.

At OpinionFacts, it's optimizing the content. That doesn't mean making the reporting better, it means making it more clickable. The data indicates the click rate is actually highest on short articles and lower on long articles, so the VP of sales gives the editorial guys a directive: cut the length of articles to improve traffic monetization. The site's filled with short shallow stories, with clickbaity headlines designed to hook more fish.

The sales team recently did a deal with Taboola, one of the sponsored content guys, and it's working great. Revenue from each click is 50% higher than average. But now the editors have dialed in how to craft stories that get more clicks, the sales team is talking to another ad network who's promising 15% higher revenue in return for reselling rights, offering OpinionFacts' rectangles to even more advertisers who will compete for the placement. It'll bring even more third parties' tracking codes and cookies onto their page to mine reader data. It's a good opportunity, and 15% is great money.

Using a new analytics tool that examines behavior inside the video content and how long people watch, the gear heads figured out that videos shorter than 237 seconds generate 11% more clicks. The editorial team is making the adjustment so all future video content adheres to this new, more hard hitting format.

The social media sharing buttons, newly redesigned last year, are working great too. The top 100 articles being shared each day have seen a huge boost through social media sharing. Traffic back to the site is significantly up since they made it easier for folks to express their outrage.

OpinionFacts is totally on fire.

Meanwhile over at DullEvidence, the sales team is answering customers' questions, like how to subscribe, and how to cancel print and subscribe to the digital content only. Paying customers are so needy. To increase subscriptions, the VP of sales has a meeting with the CEO to discuss launching a subscriber promotion to boost signups by a whole 5%.

Lots of effort is being put into research. Reporters are travelling to political hot spots and doing in-depth interviews with multiple sources to corroborate their evidence. All of which is expensive, but it's worth it to create the kind of meaty, long-form reporting that readers expect.

DullEvidence recently received a pitch from a data harvesting company. In return for placing a tracker on all pages, DullEvidence would get a cut of revenue generated from selling readers' personal data. It's good money, way easier to manage than needy subscribers, and would help offset the cost of creating the kind of journalism the brand's known for.

But DullEvidence declines. It can't afford the hit to its reputation—once readers found out they were being farmed, subscriptions would suffer. Social media sharing is barely a thing for DullEvidence. The articles simply aren't that emotionally charged—and anyway they're behind a paywall.

And so it goes on. OpinionFacts is blazing a new trail with hugely popular, emotionally divisive, highly targeted opinion content that's shared on social media. DullEvidence committing to crafting insightful and emotionally neutral factual content, as they have for 150 years.

TELLING FACT FROM OPINION

Are we going to consider ourselves informed citizens and make important decisions about politics and society, about legislation and law? Are we going to participate in our democracy as an informed citizenry? If so, we need to be able to tell the difference between factual content and opinion content.

But can we?

Research shows that we can't. Not very well, anyway.

Amy Mitchell, the Pew Research Center's director of journalism research, explained how a 2018 Pew study was designed to measure exactly that: the American news consumer's ability to differentiate "factual statements – ones that can be proved or disproved with objective evidence – from opinion statements, which are expressions of beliefs or values." It's critical, she said, for consumers of news to hone this skill if they're going to "undertake some of the other tasks being asked of them as news consumers, such as fact-checking or differentiating straight reporting from op-eds."

The study showed that not only do Americans have a moderate ability to tell the difference between factual statements from opinion statements, but they also have a tendency to "feel worn out by the amount of news there is these days, and to dip briefly into and out of news rather than engage deeply with it." So, even if you're better than the average bear at telling fact from opinion, you may be too exhausted by all the noise to work very hard at it.

Yikes. So most of us get our news for free online, and free online news—because it's ad driven—is inherently crafted to lean into emotions and opinions, rather than evidence. Our lizard brains can't tell the difference, so as far as we know opinions are facts.

It's entirely possible that we've never even seen evidence based reporting. Assuming we could recognize it, how would we describe it to a friend?

Turns out we actually do have a real-life example, and most all of us have heard of it at one time or another. Maybe you've even read it, without realizing what it was.

DullEvidence Based Appliance Reporting

In the United States as of 2020, it is actually possible to find that opinion free, DullEvidence based reporting you need to research and purchase almost any kind of consumer good. And the evidence comes from that credible institution named *Consumer Reports*.

Since 1936, their mission has been clear: "CR was created to equip people with the credible, trustworthy information they needed to make informed choices." At the time that they were founded, "consumers had very few options to gauge the value, quality, or authenticity of goods and services. It was an era of unfettered advertising claims, rapid technological progress, and patchwork regulations."

To push back against unregulated and outlandish advertising claims, it actually buys and tests thousands of products every year "to generate reviews and ratings to help consumers, support our investigative journalism and trusted consumer guidance, and advocate for consumer-friendly marketplace practices."

"Investigative journalism"? Make no mistake about it, that's what Consumer Reports delivers. While the reporting may not be about politics—the publication is decidedly apolitical—it's quite possibly the very best example of opinion free, DullEvidence based reporting on the market today. And it has maintained that standard for 84 years.

The site is filled with well-researched reporting, uninfluenced by ads or sponsored content. The About page says it's a non-profit organization, doing "rigorous, independent testing and research." its goal is to "empower consumers, inform people's purchasing decisions, influence businesses to improve the products and services they deliver, and strengthen norms, laws, and regulations through science, evidence, and data."

Obviously, back in 1936, there was no internet. But Consumer Reports has proven a success at transitioning from being a classic wood-pulp and print publisher to a reliable online presence, all the while maintaining its focus on facts and avoiding emotion and opinion.

How did it manage to survive the transition from print to online when so few others could? Why did it remain a universally trusted source of objective evidence, when everyone else chose to divide us with opinions? What's so special about what it delivers when anyone can put a video on YouTube showing how a fancy blender will turn bricks into a delicious smoothie?

The secret, dear reader, is *they charge for the content.* They always have. Precisely so they would never be beholden to the same advertising agenda they were committed to subverting.

"But hold on Grandad," I hear you say, "before I bought my toaster I checked reviews on Amazon. Same thing, and free, right?" Well, not exactly, no. Reviews are useful opinions, and by having lots of them you can create a convenient average star-rating. But the problem is those opinions are from people just like us.

We may observe that the toaster in front of us is good, and toasts evenly. It might even work better than any of the previous toasters we have owned, and look better too. However we don't know whether a certain toaster is objectively the best, in comparison to everything else available right now. We're not conducting such side-by-side tests, not using scientific methods to measure how crispy the toast turns out.

It's not our job, and we don't have the training, time or money. We are better served if we delegate this problem to experts, and pay them for their trouble.

Evidence That We Will Pay For Evidence

If Consumer Reports had decided to embrace Brand's assertion that "Information wants to be free" and give their reviews away online, I'm willing to bet they'd be funded by ads, optimized and opinion-driven like everything else.

We have a real-world example of what that looks like, because you can watch product unboxing videos on social media. There are people who actually make a living, and sometimes a great living, simply filming themselves opening boxes and expressing all kinds of emotions and opinions about their newest widget.

I'll be the first to admit unboxings can be highly entertaining. They're also very profitable—either funded by ads, or directly by the widget maker—and they're ridiculously cheap to make.

Thankfully, Consumer Reports knew their research and information had real value, and chose to embrace the other half of Brand's claim, "Information also wants to be expensive." They've built a process and gathered the staff to source the gear, run tests over an extended period of time, write coherently and publish their results to an audience willing to pay. Today, 84 years later, Consumer Reports remains trusted by just about everyone. I think the only complaint one could make, besides the fact you have to pay, is ... it's dull. Not much emotion, barely entertaining, just a bunch of evidence with a sprinkling of opinion.

And that is exactly the point.

Consumer Reports proves that real quality investigative journalism can be done—and done well—offline and online. And it proves that people are willing to pay for that DullEvidence reporting when they're engaged in the important work of choosing the right dishwasher or blender.

If publications are capable of providing this kind of reporting, and we're willing to pay for it to get quality appliances, can it also be done for news—to inform our democracy? Is there anyone still providing DullEvidence news reporting online? If so, is anyone paying for it? If they are, is the quality of their content they're getting truly better and more trustworthy than ad-driven OpinionFacts?

Pew fears we wouldn't be able to tell the difference. If that's true, how would we even begin to compare the two?

With evidence.

THE EVIDENCE

As you can tell, I've spent a lot of time thinking about our online lives and the quality of the information we seek, consume and share. But who the heck am I?

I actually worked at Netscape, the first real browser company, in 1997. Then in 2001 I invented some statistical analysis software that measures online behavior. I sold that business and launched another startup to teach companies about making effective use of such data and constructing evidence to make business decisions. After selling that one I created a product that automatically built the kind of targeted ads we're talking about here.

In short, not only do I have opinions, but I also have the depth of expertise necessary to form those opinions.

But they're just opinions, and the proof isn't in my emotional OpinionFacts, well-informed or not. The proof is in the DullEvidence. Evidence is discoverable and measurable and can help us identify true, quantitative differences between OpinionFacts and DullEvidence.

But don't take my word for it. I'm just one guy. In cases like this, I turn to people smarter than me.

So here we go.

Measuring News Bias And Reliability

Ad Fontes Media is an organization dedicated to the task of quantifying media bias and reliability. Its "Media Bias Chart" is considered the gold standard today in ranking the bias and reliability of news organizations both online and off.

Founder Vanessa Otero was inspired to start the research by her personal experiences online in the run up to the 2016 elections. She found herself concerned about the memes and bumper-sticker phrasing of biased political opinions being thrown back and forth among people on social media.

As she puts it, "Somebody conservative would say, 'this proves my point. Look at this article from The Blaze.' And somebody liberal would say 'this proves my point, look at this article from Slate.' And they would fail to convince folks from the other side and not really understand why." The more she thought about it, the more she realized that, while there might exist a space somewhere for advocating for your beliefs with reason, "there's this other world out there that's just really hyper-polarizing. I'm a patent attorney. My whole world is about explaining complex things in words and pictures. So I wanted to convey that in an image."

The organization's mission is "to make news consumers smarter and news media better." It fulfills that charter by rating a wide variety of news sources for reliability and bias "to help people navigate the news landscape." Its analysis is focused on measurable metrics of bias and reliability. "We are not measuring consumer opinions, clicks and views, or 'user engagement.' Plenty of other companies do that in order to sell ads, and we think that is part of the problem we face in the current media landscape. Ad Fontes Media does not sell ads to make money, and in fact, we believe news content ratings will be a key to fixing the way advertisers inadvertently help junk news sources proliferate."

Generating The Data

The rating system and methodology was initially created by Otero herself. "I looked at a lot of sources. I created a methodology and I was really refining how am I defining the top to the bottom? And how am I defining the left to the right? And when I'm looking at each individual article, how am I classifying it in the system? So it's really two things. It's a taxonomy of what the media is, and it's a methodology for placing the sources on that taxonomy."

The chart was an instant hit, and she knew that to make it even more valuable she would need to review more stories, and bring more people on board to better control for bias. At the outset of the project, 20 analysts with differing political views rated about 370 articles and about 17 TV shows each. Plus each of them rated approximately three articles from 100 news sources, for a total of nearly 7,000 individual ratings.

Today, the data is generated by a large team of analysts and is updated regularly. "The ranking methodology is rigorous and rule-based," says the organization. "There are many specific factors we take into account for both reliability and bias because there are many measurable indicators of each. ... The ratings are not simply subjective opinion polling, but rather methodical content analysis. Overall source rankings are composite weighted rankings of the individual article and story scores."

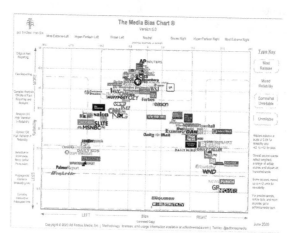

Reading The Media Bias Chart

Ad Fontes' Media Bias Chart has two axes: Bias on the X and reliability on the Y.

You'll see that the upper end of the chart is occupied by well established classic news brands that spent decades investing in the staff and processes needed for the collection of evidence. Then notice how strongly it becomes biased as we stray further down and away from evidence towards opinion, finally reaching total fabrications at the bottom.

Finding Neo-news On The Chart

The brands at the extreme left and right sides of the chart are the neo-news, and that's where you can see the online ads business model at work:

1. Create divisive content based on opinions
2. Show ads
3. Apply optimization methods
4. Get the audience to amplify it

It's About More Than The Ads

Sure, because you're the product there's ads, but it's not just about the ads.

Let me say that again, because it might sound counter intuitive, given how much we've harped on about advertising through this whole book: It's not just about the ads.

Perhaps more importantly, it's that the news itself has been edited, tweaked, tested, crafted, injected with opinion and emotion and optimized for you. That was done at the expense of neutrality and truth—because that's how we're best divided and sold profitably. That's why it doesn't matter if you use an ad blocker—*information wants to be free,* and all that.

It gets worse: You need to be sold on each and every page you look at. Every article and headline is designed to drive emotion and provoke clicking or scrolling and consuming more stuff.

Meanwhile, over on sites like DullEvidence, the subscriptions grow each year because, well, *information also wants to be expensive.*

Why Ad Blockers Don't Matter For Neo-news

It might be tempting to think that using an ad blocker would make it safe to slum it in the fringes of the chart with the neo-news providers and be safe from this business model, but you'd be wrong. All the ad blocker does is remove one step of the model:

1. Create divisive content based on opinions
2. Show ads
3. Apply optimization methods
4. Get the audience to amplify it

While you might not be getting the ads, you're still consuming that optimized content. The content that has emotional opinions baked in. The content that was tweaked and tested and crafted to suck you in—so they can sell your activity to advertisers. This is the content you're likely to share with friends on social media.

So congratulations! You're still helping them manipulate minds for their own purposes.

Do You Recognize Your News On The Chart?

What does your favorite source of news look like?

Maybe it looks like an episode of The Three Stooges, with eye gouges and pratfalls and punches thrown. You love it when Moe pulls the saw across the other team's heads. Maybe you mix in some Laurel and Hardy so you get a view from the other side, just to make sure you're fair and balanced. It's all good fun and very entertaining, and best of all free.

If you see your favorite online news among the neo-news on the left or right edges of the chart it might come as a shock. Maybe you thought you were getting fair and balanced facts because it's the other guys who bend the truth, not your guys. But neo-news appears on both sides of the chart because it's not limited to either left or right ideologies... you'll find plenty of neo-news designed and crafted to satisfy both liberals and conservatives.

But none of it is evidence.

So where are your favorite brands? Do you prefer opinion, entertainment and clickbait, or do you prefer evidence? Either one is okay, so long as you know what you're getting.

Maybe after considering all this, you've realized your favorite kind of news is OpinionFacts and you're not going to change. That's fine, go ahead with your Three Stooges—nothing wrong with that so long as you're *making an informed choice.*

I love a sideshow too. But know going in that it's not evidence, it's not informative, and it's not going help you understand policy choices, nor the other things a functioning democracy needs you to grok. (Hell, it won't even help you choose a new dishwasher.)

On the other hand, if you've decided that it's evidence you want, you'll find it living somewhere near the top of the chart, where the news is expensive and far less entertaining. (And that's where Consumer Reports would be on the chart.)

And if CR was reporting the news, I'd be the first to subscribe.

Finding The Current Ad Fontes Chart

The Ad Fontes chart is updated regularly, so take some time to check out the latest version online, in full color. Here's 3 different ways to find it:

1. Search for "Media Bias Chart"
2. Go to adfontesmedia.com (watch the spelling)
3. Go to freeisbad.com and click charts:media bias

MEASURING WHO THE CUSTOMER IS

I love the Media Bias chart. I trust Ad Fontes' methodology and I think the results are as accurate as it gets.

It's great at showing which publishers have what bias and how reliable they are—and the link between the two. But it doesn't measure the business model: It doesn't answer the question, "Who is the target customer, really—us or the advertisers?"

Wouldn't it be great if we not only knew where a news provider fell on the "bias and reliability" scale, but could also determine whether we're the customer or if we're the product.

Turns out, that can be measured too.

The Ad Shenanigans Chart

Remember how it's accidental that the empty rectangles in the web pages can be sold by third parties? Well, there's another accidental detail about websites: you can see evidence of the business practices, right there in the page.

It's not necessarily easy, but it's all there, if you know how to read the HTML code. Even better, you can actually quantify just how much shenanigans is going on.

In other words, we look at the information being published, and ask it whether it wants to be free or to be expensive.

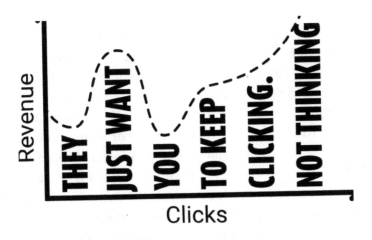

How We Measure Shenanigans

Now this is going to get a little geeky, but just as with Ad Fontes I think it's worth understanding the details of how we arrived at our chart.

Our data was collected using Chrome and we looked at the desktop website (not mobile, nor publisher-specific apps). Using a combination of software we wrote and some openly available tools, we took 87 news websites and ran them through a scoring system as follows:

1. Count the instances of paid content like Taboola. These are important revenue drivers.
2. Count the number of links pointing to external sites, reflecting the revenue from clicks via ads, sponsored content and hidden crap. We excluded links that go to the publisher's social media profiles, author bylines etc.
3. Count the number of trackers in use. While not visible to you when you're viewing the page, your data is nevertheless being collected and sold.

We averaged these values for two different story pages, not counting the home page or the category pages.

Finally, we wanted to know how many ad networks the publishers were willing to turn their traffic over to. Luckily we're able to see that pretty easily, because they all maintain a public record of all the networks they're partnered with—the so-called *ads.txt* file. A count of the records there shows us how much control the publisher wants over their reputation. A smaller number means more control.

The three values were normalized to a range of approximately 0-4 and then added together. This results in a score for each of the 87 sites, representing the degree to which you are the product being sold. The more opportunities the publisher gives us to click away and go to someone else's site, the more they are interested in turning us over to whoever their customer really is—rather than keeping us onboard and providing us with value.

Almost every news site carries ads—even for subscribers—so we don't have binary categories of "ads or no ads," but rather, "businesses that operate more like OpinionFacts or more like DullEvidence." That means considering other business model clues aside from just the number of offsite links. DullEvidence businesses also often generate revenue from subscriptions, and in many cases that's the majority of revenue, so we need to factor in that.

Luckily that's easier to measure: Subscriptions are priced right there on the website, as is the number of free articles available, if any. So we took the digital-only subscription, ignored special introductory deals, and figured out the weekly cost. In a small number of cases, publishers offer both a subscription and unlimited free articles, or perhaps some claimed "special content" for subscribers. We ignored these and treat them as free, because we assume nobody will pay without being forced to via a paywall (Consumer Reports proved that).

There are a few exceptions to subscriptions that we needed to handle: Taxpayer funded and industry funded.

US based taxpayer funded web publishers, such as the news websites of NPR and PBS, are in part "funded by the American people," via the Corporation for Public Broadcasting and other routes for budgeting taxpayers' money. For those, we took the amount of tax funding divided by the US adult population (we ignored donations and sponsorship, considering these to be voluntary or small in the context of operating their news websites).

For non US based, like BBC and CBC, we ignored the tax payer funding and treated them as 100% ad funded, which they are for US audiences.

The key industry funded publishers are Associated Press (AP) and Reuters. They are funded by a pool of contributions from classic news publishers, to whom they provide reporting services. In addition they have consumer facing sites carrying ads. We treated the industry pool funding like a subscription, and divided the total annual revenue figure by the US adult population.

The Charts

Presenting this data across 87 news publishers makes for an overwhelming quantity of data, so we broke it down into 3 categories, represented in three charts:

1. National brands that are free
2. National brands with a paywall and subscription
3. Local brands—i.e., large local markets supporting a significant news operation, but excluding brands that are now considered national.

The left side of the graph is the quantity of ad shenanigans, or the extent to which you are the product—i.e., the more offsite links there are, the more they're asking you to click on things they get paid for.

Where applicable, the right side is the subscription price, and the degree to which you are the customer, because you're directly paying for the news content, and you're an important source of revenue.

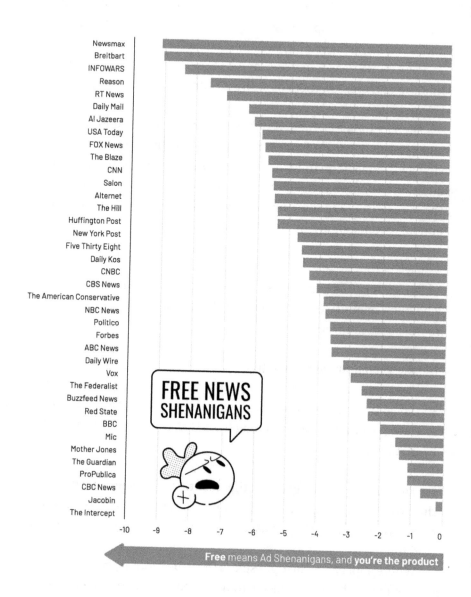

FREE NEWS
SHENANIGANS

Free means Ad Shenanigans, and you're the product

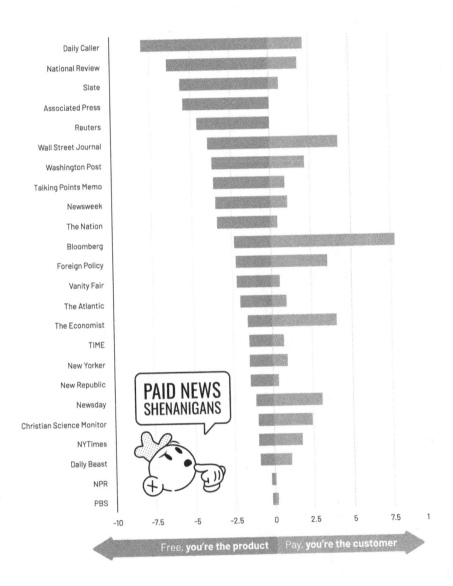

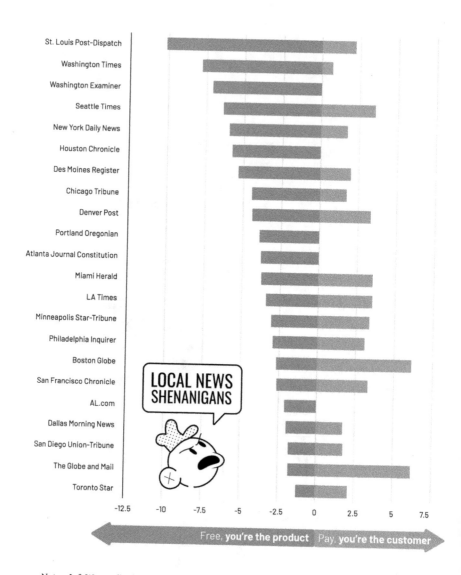

Notes: InfoWars sells their own brand products, like ingestibles. The ads are standard size & format, and there is ad sales information, but no external advertisers. We used data from Breitbart as a proxy.

Finding Your News On The Chart

As you did with the Ad Fontes chart, take a moment to find the ranking of your favorite news publisher. Are you surprised? Dismayed? Do you believe it? Do you even care?

Maybe for a second time you'll reject the evidence and decide that your OpinionFacts is far better than that DullEvidence garbage. Okay, maybe that's true. I'm sure the sales team at OpinionFacts would agree with you.

We've said it before: If the news you get is free, then you're the product, because the revenue comes from the advertiser. And now the data shows the situation clearly, thanks to all the embedded ad shenanigans.

No matter how legit the site and content might appear, OpinionFacts' revenue isn't coming from you, so OpinionFacts' motivation is to please the advertisers (and not so much please you).

Enough Numbers Already! Observing The Brand Promise

I get it. That's a lot. There's numbers and math and normalization and code and ... and maybe you find my data overwhelming.

So let's look at another type of evidence from the websites in question: Let's look at the brand promises they make to their customers.

When publishers charge for subscriptions, the subscriber is the customer. It's pretty easy to find the brand promise they make: They state it right on the subscription pages at the point you're about to hand over money.

Here's what some brand promises look like when they're targeting the person who pays for the subscription:

New England's most trusted news source
Stories You Need, Analysis You Trust
Authoritative insight and opinion
Reliable Reporting. The Right Opinion
All the News That's Fit to Print.

Those are messages that speak to the quality and trustworthiness of the content. They're telling us that in exchange for contributing to their revenue, what you'll get is "trusted analysis that's authoritative and reliable and worth printing." That's all stuff that's important to subscribers. Not to advertisers (with few exceptions). Thus, the subscriber is the customer.

But when the brand promise is aimed at a different customer, the messages are very different. To find them, we need to dig a little deeper. It's not on the publisher's website at all, because that's not where customers hand over money. Instead we need to look at the advertising networks because they write the checks.

So here are real examples of the sales pitch you can find on the ad networks' sites:

Use your data to drive valuable engagement and monetization
Manage, Control & Monetize Your Content on the Open Web
Monetize. Engage. Acquire
Monetize your traffic at 30-50% higher rates than other platforms
Maximize revenue from native ads

You can see the promise the networks, as proxies for the publisher, are making to the customer: "To drive engagement and monetize content by delivering traffic at higher rates to maximize revenue." That's all stuff that's important to advertisers and publishers. Not to readers—we're just "traffic" to be "delivered." They're literally broadcasting in plain sight who they really want to satisfy—and it ain't you and me.

Am I making you queasy by showing you inside the sausage factory? Sorry, but if you insist that information should be free, you need to understand how the free gets made.

Those Three Stooges antics need to be scripted and produced, and the web servers need to be kept humming. There's investors and a whole cast of extras to be paid.

And it's the real customers who pay them, not us.

FREE IS BAD

We have to just come out and say it again.

Free is bad.

The Ad Fontes data shows us that classic news providers who are still invested in evidence based journalism are more reliable. And the Ad Shenanigans data shows us that, by and large, those same providers are less likely to collect and sell our data to monetize their efforts, and more likely to embrace *us* as their customers.

The evidence clearly shows that, if we're willing to pay for things, we'll get better things. Now, if the thing is a cat meme, we can make a judgment about whether a better cat meme is worth paying for. I'd suppose it's not—I'm happy to get my cat memes from my free Facebook.

But when the *thing* is news—the information we need to be a member of the informed populace who keeps democracy chugging along—maybe it's worth paying for. That's important stuff.

Team OpinionFacts clearly values emotional, divisive clickbait headlines over quality evidence based information. Forming a more perfect union isn't on their radar.

It's really not in anyone's best interests to turn democracy over to the ad-tech guys and the neo-news providers. It's just not.

Yet here we are.

Whose fault is that?

THE BLAME GAME

This sucks. We need someone to suffer 15 minutes of blame. Someone to boycott, to picket, to chase with torches.

So whose fault is it?

It's not Google's fault, or Facebook's, or "The Media's." It's not the fault of some unintended side-effect of web browsers.

It's our fault.

Let me say it again for the folks in the back: It's *our fault*. Every step of the way, these were choices *we* made, demanding our information for free.

John Brockman, editor of Edge.org, observed that we've forgotten the second half of Brand's quote, and as a result "information wants to be free became a mantra, it became an ideology. For some, it's a religion. ... But I've always been wondering about the tension of the two fighting against each other and what happened to one half of the fight?"[137]

What happened was we faced a fork in the road, with one direction labeled "information wants to be free," and the other labeled "information wants to be expensive." We chose free.

Free search, free browsers, free email, free social media. We even demanded free news and facts, and the internet delivered on our choice.

Publishers had to sell empty rectangles to pay the bills. They hijacked our lizard brains and used them to silence our frontal lobes. They architected the web to feed our hard-wired nature to forage shallow and wide. They manipulated the content with emotional opinions that reinforce our biases. They triggered the endorphins and dopamine we love so much.

We're no longer just swapping Seinfeld for a few seconds of glancing attention on our way to the bathroom during the commercial break. As Bob Hoffman wrote: "Today, the ad industry gives us fake news, clickbait and cat videos and we voluntarily give them our names, addresses, health history, sexual predilections, banking information, psychological profiles, credit history, and dozens of other tidbits of personal information. And they sell it to whomever they please."

We let them do it, because it was free. We made the choice to sell ourselves in exchange for something to click.

Oh, and at the expense of evidence, facts and critical thinking. As a result, we created a poorly informed citizenry who can't even tell what's quality any more.

BUT WE CAN FIX IT

We can't be blamed for our biology—specifically, we can't be blamed for how easily manipulated our biology is. That's just life.

But once we know how to recognize the manipulation, we *can* be blamed for letting people manipulate us.

The good news: We can now recognize the manipulation, because the evidence and the data show us how. Now we know that bias and reliability are measurable, we have the tools to identify the providers who manipulate us.

Now that we can measure the degree to which publishers consider us the customer, we have the tools to recognize the business model. We can make intentional choices about when to allow them to manipulate us, and when to avoid it (the first for entertainment, and the other for evidence based information).

When our washing machine is leaking all over the floor, we know that Instagram celebrities aren't going to give us reliable advice, and we should instead pay for Consumer Reports.

Thanks to the data, we can identify the providers and distributors that are likely to hijack our lizard brains and sell us into ad-tech servitude.

WHAT NEXT?

It's all well and good to be able to find news providers on a chart. The trick is to make smart decisions based on what that tells us.

We can't fix the business model of OpinionFacts. The economics of selling emotions are too powerful for me and you, and likely would withstand any attempt at legislation.

However, what we can fix is our news consumption.

It's clear that good quality news is expensive to create, so we're going to have to pay some money. That can feel like a big commitment, but I'll help you get there in a way that's relatively painless.

I'll offer you my best advice based on everything we've learned. I'll share my recommendations for choosing news outlets, and eliminating bias and manipulation from our online lives.

And I'll give you my favorite alternative tools and resources for identifying the evidence based facts you need—so you can be an informed and effective participant in a complicated world.

That's the next step. So let's get started.

8. FIXING NEWS

Based on everything we've learned so far, we should now have a pretty good sense of what we're looking for: *evidence based reporting and analysis* (in the style of Consumer Reports).

And we know what to avoid: attention grabbing breaking newsy emotional lizard brain bias.

Unfortunately, they both show up on our devices, and they look pretty much the same. So how do we break through the mess and find a reliable path to the evidence based news we want? It'll be easier if we divide the problem into pieces and tackle them individually.

HOW DO YOU CONSUME NEWS?

First, think about how and where you consume news. Do you prefer to watch, listen or read? Do you want it delivered to you, or do you prefer to wait until you're in the right frame of mind?

It's often driven by the time you have available. A busy working mother will have very little time to grind through websites on a quest for news, while a retiree might spend several hours in front of the TV.

Commuting by public transit is often an ideal time to read, whereas driving dictates an audio format.

So let's start by defining how you want to consume news and we can let that drive an appropriate choice for who you get it from. I'm ignoring old-school news distribution models like print newspapers or cable/broadcast TV because I assume you do too.

Watching TV News Online

TV stations have had websites since roughly the dawn of time—starting of course with text articles. As soon as the technology permitted, they added streaming media players to the web pages, making use of their expertise in well scripted opinions delivered by plausible spokesmodels straight from central casting. Adapting this to fit onto portable devices was simple.

As you might guess, I'm not a fan. In the absence of subscriptions, these publishers are forced to do what they have done for 30 years: create divisive emotions so we can be more precisely targeted and sold. The *customers* of TV love it, but it's not worked out so well for *us*.

Listening To News Online

Listening to news is so convenient that it's won many converts recently. You can drive, or wash the dishes or exercise and get your daily dose at the same time.

Smartphones have been the catalyst because they're always in our pocket, and as Reuters Institute explains, "A desire to get away from screens may be one factor driving the current boom in audio listening."

Premium News Publisher Apps often have audio versions of subscription news stories, with professional voice talent reading the original written articles,. They provide busy people with the same quality content in a convenient form. As we've discussed, they're a great source of evidence based reporting and opinion. If you prefer to listen rather than read, this is a great option.

Free Audio News Apps, even from publishers you know and enjoy, are to be avoided. They have to make money somehow, and the shenanigans they play are even worse inside an app than they can get away with on websites. If you're going to use an app, use apps only from companies that have an obvious revenue source, like subscriptions, or maybe donations.

Podcasts initially grew out of radio shows, and their low cost of production has caused a proliferation in the last few years. As entertainment they are often wonderful, covering interesting topics and unique, niche interests that could never have received attention 20 years ago. However there's a big practical problem that makes podcasts unsuited to news.

Although we talk of "subscribing" to a podcast, it's usually free of charge. In the classic podcast world, it's impractical to restrict access to those who've paid. While podcasts do theoretically support a login/password, most podcatcher apps either don't support it or make it too hard for non-nerds (e.g., Apple makes it hard, because it can't slice off its 30%).

In practice, that means "sponsorship" advertising is the only revenue available. The most successful podcasts started as radio shows with an existing funding model—NPR for example—or brought along a tightly defined demographic and a close relationship with advertisers—think: Rush Limbaugh.

On the plus side, although ads can be dropped in at the time of download, podcasts don't suffer from micro-targeted ads, and obviously with nothing to click there's no clickbait. However the economics will tend to nudge them towards lizard-brain-tweaking opinion or entertainment.

This isn't meant as a criticism. I subscribe to more than 10 podcasts and enjoy them. Some are definitely entertainment, like Hidden Brain and Planet Money. Others are opinion or what used to be called "current affairs." However none of them in my experience provide evidence-based news. At best they are opinions that reference other evidence based publications.

Pandora/SiriusXM and Spotify claim to have news channels, and while I've not listened, I can't imagine there's the levels of staff needed for reporting objective evidence. They restrict themselves to opinion and entertainment.

Reading News Online

It shouldn't come as a surprise that this is where I believe we get the best and most productive experience gathering and absorbing quality information. Text is the basic language of the web, as conceived by Tim Berners-Lee, and those underpinnings are still visible today with the majority of news sites structured around long form copy.

Reading lends itself to evidence based reporting, because the reader can take time to interpret a chart or a table, or cross-check a citation. In that environment, emotions are kept in check. Opinions can be digested, or rejected, because the reader is in control of the rate of information flow.

Reading the news is a powerful tool for those with the time, and the ability to pay for evidence based research. But how?

News Publisher Apps: my go-to recommendation, for the simple reason that the quality ones contain a paywall, so the business has a consistent revenue and is less beholden to advertisers and emotion. You're the customer, not the product, so you're helping to pay for the researchers and trained journalists who are needed for evidence based reporting.

The user experience and layout are controlled by the publisher too, allowing them to change the emphasis and order, depending on editorial decisions, and content can be updated as a story develops. The paywalled names are a who's-who of quality, classic news, which have spent decades building the research teams and the organizational structure to seek out evidence and then report it. That's what you want, right?

(A bunch of bottom-feeders have figured out they can achieve a veneer of quality by shoving out a flashy app, but you can spot them because they're free. So don't be fooled.)

Aggregators: If you want more sources delivered to you in an organized fashion, aggregators may be your answer. As you recall, there are three main aggregators that really matter:

- *Apple News (and News+)* is curated by humans—and it shows. They deliver balanced, quality stuff, from quality sources. You'll see tolerable ads that are opaque to targeting shenanigans, with Apple promising no privacy compromises. Better still, you can subscribe and you get access to a large number of publishers for a single price. For the casual reader wanting a range of evidence and opinion from multiple sources, and more besides, it's a good option.
- *Google News* chooses its articles algorithmically, but the clickbait nonsense is filtered out. You'll only see the headlines and a summary—to read the whole article you'll need to click through to the publisher's website where you're served ads by Google, Taboola, et al. However, subscriptions aren't encouraged.
- *Facebook News* is new and it's still early days. It feels less like a news service and more like an attempt to stave off congressional action. The hand curation eliminates the complete garbage, but the pages open in a regular browser not the Facebook app, so they don't get any revenue except perhaps through expanding their profiling of you. Subscriptions are obviously absent.

Email: It just won't die. And publishers know it's a gateway to building a long term readership, so signing up for regular email updates and newsletters is still an option for lots of them. Email delivery can support subscription content as well as free, so choose your poison. Like Google News, the summary form of articles works okay for headlines, but for the details you'll be clicking through to the website, which brings us to....

News Publisher Websites: This is where the whole mess started going wrong in 1997, when ad-tech and surveillance capitalism pumped steroids into the monster and spawned neo-news. Evidence based reporting exists on the sites, but it's drowned out by opinion, which is swamped by entertainment, which is stirred up by Russian and Chinese clickbots.

Controlling the urge to forage: If you're finding yourself heading to publisher websites, the urge to graze from one patch to the next can be strong, and we can find ourselves munching on the shallow sugary stuff pretty easily.

I know people claim to find value in getting "a lot of opinions from across the spectrum," and truly believe that while they're foraging across multiple sites they can separate opinions from fabrications. I doubt that. I acknowledge I'm better off paying an expert to figure out unbiased fact from right- or left-leaning fiction. The experts I pay are called reporters.

I'm also ready to admit that—even when I seek the safety of the paywall and restrict myself to websites I pay for—bright, shiny objects keep popping up, and opinions are shrieking for my attention. Sometimes, I just can't help myself from clicking away.

However, I have found a couple of tools that suppress the emotional craving should I want to forage.

- **Scroll** and **PrivacyCloud** have deals with select publishers that remove ads from the content in return for other payment. For Scroll it's subscriptions, while for PrivacyCloud it's ads via email.
- **NewsGuard** is a browser plugin. If you insist on foraging, it's a great way to view the nutritional information as you gorge yourself on free stuff. It reviews the domain you're looking at, finds all the links leading to other pages, and tells you if they're junk or credible. They don't attempt to differentiate bias, just

reliability. In other words, it's like looking at just the vertical axis of the Media Bias Chart.

Finally, SMS. Yes, really. If you agree that less is more, then the brief summary format enforced by text messaging might be just right. A new provider, appropriately named *The New Paper* offers just this. Recognizing that ads inside SMS are an impossibility, the company has committed itself to subscriptions, and there's no free option beyond a seven-day trial. So far, reactions from customers look very positive.

What About Local News?

National news seems to have solidified around a few big brands that have the staff and infrastructure for gathering and distilling real evidence, and I feel confident in recommending you should spend your hard-earned money there.

But we do need to know what's going on in our own back yard. The trouble is—as we've seen with news deserts and the proliferation of faux local news websites—your access to legitimate local news very much depends on where you live. Established publishers in bigger cities might survive in a form strong enough to provide real community reporting, but for smaller cities the legacy vendors are up against serious financial challenges.

Ken Doctor, long-time Knight Ridder executive and more recently the founder of Lookout Local, says there are three financial milestones that news organizations must pass to successfully transition to digital:

First, they have to make the majority of their revenue from digital sources.

Second, the majority of that digital revenue needs to come from readers, rather than from advertising—meaning subscriptions.

Third, they have to somehow manage to achieve net growth from digital dollars more quickly than losing it from print dollars.

That sounds like a simple formula on the face of it. As I say, some of the big publishers have managed it. But it's tougher to do with the smaller market of a local publication. So your local classic newspapers may be struggling to stick around—if they're not gone already.

So what can you do to get your local news?

Emerging Alternatives To Classic Local Papers

There do seem to be some interesting community focused alternatives rising from the ashes of the local papers. As I mentioned earlier there are displaced journalists who remain committed to their communities, trying to muster the resources to start up their own local publications, and many communities seem receptive.

From *Mountain State Spotlight* to *Block Club Chicago*, *Michigan Advance* to the *Colorado Sun*, journalists are working hard to fill the void in local news. And they're not just printing old school on woodpulp. They're using podcasts, email newsletters, online news portals, and more.

As Thomas Baekdal writes, "Local communities want news, but they want it from journalists who are not just doing things the old way. They don't want a package of random content designed for the 1980s, they want the journalism itself."[138]

I live in California, in the small-ish city of Santa Cruz, on the periphery of Silicon Valley. What I've seen happen to my local news—good and bad—has parallels across the nation.

Our local paper, *The Santa Cruz Sentinel*, is surely not long for this world. For a while it seemed that Patch Media might step into the breach, but our section of patch.com never really gained traction: It simultaneously lacks deep roots in the community and has a charmless corporatism. Fortunately we have driven, creative citizens who recognize the problem and have stepped up, forming not one, but *two* alternatives.

Santa Cruz Local, founded in 2019, is "a local news podcast, newsletter and website about public policy in Santa Cruz County." The founders are young and energetic, and started the company "because we saw holes in our county's news coverage, and we believed our community deserved better."[139]

Lookout Local was recently launched by seasoned local news veterans, and is already getting national attention due to their ambitions to roll their model out to other cities, and to avoid the mistakes made by Patch.[140] It's got plans to bundle local news into subscriptions from larger regional players like the LA Times or even national brands like the Washington Post. At the same time they recognize that, "A local news site will live or die through its relationship with local people."

Lookout also draws a healthy distinction between generic advertising and sponsorship of local news by local companies. This may be anathema to ad-tech, which wants to treat us all like the product, but since we do live our lives in our local communities, I think they might be onto something.

Interestingly, both of these companies choose to describe themselves as driven by *memberships* instead of subscriptions, and *sponsorships* instead of targeted ads.

Other Local Models

Looking further into the future of local news, there are still more alternative models showing promise. Tony Haile, CEO of Scroll, recently wrote about this in the Columbia Journalism Review. He explains how local publishers might form coalitions, giving readers a network of publications under a single subscription.[141]

One way that might work is with a "Hub-and-Spoke" model—where larger publications such as the Washington Post bundle subscriptions with local papers, splitting the revenue depending on how much of the readers' time each publisher earns. The trick here is finding partners who don't cannibalize each other's audiences.

Or several smaller local papers might share content through a One-Slot Paywall. With a single subscription, multiple local publishers might share some common content like business, lifestyle, food or travel across all their properties, freeing them to focus their in-house reporting efforts on local issues.

Mark Glaser wrote about five other innovative business models for local news:[142]

1. Cooperatives allow community members to buy a stake in the paper.
2. Some publications convert from for-profit businesses to non-profits.
3. There's some experimentation happening with government supporting local news in the hopes of encouraging civic participation.
4. Public media stations like NPR and PBS are merging with digital media startups, combining their scale and mature business models with new ideas and technologies and younger, more diverse audiences.
5. State-level organizations can serve as hubs, supporting local news through collaboration, cost-saving shared infrastructure, and community outreach initiatives.

An example of local news outlets banding together is the *Rebuild Local News Coalition*, an alliance of 3,000 local newsrooms across the country. The group recently presented an extensive proposal that combines a number of these ideas. The hope is to urge government to "dramatically help local news while maintaining strong First Amendment safeguards."

The proposal is built around six broad categories, including the support of nonprofit local media, increased coverage of marginalized communities, and safeguarding nonpartisanship. The plan hinges on tax credits for consumers, aimed at supporting local news through subscriptions or donations—a variant of the bipartisan Local Journalism Sustainability Act. The president and co-founder of Report for America, Steven Waldman, coordinated the proposal, saying, "The collapse of local news fundamentally threatens democracy and the health of communities. The country must confront this crisis."

It's an fascinating development, and I like the idea of funneling funding through subscriptions and donations from consumers. It maintains the integrity of the relationship between consumer and publisher, and keeps us mindful of the need to pay for quality news. I'm hopeful they'll succeed.

 # You have The Power

READY TO MAKE AN INTENTIONAL CHOICE?

You don't need your doctor peering into your fridge and telling you which brand of juice to drink. Her job is just telling you to buy quality juice (with no corn syrup nor motor oil added). From there, it's on you. Luckily, you just need to read a nutrition label.

Likewise, you don't need me to complain about what you choose to read and watch and listen to on your device. We're all grown-ups here, with busy lives and choices to make. If you've had enough and just want to grab a pizza, turn on your device and be entertained, I completely understand. I like entertainment, I share memes on Facebook, and I don't want some geezer telling me I shouldn't.

But you're looking for that "nutrition label" for your news—to help you avoid the shallow sugar. And now you know the differences between evidence, opinion and entertainment, the economics of creating and publishing them online, and the different motivations publishers follow.

So now I feel duty-bound to tell you how to find the stuff that won't clog your brain.

Free Is Bad

It begins with the core of our thesis. You remember it: *Free is bad.*

The task at hand is to find your way to the right paid content. The content that gives you the quality, evidence based information you need—so you can make intelligent and informed choices (without poking your lizard brain with sticks).

A Simple, 3-Step Process

1. Make A Commitment To A Classic News Brand

First, I'll ask you to form a monogamous relationship with a classic news publisher.

If you've spent the past decade foraging and fiddling around among OpinionFacts, the idea of settling down is going to be a shock—I get it. You might even be tempted to think you'll need multiple classic news subscriptions to maintain some diversity in your news.

The reality is, most folks are fine with just one. As the Reuters Institute pointed out, most people will only subscribe to one news source. Rather than being a limiting choice, it's actually a good thing.

By narrowing your attention down to one you will more readily understand its biases and peccadilloes. The consistency of opinions helps prevent you jumping around seeking to affirm your emotions.

To choose your classic news source, I recommend taking another look at the Ad Fontes Media Bias Chart in the previous chapter. Notice again that the central, upper reaches—low bias and high quality—are dominated by classic-news publishers, while the lower quality biased extremes are dominated by neo-news. We've seen the economic and psychological reasons for this, but in this diagram you can see so clearly what's going on: Classic-news sells evidence and neo-news gives away entertainment.

For a second opinion, take another look at my own "ad shenanigans" research data. Media businesses are telling us how they make money—who their customer is. It's right there in the code of their web pages.

If you don't like being the product, then you're going to have to become the customer. So now it's time to make a choice. Pick just one classic news publisher whose bias you like—or at least can live with—that appears near the top of the Media Bias Chart.

Is your choice classic or neo? Classic, right? That's good. Now take a look at my chart and find that news provider there. Are you the customer or the product? You get the idea.

2. Install Its Classic News App.

Whichever you choose, your next step should be installing their app. That's a commitment you should be willing to make in your new monogamous relationship with news. You've matured, after all, so no more foraging for you.

Don't worry, you can change the terms of the relationship later—even break it off if it's truly unbearable. But start as though you mean to stick around: Place that classic news icon on the home screen of your device, just like an engagement ring.

The presence of this icon will serve to prompt your brain for "top down" information gathering. As Gord Hotchkiss said: When we go directly to an information source we trust, "The entire brain focuses on the task at hand and things like reliability of information become much more important to us."[143] The urge to forage "bottom up" by chasing random stimuli is reduced, and we're less susceptible to the priming that sends us down unrelated rabbit holes.

3. Use The App Intentionally

Maybe it goes without saying (but it's my book, so I'll say it anyway): Steps one and two don't matter if you fall right back into your old habits.

But I'll admit, it's easy to do. So step three is easy, too: Train yourself to use the app.

Go there when you're in the mood for news, when your interest in a subject or breaking news story is piqued and you're ready for some focused, top-down activity.

Go there to vet the wackadoodle stories your very emotionally triggered friends are sharing willy-nilly on social media.

Go there to educate yourself about important issues that affect your life in meaningful ways—issues that only carefully considered, evidence based investigation can illuminate.

But *don't* go there as a response to emotional triggers. That means you must turn off notifications for the app. Even classic news uses these notifications to try and out-compete the other voices. You don't need that, because you're going to pay attention on your schedule, not theirs.

And don't be discouraged or bored by the lack of passionate exposition. *That's kind of the point.*

The Secret You Should Know: You Are Not Alone

Most likely the classic news app you installed has a paywall. I'll let you in on a secret: Life is good behind the paywall.

Like I said, it's a big commitment and I get that, but trust me, it's totally worth it for the restoration of sanity and clarity of thought. Life behind the paywall is rational, quiet, and populated by an informed citizenry.

There are a ton of interesting articles on a wide range of topics—and if you don't have time to read them, maybe you can listen to them. We get the information we need and no more so we can get on with the rest of our lives.

The Reuters Institute study found that subscribers say the number one reason they join is because it's "better quality than I can get from free sources."

Better yet, we've left the world of ad-tech surveillance and divisive opinion. The classic news providers have no economic incentive to optimize stories and sell rectangles, jerking our emotions this way and that to satisfy the needs of advertisers, because we hand over money once a month.

Sure, it's another $9.99 on our credit card statement, right alongside Netflix and Hulu and Amazon Prime, but that's okay. We've spent enough time with the alternative and we sure as shit don't want any more of that.

So come on in, the water's fine. The quality's great, you can read or listen, and you're not treated like traffic because ... wait for it ... you are the customer.

The Other Secret You Should Know

Nobody wants to be the only schmuck paying when everyone else gets the same stuff for free. But don't worry: Smart people like you are subscribing in ever growing numbers.

PROPORTION THAT PAID FOR ANY ONLINE NEWS IN LAST YEAR (2014–20) – SELECTED COUNTRIES

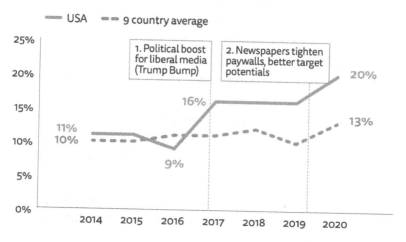

Credit: Digital News Report 2020, Reuters Institute for the Study of Journalism, Oxford University.

The trend is being driven from both directions: consumers are willing to pay to escape the circus, and quality publications are raising paywalls because they have confidence in that growing willingness.

The New York Times has been transparent in sharing their subscriber growth: "The company added 669,000 net new digital subscribers, making [Q2 2020] its biggest ever for subscription growth. The Times has 6.5 million total subscriptions, a figure that includes 5.7 million digital-only subscriptions."[144]

Over at The Atlantic, it's a similar story: "Over the past 12 months, The Atlantic has amassed over 300,000 new subscribers."[145]

Classic news publishers are embracing this trend because it fits their historical commitment to providing their subscribers, and society at large, with real evidence based journalism.

As the Washington Post's chief revenue officer Joy Robins puts it, "Our first priority can't be to sell advertising."[146] On which, my friend Gam Dias commented: "This realization, from an innovative publication like the WP may lead the way for a different set of revenue models that will not compromise societal values."[147]

What If I Prefer All The Divisive Free Stuff?

Some of us really love our free neo-news. It's exciting and emotional and weirdly satisfying to wallow in. But it's not *facts*—and news is supposed to be facts.

That's the entire point of this lengthy exercise. But if you just can't bring yourself to quit the emotional dopamine rush of neo-news, then maybe classic news simply isn't for you.

That's okay, as long as you understand what you're choosing. Plenty of people buy a washing machine based on the winning smile and firm handshake of the salesman or the algorithmic averaging of random, sometimes-fake Amazon reviews, without even glancing at Consumer Reports and its nerdy charts and multi-year studies of reliability.

What If I Can't Pay?

Maybe that $9.99 is a genuine hardship, but you're still really interested in finding quality news from a classic source.

If it's truly not possible to pay for a subscription, the important thing is to escape the ad-tech shenanigans of neo-news, OpinionFacts and the Three Stooges. There's a handful of classic news publishers in the top portion of the Media Bias Chart that don't directly require payment from you because they're funded in other ways (they might nag you for donations, but hey, that's between you and your bathroom mirror

What If Monogamy Isn't For Me?

Eventually most of us want to settle down, but not everyone. And maybe not you.

A news aggregator will be your best bet, because it brings all the plausible candidates to you in one place. Kinda like using Tinder instead of asking random strangers on the street for a date.

Just remember that ad blockers are no protection from the bad stuff. It's not the ads that are infectious, it's the whole machinery of divisive opinions upon which those ads are carried. Don't get intimate with just any old website that seems attractive.

What If I Still Want To Flirt With Neo-news?

If you've made a commitment to classic news, installed the app, and are enjoying the peace that comes from escaping ad-tech, why not take a peek over in the seething cauldron of festering opinions? Just don't say I didn't warn you.

MAKE THE CHOICE THAT'S RIGHT FOR YOU

I said this earlier, but I'll say it again for the record: I'm happy with whatever news source you choose, with whatever inherent bias it has.

I'm not here to change your politics.

What matters to me is that you see the dangers of news content that's emotionally driven. It's optimized to enrage and divide—just to sell ads.

That's just a bad thing—I would hope we could all agree.

So it's my hope you'll make intentional choices about where you get your news, and you'll find a source that speaks to you, while also avoiding the manipulations of ad-tech and all its foul machinations.

Because all I really need is to see my fellow citizens freed from the tyranny of free news.

9. CONCLUSION

The early promise of the internet was the free distribution of information. But "free" has several distinct meanings:

- *libre*—not under the control of another
- *unimpeded*—not physically restrained, obstructed, or fixed
- *gratis*—available without charge

Perhaps, back then, we were confused about what free really meant. Or, in our idealism, maybe we assumed it could mean all three things at once.

By now, I hope you agree that the first two meanings remain true, at least in Western democracies. But "without charge" has never been true of the internet. It's simply not possible to provide useful information at no cost.

Even ignoring the cost of research and writing, merely displaying the simplest information in our apps requires huge numbers of internet-connected servers, and smart people to program and maintain them. We access the information "in the cloud" but forget the substantial and growing cost of storing it there. Someone needs to pay.

The Xanadu project recognized the problem of payment, and even in the 1960s had a vision for how it might be solved. Unfortunately, the web we ended up with dodged the question of payment completely. Now here it is, 30 years later, never having really grown up, gotten a job and moved out of the house.

We're still stuck with it raiding the fridge and inviting noisy friends from ad-tech over. We like the web and the fun stuff, and we want the information, but man, those ad-tech guys are just awful. They make so much noise, and they read our personal mail—and who invited them anyway?

No wonder we turn to ad blockers, even if they don't really work.

Long Range Solutions

Yet somehow we have to solve the payment problem if we want to solve fake news, the erosion of privacy, and maybe save democracy itself. But how?

My preference would be that we pay, because it's simple and elegant and seems most likely to reward quality journalism. That's why I gave you my ideas for how to make that work for you.

But that's not really a long range solution. It can't work for every website we visit. While more and more people are willing to pay a subscription for better online news, they're very rarely willing to pay for more than one. So if we want recipes, dog toy reviews and celebrity gossip we're going to need something we don't currently have.

We either need better ad-tech, or better payment options. Either one of which is a big, messy, complicated undertaking that won't happen overnight.

Nevertheless, it's nice to think we might get there one day. So let's take a quick look at them both and where they might lead us.

Ad Industry Self-Regulation

The main industry body that guides online ads is the Interactive Advertising Bureau (IAB). It has various codes of conduct for data collection, targeting, etc. It also defines standards such as the sizes of the empty rectangles that publishers fill with ads.

But it's all just recommendations. The IAB is unable to stop this ad-tech crapfest juggernaut: The flow of money has just been too huge and too quick.

Once the loopholes inherent in the decentralized planning of web technologies were discovered, nobody could have stopped it. We've seen the failure of minor tweaks within browsers, like P3P and "Do Not Track" (there's a reason you haven't heard of them, by the way: They didn't work).

Optimism For Better Adtech

Some publishers thrive by renting the empty rectangles on their pages to unknown third parties. A toothless IAB suits them just fine: The money rolls in while giving them plausible deniability about ad-fraud bots and shenanigans.

On the other hand, plenty of publishers have always disliked those empty rectangles—because of the lack of control, and the hit to the perceived quality of the adjacent words they carefully crafted. If the IAB keeps itself occupied with fiddling around the edges with cookie consent policies and the like, then this creates an incentive for quality publishers to step aside and experiment with something new.

A publisher might not control exactly *what* fills those empty rectangles on the page, but they can control *who* gets to fill them. Rather than treating that decision as a transactional highest-bidder sale, I'm seeing a more enlightened approach where the sales are handled by companies promising quality. For example, The Ozone Project in the UK is an ad network promising a "privacy by design" platform, which "is built for transparency, brand safety and ease of access."

A slightly different refinement is proposed by PrivacyCloud, which I mentioned in an earlier chapter. They work with publishers who are willing to completely remove the ad-tech from their pages, in return for the ability to deliver ads elsewhere. "We unbundle the media – the content from the ads, " says CEO Sergio Maldonado. "We give the user control over what they consume. We let the consumer choose." Rather than seeing the ads inline and in competition with the content, they're delivered to the consumer in a way that doesn't interrupt, and when the consumer is more likely receptive to the message: via email. There's much to like about this sponsorship concept and I'll be watching progress.

A different take is from Scroll, which we've also discussed. Essentially it acts as an intermediary between readers and publishers, like ad networks do. However instead of funneling money through ads they take payments from consumers and share it directly with publishers. No ads appear in the pages—just like blocking, but without the guilt. Their deal with browser maker Firefox is also a good sign.

Refining ad-tech would mean keeping those empty rectangles in play—and the third party companies that sell them—but placing limits on data harvesting, and possibly letting us individually define limits on how much privacy we're willing to give up.

I'm cautiously optimistic.

Other New Technologies

There's a bewildering array of startups trying to solve privacy, identity, data storage, brand management—even something called attention management.[148]

Here's my best attempt at understanding the big categories:

Personal Data Stores would be a vault for your data that you control—only you can give someone the key to come and look inside. Say, for example, when you're applying for a loan. The best example is Sir Tim Berners-Lee's Solid (you'll recall he invented the web). It's a clever idea and would fix many problems, but would drastically alter the plumbing of the web. Publishers would need to overhaul their website code, probably browser makers too. Worse, us consumers would have to change our behavior and learn how to manage our data. I don't see the economic incentive for that.

Declared Data Platforms are an ad-tech innovation, capturing personal data, storing it in a secure, private cloud, and selling insights into the aggregate data. CitizenMe is an example where consumers share their data via surveys, providing valuable market research. The publishers, advertisers and browsers would not need to change, and the consumer's data—or at least a fragment of it—remains their property. Yet this is an additional use of data rather than a replacement for the current broken model.

Data Mobility Platforms enable compliance in a world where legislation is tightening, by providing mechanisms for companies that already store our data to gain our permission to hold, process and share our data, in a granular way. JLinc and Irma are protocols that consumers will never see, except when you visit a website and it asks permission. Like Personal Data Stores, these tools require changes to websites code their user experience, to ensure we aren't inundated with pop-ups every time we make a click.

I'm not hugely optimistic about any of these new technologies. They seem far too ambitious—even for a nerd like me. And they depend a lot on us consumers taking on new responsibilities for things most of us don't understand.

As the saying goes, "Data is the new oil," so some people like to think we might be able to make money from selling access to our data. But oil becomes most valuable when it's refined—I simply don't see us all running our own personal oil refineries, mucking about managing our personal information, filling out surveys, or even clicking *yet another button* to grant use of our data. It's just more work and that's not going to turn out well: Optimizing data isn't how we want to spend our time, even if we had artificial intelligence helping us.

Ultimately, if we're not figuring out who pays the publishers, they'll turn to the ad-tech spigot, even though it might be distasteful.

Consumer Pressure

We're tired of dealing with surveillance and a poor user experience while we're accessing our free stuff, so we're fighting back with the only tool we have: ad blockers. We hope our ad blocker acts like a little virtual protest march.

We're there with our friends, striding arm in arm, chanting "free is good." Some publishers notice our raised fists, and the corresponding decline in ad revenue. What do they do in response? Block our blockers or raise the paywall. (Remember the Facebook example? It actually got *better* at circumventing ad blockers.)

Other publishers simply ignore our little protests because humans are irrelevant. The real money makers are fraud bots and they outnumber us and our puny ad blockers 100:1 and the money keeps flowing despite our feeble protests.

Perhaps some publishers understand that we'd accept a quid pro quo, if only the ads were nicer. Ad-blocking company eyeo is behind Acceptable Ads, saying its ads "are respectful, nonintrusive and relevant." It's true that such ads are better, perhaps even reaching the low bar of being "acceptable." Combined with other efforts maybe it can tip the balance?

Consumer pressure can also come from the tech we use to access the internet. Apple continues to build its brand on privacy, and is immune to the ad-tech companies' whining that this will lead to the end of free stuff. Apple has customers that clearly want privacy, and it owns the necessary parts of the ecosystem to solve it—so long as it resists the temptation to be the one making money off you as the product, merely replacing one ad-tech for another.

Microsoft's retreat from smartphones makes it less relevant to the delivery of solutions, even though it too has customers who value their privacy.

Legislation

Responses to a 2019 survey conducted by the Network Advertising Initiative (NAI) indicate strong consumer support for federal privacy legislation, with 67% of respondents stating that Congress should enact laws to protect the data privacy of American citizens. This contrasts starkly with the combined 15.7% who believe state or local governments should be primarily responsible for protecting consumer privacy.[149]

The European Commission is further down the legislation road, where the GDPR legislation has been in place since 2018, and an earlier form since 1995. Aurelie Pols, a data governance and privacy engineer, based in Spain, explained that GDPR is good because it brings transparency "which is a benefit. Consumers can make choices that are more informed. It fosters trust. It's about agency of your life. Data is going to impact your life more and more. Are you going to get into university? Social benefits? Insurance? Driving license? They all depend on data and trust."

I can't say I disagree with any of that. Here in the US, the closest we have to GDPR is CCPA, but that's just in California. Facebook and others quickly found loopholes in it, so there's a new version on the ballot, designed, as Gilad Edelman put it, "to patch the holes currently making the CCPA such a leaky privacy vessel."[150]

The biggest problem with legislation is that tighter privacy rules could well lead to dramatically lower ad revenue, which would need to be made up via direct consumer payment. Edelman interviewed ACLU attorney Jacob Snow: "Privacy becomes a luxury that rich people have but poor or economically struggling folks don't have access to." CCPA is weak because, "We didn't want to put a law into effect that's going to crush an already crushed business. They call it 'pay for privacy'; we call it 'preserve the free press.'"

I asked Pols to imagine really tight privacy laws—of the sort that might exist in more extreme policy decisions—and what would happen to free services, such as Gmail, search, Android and news aggregation. She said that, if privacy laws really had teeth, Gmail would become a paid service. Search would be like DuckDuckGo, with no history of previous searches. Android would need to become an open source utopia, like Linux but without the grown-ups. And ads within news would be targeted to the content, not the individual.

That doesn't sound so bad, if you ask me.

Forcing Payment Somehow

There have been growing voices calling for Google to pay publishers for articles appearing in Google News and other places. Some countries—notably Australia, Brazil and Germany—have enacted legislation accordingly.

It creates a tricky situation, because search has always relied on the "fair use" legal doctrine to justify the lifting of summary text from a web page and presenting that in search results. Much the same thing happens in this book, when I find a relevant article: Copyright law allows me to use quotes from it—under certain conditions, which include me not reducing the revenue they might otherwise make.

So, Google argues, why is news any different? Publishers argue back that the reader is getting value just from that summary and aren't clicking through to their sites. And they have seen a measurable decline in visitors, so perhaps they have a point.

However, I suspect that readers have figured out that publishers are in fact writing shorter articles with clickbait headlines. There's no reason to click into the article, because the story *is* the headline and summary—we won't find added value at the publisher's site. Publishers have trained people not to click through, so it's really their own fault.

Publishers dependent on clicks are in a race to the bottom, and I don't see how that will change if Google is forced to pay them. I believe subscriptions would fix it more fairly, and so far I'm not seeing anything that'll change my mind anytime soon.

Of course, as we've discussed before, Google's betting that if it *chooses* to pay before it's *forced* to pay, it can save some face and retain news traffic within its walled garden. Its recent billion dollar initiative that pays publishers to curate content for Google News story panels is something of a Trojan horse. It looks like a gift for the news industry, but it's really filled with ulterior motives that assuage publisher complaints and keep users inside Google's walls.

The Trend Is Towards Payment, Somehow

We can wait for the ad industry to self regulate in response to consumer pressure. Or we can wait for better ad-tech, or for privacy technology to save us, or for legislation to protect our best interests. All of those things are slow processes. So they won't help when you wake up tomorrow and fire up your cellphone in bed.

The thing that *can* make a difference—now, in the online world we live in—is paying for content. Because ... say it with me ... *free is bad.*

You and I might be ready to see that elephant in the bedroom and make that commitment. But is there a meaningful trend in that direction among consumers? Enough to shift the industry at large?

The NAI survey shows that people are concerned about data collection, yet also believe they should get their stuff for free. But we can't have both data privacy *and* free stuff. If we rein in data mining and targeting, we reduce the flow of money from ad-tech to publishers.

Publishers need cash to come from somewhere. So get used to the advertising.

To get rid of advertising, we need to reach a tipping point where our collective concern for privacy outweighs our desire for free stuff. And maybe we're getting close. There's a report from the McGuffin ad agency that indicates around 70% of us are willing to pay a modest monthly fee for services like Google Maps and Instagram.[151]

Perhaps our willingness to pay for quality news is not far behind. I remain optimistic. After all, just 30 years ago organic food was a fringe obsession for hippies. Today it's a mainstay at Walmart and we pay more because it's better than the alternative.

It is a ray of hope that already, ad-tech isn't delivering all the revenue answers. An example that's close to home is my friend Avinash Kaushik. He currently works at Google as the digital marketing evangelist. And he publishes a newsletter with online marketing tips and advice, for which he recently started charging a subscription.[152]

You heard me right—an online marketing email newsletter, via subscription, from a Googler. Proving that people are willing to pay for valuable, authoritative content from sources they trust.

Today the options to pay for news are sparse, but they're growing. Obviously classic news publishers have been there, to a greater or lesser degree, from the start with subscriptions and premium content. And we've already discussed how paid aggregators like Apple News+ and Scroll let us pay a single subscription to access multiple publications. I expect the number of publishers in those kinds of services will grow, and might even expand beyond what we presently think of as news and magazines.

Apple and Google are uniquely positioned to offer these aggregated payment systems, because they control both the browser tech and the wallet systems for payment. And because of their deep, deep pockets and established reach. Of the two, my money's on Apple because it's not in the ads business.

As the desire and willingness to pay grows, I imagine still more creative and granular options coming down the line, like micropayment technologies based on Bitcoin or something even Ted Nelson couldn't have imagined.

One can hope.

Pay For The Things Worth Paying For

Ad funded entertainment has been with us for more than a century—and I'm okay with that, really. It's the information I'm concerned about.

Since the late 1990s, when the web went mainstream, we've lived in a world where information wants to be free. But now there's a change in the wind. Disinformation, fraud and shenanigans are eroding the foundation of democracy.

Yet all the while, the answer was right in front of us: *Information wants to be expensive.*

Maybe we don't need to pay for everything, but we should be willing to pay for important facts—like when it comes to buying washing machines or choosing which politicians to elect. The idea of payment is, after all, as old as humanity and it's deeply embedded in our culture—perhaps in our brains. It brings transparency. It aligns interests. And we understand it.

If you're concerned about privacy and surveillance capitalism then there's steps you can take right now: Avoid neo-news, subscribe to classic news. Use DuckDuckGo. Dump Gmail.

Your credit card statement will see a fractional increase. Your cortisol levels will see a big decrease.

Be the change you want to see.

ACKNOWLEDGEMENTS

This book exists only because of the love and support of my wife, Lisa. It's been 25 years of adventure and creativity, and every day is a delight. I'm always striving to become the man she thinks she married.

Special thanks to my ghostwriter Chip Street, and my editor Richi Jennings. They turned my scattered ideas into a coherent narrative. Thanks also to my researchers Dr. Andrea Pampaloni and Austin Woods. The illustrations from Manuel Berbin always make me smile.

I spoke to a number of experts who provided vital insight into complex topics. My sincere thanks to Aurelie Pols, Andrew Goodman, Brad Geddes, Craig Vachon, Matt Bailey, David Szetela, Jim Brock, Dana Todd, Andy Atkins-Kreuger, Marshall Simmonds, John Shehata, Ben Williams, Tony Haile, Sergio Maldonado, Gam Dias, and Ashley Friedlein. Three people really deserve acknowledgement, not just for the time they gave me, but also the encouragement to pursue the topic. Big thanks to Vanessa Otero, founder of AdFontes Media for letting me include the Media Bias Chart, Dr. Augustine Fou, ad-tech fraud expert, for reviewing my analysis and charts, and Gord Hotchkiss for his guidance and support.

ENDNOTES

INTRODUCTION

[1] en.wikipedia.org/wiki/Wikipedia:Funding_Wikipedia_through_advertisements

1. SEARCH

[2] infolab.stanford.edu/~backrub/google.html

[3] web.archive.org/web/20040919085727/http://news.com.com/
Pay-for-placement+gets+another+shot/2100-1023_3-208309.html

[4] medium.com/@shareablelife/
is-google-search-a-walled-garden-6162f8fa021a

[5] theamericanconservative.com/articles/
the-death-of-the-internet

[6] gizmodo.com/
what-did-people-use-before-google-to-search-the-web-1843750339

[7] pewresearch.org/fact-tank/2016/09/21/
the-state-of-privacy-in-america

[8] medium.com/@docjamesw/why-i-left-google-c170e6165f2a

[9] medium.com/@docjamesw/
why-i-left-google-redux-f83353a7e568

[10] nytimes.com/2020/06/19/technology/google-neeva-executive.html

[11] searchenginejournal.com/google-vs-duckduckgo/301997

[12] spreadprivacy.com/duckduckgo-revenue-model

[13] support.startpage.com/index.php?/Knowledgebase/Article/
View/180/20/how-can-startpage-be-free-how-do-you-make-money

[14] blog.mojeek.com/2018/10/search-that-does-not-follow-you-
around.html

[15] info.ecosia.org/privacy

[16] betterinternetsearch.com

[17] swisscows.com

[18] searx.me

2. EMAIL

[19] variety.com/2017/digital/news/
google-gmail-ads-emails-1202477321

[20] bbc.com/worklife/
article/20200707-why-email-loses-out-to-popular-apps-in-china

[21] hushmail.com/personal

[22] protonmail.com/about

[23] hey.com/the-hey-way

[24] help.smallbusiness.yahoo.net/s/article/SLN29633

[25] payments.mail.yahoo.com

3. AD TECH

[26] xanadu.com.au/general/faq.html

[27] xanadu.net/xuWeb.html

[28] hbr.org/2013/02/stop-selling-ads-and-do-someth

[29] lumapartners.com/content/lumascapes/
display-ad-tech-lumascape

[30] buysellads.com/advertisers

[31] airpush.com

[32] survata.com/brand-campaign-measurement

[33] us.epsilon.com/epsilon-peoplecloud-overview

[34] optinmonster.com/features/adblock-detection

[35] monetizepros.com/guides/adsense

[36] ftc.gov/tips-advice/business-center/guidance/
native-advertising-guide-businesses

[37] mediaplanet.com/us/blog/insights/7-great-examples-of-sponsored-content

[38] propublica.org/article/own-a-vizio-smart-tv-its-watching-you

[39] cnet.com/news/privacy-advocates-rally-against-doubleclick-abacus-merge

[40] engadget.com/google-antitrust-hearing-double-click-200745163.html

[41] propublica.org/article/google-has-quiet-ly-dropped-ban-on-personally-identifiable-web-tracking

[42] adsbydomain.fouanalytics.com/q/people.com

[43] wired.com/story/how-digital-ads-subsidize-worst-web

[44] wired.com/2017/02/veles-macedonia-fake-news

[45] medium.com/@vanessaotero/advertisers-cant-differentiate-between-polarizing-junk-news-and-good-journalism-48c1f346d276

[46] sparktoro.com/blog/on-serp-seo-the-infuriating-reality-of-searchs-future

[47] seroundtable.com/google-sites-taboola-or-outbrain-links-23165.html

[48] time.com/5549635/tim-berners-lee-interview-web

[49] linuxjournal.com/content/what-surveillance-capitalism-and-how-did-it-hijack-internet

[50] linuxjournal.com/content/privacy-mine-right-individual-persons-not-data

[51] forbes.com/sites/ashoka/2020/07/23/from-surveillance-to-agency-how-to-center-the-internet-on-humanity

[52] nsslabs.com/tested-technologies/web-browser-security-wbs

[53] opera.com/secure-private-browser

[54] brave.com/about

[55] acceptableads.com/standard

[56] eyeo.com/about

[57] betterads.org/standards

[58] epic.org/reports/prettypoorprivacy.html

[59] dl.acm.org/doi/10.1145/3319535.3354212

4. SMARTPHONES

[60] macworld.com/article/2047342/remembering-the-newton-messagepad-20-years-later.html

[61] wsj.com/articles/SB10001424052702304388004577531002591315494

[62] web.archive.org/web/20120315185427/http://blog.t-mobile.com/2012/03/12/the-hidden-cost-of-device-subsidies

[63] wired.com/2008/01/ff-iphone

[64] theverge.com/2017/6/13/15782200/one-device-secret-history-iphone-brian-merchant-book-excerpt

[65] cio.com/article/2448257/collaboration-gone-bad--lessons-to-learn-from-the-rokr-phone.html

[66] web.archive.org/web/20110205190729/http://www.businessweek.com/technology/content/aug2005/tc20050817_0949_tc024.htm

[67] gizmodo.com/lg-says-apple-copied-the-prada-phone-also-apples-moth-235933

[68] marketwatch.com/story/blackberry-co-ceos-were-stunned-when-steve-jobs-showed-what-iphone-could-do-2015-05-24

[69] thoughtco.com/history-of-smartphones-4096585

[70] arstechnica.com/gadgets/2015/08/waiting-for-androids-inevitable-security-armageddon

[71] theglobeandmail.com/report-on-business/blackberry-says-it-is-exploring-strategic-alternatives/article13708618/

[72] computerworld.com/article/2503385/carriers-desperate-ly-seeking-windows-phone.html

[73] reuters.com/article/us-verizon-microsoft-idUSBRE83I1B820120420

[74] HYPERLINK "https://arstechnica.com/gadgets/2015/10/new-lumias-continue-windows-phones-frustrating-carrier-situation/"arstechnica.com/gadgets/2015/10/new-lumias-continue-windows-phones-frustrating-carrier-situation

[75] computerworld.com/article/2503385/carriers-desperate-ly-seeking-windows-phone.html

[76] androidcentral.com/project-mainline

[77] wired.co.uk/article/duckduckgo-android-choice-screen-search

[78] statista.com/chart/5824/ios-iphone-compatibility

[79] apple.com/ios/app-store/principles-practices

[80] reuters.com/article/us-google-apple-idUSKBN2440UY

[81] android.com/one

[82] gadgets.ndtv.com/mobiles/features/meet-hmd-global-the-team-bringing-nokia-phones-back-1633189

[83] techradar.com/in/news/android-11-update

[84] wired.co.uk/article/duckduckgo-android-choice-screen-search

[85] theverge.com/2020/2/20/21145595/
google-app-ban-ads-play-store-android-user-experience

[86] android.com/play-protect

[87] securityboulevard.com/2020/08/
chrome-web-store-fail-300-more-scam-browser-extensions

[88] web.archive.org/web/20120315185427/http://blog.t-mobile.
com/2012/03/12/the-hidden-cost-of-device-subsidies

[89] arstechnica.com/tech-policy/2020/09/att-wants-to-put-ads-
on-your-smartphone-in-exchange-for-5-discount

[90] arstechnica.com/information-technology/2020/08/snapdrag-
on-chip-flaws-put-1-billion-android-phones-at-risk-of-data-theft

5. SOCIAL MEDIA

[91] web.archive.org/web/20030214100703/http://www.makeout-
club.com/

[92] danah.org/name.html

[93] danah.org/papers/FriendsterMySpaceEssay.html

[94] cio.com/article/2445154/google--myspace-link-up-in-search-
deal.html

[95] latimes.com/archives/la-xpm-2009-jun-17-fi-ct-myspace17-
story.html

[96] businessinsider.com/2008/10/
zuckerberg-facebook-will-have-a-business-plan-in-three-years

[97] techcrunch.com/2016/08/09/facebook-will-bypass-web-
adblockers-but-offer-ad-targeting-opt-outs

[98] techcrunch.com/2016/11/02/add-cash-plus

[99] facebook.com/business/help/407108559393196?
id=369787570424415

[100] facebook.com/business/marketing/audience-network

[101] facebook.com/business/help/788333711222886?
id=571563249872422

[102] facebook.com/help/186325668085084

[103] techcrunch.com/2016/08/09/facebook-will-bypass-web-ad-
blockers-but-offer-ad-targeting-opt-outs

[104] cnet.com/news/facebook-zuckerberg-faces-more-cam-
bridge-analytica-questions-on-capitol-hill-congress-senate

[105] techcrunch.com/2018/04/28/
facebooks-dark-ads-problem-is-systemic

[106] forbes.com/sites/petersuciu/2019/10/11/more-americans-are-
getting-their-news-from-social-media/#5e5c64373e17

[107] diasporafoundation.org

[108] web.archive.org/web/20111002003516/http://blog.diaspora-
foundation.org/2011/09/21/diaspora-means-a-brighter-future-for-
all-of-us.html

[109] joinmastodon.org

[110] maketecheasier.com/facebook-alternatives-social-networks

[111] web.archive.org/web/20141007061300if_/https://ello.co/
request-an-invitation

[112] ionos.com/digitalguide/online-marketing/social-media/
the-best-facebook-alternatives

[113] vero.co/values

[114] theverge.com/2018/3/2/17067610/
vero-social-media-ayman-hariri-downloads

[115] mewe.com/about#bill

[116] vator.tv/news/2019-07-17-mewe-ceo-mark-weinstein-on-how-
his-company-is-positioning-itself-as-the-anti-facebook

[117] foundation.mozilla.org/en/blog/how-tell-fact-crap-newsfeed

6. NEWS

[118] macalester.edu/news/2017/04/how-news-has-changed

[119] journalism.org/2013/03/17/the-changing-tv-news-landscape

[120] time.com/3712579/rush-limbaugh-radio-history

[121] niemanlab.org/2016/01/20-years-ago-today-nytimes-com-de-
buted-on-line-on-the-web

[122] niemanlab.org/2016/01/20-years-ago-today-nytimes-com-de-
buted-on-line-on-the-web

[123] tinyurl.com/y52syf8l

[124] ijoc.org/index.php/ijoc/article/view/5096/1715

[125] nytimes.com/2011/03/18/business/media/18times.html

[126] archives.cjr.org/the_audit/audit_interview_alan_d_mutter_1.php

[127] newsosaur.blogspot.com/2009/02/mission-possible-
charging-for-content.html

[128] baekdal.com/newsletter/the-problem-with-newspaper
-jobs-and-how-we-get-polls-wrong

7. NEWS TODAY

[129] reutersinstitute.politics.ox.ac.uk/sites/default/files/2020-06/DNR_2020_FINAL.pdf

[130] mediapost.com/publications/article/353880/how-we-forage-for-the-news-we-want.html

[131] mediapost.com/publications/article/86382/foraging-for-information-with-search.html

[132] mediapost.com/publications/article/354866/our-brain-and-its-junk-news-habit.html

[133] blogs.lse.ac.uk/polis/2015/09/10/how-journalism-is-turning-emotional-and-what-that-might-mean-for-news

[134] mediapost.com/publications/article/327647/why-marketing-is-increasingly-polarizing-everythin.html

[135] swordandthescript.com/2019/12/marketing-predictions-2020

[136] hal.inria.fr/hal-01281190

[137] edge.org/conversation/john_brockman-stewart_brand-george_dyson-kevin_kelly-edgedld-an-edge-conversation-in

8. FIXING NEWS

[138] baekdal.com/newsletter/the-problem-with-newspaper-jobs-and-how-we-get-polls-wrong

[139] santacruzlocal.org

[140] digiday.com/media/this-is-not-your-grandfathers-patch-look-out-local-wants-to-be-the-modern-local-news-of-santa-cruz

[141] cjr.org/analysis/nytimes-subscriptions-local-publishers-compete.php

[142] knightfoundation.org/articles/5-business-models-for-local-news-to-watch-in-2020

[143] mediapost.com/publications/article/354866/our-brain-and-its-junk-news-habit.html

[144] nytimes.com/2020/08/05/business/media/nyt-earnings-q2.html

[145] digiday.com/media/weve-really-reset-our-floor-how-the-atlantic-gained-300000-new-subscribers-in-the-past-12-months

[146] thedrum.com/news/2020/05/18/our-priority-can-t-be-sell-advertising-washington-post-rethinks-revenues-lockdown

[147] privacyforprofit.com/2020/05/18/our-priority-cant-be-to-sell-advertising-washington-post-rethinks-revenues-in-lockdown

9. CONCLUSION

[148] privacyforprofit.com/privacy-tech

[149] networkadvertising.org/sites/default/files/final_nai_consumer_survey_paper_22oct2019.pdf

[150] wired.com/story/california-prop-24-fight-over-privacy-future

[151] mcguffincg.com/what-consumers-would-pay-for-popular-free-apps

[152] kaushik.net/avinash/marketing-analytics-intersect-newsletter